The Talmud
of the
Land of Israel

Chicago Studies in the History of Judaism
Edited by Jacob Neusner

The University of Chicago Press
Chicago and London

The Talmud of the Land of Israel

A Preliminary Translation and Explanation

Volume 34

Horayot and Niddah

Translated by
Jacob Neusner

Jacob Neusner is University Professor and Un-
gerlieder Distinguished Scholar of Judaic Studies
at Brown University. He is the author of numerous works, including *Judaism: The Evidence of
the Mishnah,* published by the University of Chicago Press.

The University of Chicago Press, Chicago 60637
The University of Chicago Press, Ltd., London

©1982 by The University of Chicago
All rights reserved. Published 1982
Printed in the United States of America
89 88 87 86 85 84 83 82   5 4 3 2 1

Library of Congress Cataloging in Publication Data

Talmud, Yerushalmi. English.
   The Talmud of the land of Israel.

   (Chicago studies in the history of Judaism)
   Bibliography: p.
   Includes index.
   1. Talmud Yerushalmi—Commentaries.   I. Neusner,
Jacob, 1932–   II. Title.   III. Series
BM498.5.E5 1982   296.1'2407   81-13115
ISBN 0-226-57694-9 (v. 34)   AACR2

Contents

In memory of
Rafael Moshe Zaiman

1968–1980

Foreword

This translation into English of the Talmud of the land of Israel ("Palestinian Talmud," "Talmud Yerushalmi") is preliminary and provisional, even though it is not apt to be replaced
for some time. It is preliminary, first, because a firm and final
text for translation is not in hand; second, because a modern
commentary of a philological and *halakhic* character is not yet
available; and, third, because even the lower criticism of the
text has yet to be undertaken. Consequently, the meanings imputed to the Hebrew and Aramaic words and the sense as-
cribed to them in this translation at best are merely a first step.
When a systematic effort at the lower criticism of the extant
text has been completed, a complete philological study and
modern dictionary along comparative lines made available, and
a commentary based on both accomplished, then the present
work will fall away, having served for the interim. Unhappily,
as I said, that interim is apt to be protracted. Text-critics, lexicographers, and exegetes are not apt to complete their work on
Yerushalmi within this century.

The purpose of this preliminary translation is to make possible a set of historical and religious-historical studies on the formation of Judaism in the land of Israel from the closure of the
Mishnah to the completion of the Talmud of the land of Israel
and the time of the composition of the first *midrashic* compila-
tions. Clearly, no historical, let alone religions-historical, work
can be contemplated without a theory of the principal document and source for the study, the Palestinian Talmud. No theory can be attempted, however tentative and provisional,
without a complete, prior statement of what the document appears to wish to say and how its materials seem to have come

to closure. It follows that the natural next steps, beyond my now-finished history of Mishnaic law and account of the Judaism revealed in that history, carry us to the present project. Even those steps, when they are taken, will have to be charted with all due regard to the pitfalls of a translation that is preliminary, based upon a text that as yet has not been subjected even to the clarifying exercises of lower criticism. Questions will have to be shaped appropriate to the parlous state of the evidence. But even if the historical and religions-historical program were to be undertaken in the Hebrew language instead of in English, those who might wish to carry on inquiries into the history of the Jews and of Judaism in the land of Israel in the third and fourth centuries would face precisely the same task we do. No one can proceed without a systematic account of the evidence and a theory of how the evidence may and may not be utilized.

Let me now describe the project as a whole. It calls for the following thirty-five volumes to comprise the thirty-nine tractates of the Palestinian Talmud:

The Division of Agriculture

1   Berakhot
2   Peah
3   Demai
4   Kilayim
5   Shebiit
6   Terumot
7   Maaserot
8   Maaser Sheni
9   Hallah
10   Orlah and Bikkurim

The Division of Appointed Times

11   Shabbat
12   Erubin
13   Pesahim
14   Yoma
15   Sheqalim
16   Rosh Hashshanah
17   Sukkah
18   Besah and Taanit
19   Megillah
20   Hagigah and Moed Qatan

The Division of Women

The Divisions of Damages and Purities

I have used three typefaces for the translation. Each Mishnah-pericope is in an oblique typeface; citations from the Tosefta, verbatim or nearly so, are in boldface type; and all other discussion provided by the Talmud for the Mishnah-pericope at issue is in regular type. My explanations of the Talmud's materials are clearly separated from the Talmud itself.

My translation generally follows the commentary of Pené Moshe. Where it does not, I have followed my own theory of what the text says. I prefer his. The text generally is corrected to conform to the Leiden manuscript (*The Palestinian Talmud. Leiden MS. Cod. Scal. 3. Facsimile of the original manuscript* [Jerusalem: Kedem Publishing, 1970]) and the *editio princeps* (*Talmud Yerushalmi . . . Venezia* [printed by Daniel Bomberg, 1523–24; reprinted without place or date]). Since this translation is heavily glossed with bracketed language, amplifying and explaining what I believe the text has to say, the appended comments are kept brief. They deal consistently with the relationship between the Talmud's treatment of the Mishnah and the materials of the Mishnah, and, where need be, they may also extend and augment what I have already said, in the translation, about the Talmud's meaning. But there are not a few passages in which the translation suffices with a rather general picture of what the Talmud says; the principal exercise of the explanation is to follow the Talmud on the Mishnah in particular.

Let me explain further details of the translation and the decisions of the policy made in executing it.

First, the Palestinian Talmud sometimes cites pericopes also found in the Tosefta. In numerous instances there are differences in the versions of those pericopes presented in the two documents. In most of these, I have noticed, the Tosefta's version is intelligible and makes sense, and that in the Talmud of the land of Israel does not. Where I give the Tosefta's version of a pericope rather than the one now in the Talmud, I always mark the passage accordingly. I believe a bit of thought will indicate that my decision is justified by the context, which confirms that it is the Tosefta's version that is subjected to further discussion, rather than that which we now have in the Yerushalmi's manuscript and printed texts. A better text of Yerushalmi will reconcile or at least account for the differences between the two versions. Since my principal purpose is to provide an intelligible account of what the Talmud of the land of Israel appears to say, I believe that this decision, provisional at best, in favor of the Tosefta's version where it is clearer and contextually justified, is correct.

Second, the Palestinian Talmud very commonly utilizes materials more than once or even twice, so that a given discussion will be attached to pericopes of the Mishnah in two or more different tractates or chapters. Now these several points at which a single discussion is utilized may present us with texts of varying quality and even character. Rather than impose my judgment of which version of a given passage is better (or best) of the lot, I have in the main translated what is before me, however unsatisfactory that version may be, and referred the reader to other versions of the same passage. These may differ markedly and even may provide substantially more lucid, and obviously superior, texts. But, it should be noted, where one version is markedly unclear, while its parallel is more readily accessible, I give the parallel, as does Pené Moshe. Here too a critical text will solve many problems I have left for others to confront.

Third, I have in general tried to put into English what the reader is apt to find in the accessible Hebrew-Aramaic versions, that is to say, the printed text, corrected against the Leiden MS and also against the *editio princeps*. As noted, where the available Geniza-fragments, in Ginzberg as supplemented by Bokser's bibliography, provide significant alternative readings, these too are inserted. But I plead guilty to the charge of not having first established, and only then translated, the "best possible version" of the Palestinian Talmud. Rather, I give what is at present fairly widely available. At some other time a new translation will present in English a new and superior text for the original. Then others may impose their own judgment as to what version, among several that may be available, should be inserted at each of the points at which a given pericope may make its appearance. As always, the best is the enemy of the good. In all, there is no limit to how this first translation into English and brief explanation can be improved.

The commentary follows a simple pattern and takes up only a few problems. First, where necessary, I give a brief explanation of the principal issue of the Mishnah. Since I have already provided a complete translation and commentary to the Mishnah (and the Tosefta), there is no reason to do more than say what is important in understanding the Talmud's approach to the Mishnah. Second, I explain the division of the unit of the Talmud pertinent to a pericope of the Mishnah and briefly account for the unfolding and order of the Talmud's topics, one by one. Third, I proceed only when necessary to a brief précis and résumé of what the Talmud has to say, with special interest in the continuity of the Talmud's discourse, both from the Mishnah and also within the Talmud itself.

While the presentation is in accord with the division of the Palestinian Talmud along the lines set forth by the division of chapters of the Mishnah into individual pericopes, I have also included a cross-reference to the pagination of the *editio princeps* to facilitate reference.

It goes without saying that there are a great many more points of interest in the Talmud of the land of Israel than I highlight here. For example, this Talmud, like the other one, contains much information on topics of interest to philologists and lexicographers, historians and archaeologists, and others who come to all the primary sources of late antiquity with a substantial program of inquiries independent of the principal interests of those sources. Were I a Semitist or a classicist, the character of this translation would be quite different from what it is. What I promise is what I believe I deliver, an intelligible account of what the Talmud of the land of Israel says, its arguments, modes of thought, principal dialectical currents. Where I fail is when what I give is not intelligible—or (more commonly) more intelligible than the original text should allow. People looking for a version of Krauss's Greek and Latin loan-words in any case will hunt in vain here for what they seek; such information is by definition far beyond the bounds of this one document. I am not much interested, either, in explaining *realia,* e.g., what kind of wagons or road-marks the Talmud has in mind. Some give seminars in "keys and locks in Talmudic times." Mine are devoted to "the function and structure of late antique Judaism." That above all else accounts for my conception of a suitable translation of a preliminary character.

My introduction to the tractates of the Talmud of the land of Israel deals only with the substance of the law, that is, with the Mishnah. It is not feasible to introduce the Talmud as re-gards the Mishnah of each tractate, since, at this point, it is difficult to point to differences, for example, between the Tal-mud to Horayot and the Talmud to Niddah, and so through-out. Hence I am not sure what such an introduction to the Talmud of each tractate would require. At this time we lack all points of differentiation and comparison. My intent for volume 35 is to compose an account of the Talmud in general that will permit specification of points of special interest and differentia-tion of traits among the various tractates in particular. I regret my incapacity to do better than this, but, after what has al-ready been said, this hardly requires specification once more.

The abbreviations, bibliography and glossary section at the end was prepared with the help of Professor Alan J. Peck. This section serves the entire thirty-five volumes, not this part of it alone.

My student, Mr. Leonard Gordon, checked my translation against the Leiden manuscript and the *editio princeps,* and saved me a great deal of tedious work in so doing. He also uncovered more than a few points requiring attention and correction. I am grateful for his hard and careful work.

Professor Baruch A. Levine of New York University served as the critical reader for this volume. I am thankful for the many corrections and observations supplied by him, and still more, for his willingness to take time out to study this tractate and so improve my work on it. I retain full responsibility for whatever unsolved problems and deficiencies may remain.

I completed this book during my tenure as a Guggenheim fellow and during my coincident extraordinary research leave from Brown University. I am grateful to both the John Simon Guggenheim Memorial Foundation and Brown University for continued support for this research.

J.N.

Horayot

1 Introduction to Horayot

Horayot deals with inadvertent collective sin, that is, erroneous decisions unintentionally made by the instruments of government and community, as distinct from those made by individuals. Scripture makes provision for collective expiation of guilt incurred on account of collective action effected through public institutions, e.g., through government or instruction. It is this topic that is now worked out fully in relationship to, and essential as an exegesis of, Scripture itself.

The Scriptures that refer to a sin committed in error are at issue. Specifically, when the court instructs the community to do something that in fact should not be done, we have a case of erroneous instruction to which, the Mishnah takes for granted, Lev. 4:1-5, 13-21, 22-26 and Num. 15:22-26 refer. The Mishnah's problem is to define situations in which there has been a bonafide error on the part of the court. There we invoke the stated Scriptures and their provisions. If there is no court error, other Scriptures, specifically those that treat an individual's inadvertent or deliberate sin, obviously will come into operation. So, in all, the problem of the tractate is presented by Scripture, and the Mishnah's and Talmud's particular contribution is clear.

Lev. 4:1-5 state:

And the Lord said to Moses, Say to the people of Israel, if any one sins unwittingly in any of the things which the Lord has commanded not to be done, and does any one of them, if it is the anointed priest who sins, thus bringing guilt on the people, then let him offer for the sin which he has committed a young bull without blemish to the Lord for a sin offering. He shall bring the bull to the door of the tent of meeting before the Lord, and lay his hand on the head of the bull, and kill the bull before the Lord. And the anointed priest shall take some of the blood of the bull and bring it to the tent of meeting; and the priest shall dip his finger in the blood and sprinkle part of the blood seven times before the Lord in front of the veil of the sanctuary.

Lev. 4:13ff. speak of the entire congregation's doing so:

If the whole congregation of Israel commits a sin unwittingly and the thing is hidden from the eyes of the assembly, and they do any one of the things which the Lord has commanded not to be done and are guilty; when the sin which they have committed becomes known, the assembly shall offer a young bull for a sin offering and bring it before the tent of meeting; and the elders of the congregation shall lay their hands upon the head of the bull before the Lord, and the bull shall be killed before the Lord. Then the anointed priest shall bring some of the blood of the bull to the tent of meeting, and the priest shall dip his finger in the blood and sprinkle it seven times before the Lord in front of the veil. And he shall put some of the blood on the horns of the altar which is in the tent of meeting before the Lord; and the rest of the blood he shall pour out at the base of the altar of burnt offering which is at the door of the tent of meeting. And all its fat he shall take from it and burn upon the altar. Thus shall he do with the bull; as he did with the bull of the sin offering, so shall he do with this; and the priest shall make atonement for them, and they shall be forgiven. And he shall carry forth the bull outside the camp, and burn it as he burned the first bull; it is the sin offering for the assembly.

Finally, Lev. 4:22ff. say the same for the unwitting sin of the ruler:

When a ruler sins, doing unwittingly any one of all the things which the Lord his God has commanded not to be done, and is guilty, if the sin which he has committed is made known to him, he shall bring as his offering a goat, a male without blemish, and shall lay his hand upon the head of the goat, and kill it in the place where they kill the burnt offering before the Lord; it is a sin offering. Then the priest shall take some of the blood of the sin offering with his finger and put it on the horns of the altar of burnt offering, and pour out the rest of its blood at the base of the altar of burnt offering. And all its fat he shall burn on the altar, like the fat of the sacrifice of peace offerings;

so the priest shall make atonement for him for his sin, and he shall be forgiven.

The last relevant set of scriptural verses is at Numbers 15:22–29, which go over the ground of the unwitting sin of the community, but are understood in the Mishnah to refer specifically to an inadvertent act of idolatry:

But if you err, and do not observe all these commandments which the Lord has spoken to Moses, all that the Lord has commanded you by Moses, from the day that the Lord gave commandment, and onward throughout your generations, then if it was done unwittingly without the knowledge of the congregation, all the congregation shall offer one young bull for a burnt offering, a pleasing odor to the Lord, with its cereal offering and its drink offering, according to the ordinance, and one male goat for a sin offering. And the priest shall make atonement for all the congregation of the people of Israel, and they shall be forgiven; because it was an error, and they have brought their offering, an offering by fire to the Lord, and their sin offering before the Lord, for their error. And all the congregation of the people of Israel shall be forgiven, and the stranger who sojourns among them, because the whole population was involved in the error.

Now, it is clear, all of these verses take for granted that the sin under discussion is inadvertent or unwitting. Whether it is the ruler, the high priest, or the entire people, all are subject to the conception that an erroneous ruling by the court has caused this unwitting sin. The outline of the tractate follows.

The offering brought because of an erroneous decision by a court (1:1–5).

1:1   If the court gave a decision to transgress any of the commandments and an individual did what they said, he is exempt, since he relied on the court. If someone on the court knew that the decision was in error, lo, this one is liable, since he knew and did not rely on the court. He who relies on himself (and makes an error) is liable; he who relies on the court is exempt.

1:2   If the court realized its error but the decision did not reach an individual, who went and did in accord with their original instruction, Simeon declares him exempt. Eleazar: He is subject to doubt.

1:3   If a court gave a decision to uproot a whole principle of the Torah, lo, they are exempt under the rule of Lev. 4:14. If they gave an instruction to nullify part and carry out part of a rule of the Torah, then they are liable under the rule of Lev. 4:14. If the court was somehow impaired, they are exempt from a public offering under the rule of Lev. 4:14.

1:4–8   If the court and the community carried out the decision, they bring the required bullock, so Meir. Judah: Twelve tribes bring twelve bullocks. Issue: What is the political entity to which the rules apply?

The offering brought by the high priest who has unwittingly done what is contrary to the commandments of the Torah. The ruler (2:1–2:5).

2:1   If an anointed high priest made a decision for himself and carried it out, all inadvertently, he brings a bullock. If he made the erroneous decision inadvertently but deliberately carried it out, or deliberately made an erroneous decision but inadvertently carried it out, he is exempt.

2:2   If a high priest made an erroneous decision by himself and carried it out by himself, he effects atonement for himself by himself. If it was the community, he effects atonement for himself with the community.

2:3–4   They are not liable on account of a decision inadvertently violating a positive commandment or a negative commandment concerning the sanctuary, but they are with regard to one involving a menstruating woman.

2:5–6   The inadvertent violation of the provisions of Lev. 5:1–4 does not fall under the laws of this tractate.

Individual, anointed priest, community (2:7–3:8)

2:7   In the case of all the commandments of the Torah, on account of which they are liable for deliberate violation to extirpation, and on account of inadvertent violation to a sin offering,
    an individual brings a female lamb;
    a ruler brings a male goat;
    an anointed priest and court bring a bullock.
    As to a suspensive guilt offering, an individual and a ruler may become liable, but the anointed high priest and court do not become liable.

3:1 An anointed high priest who sinned and afterward was removed from office. An anointed high priest who passed from
his office as high priest and then sinned.

3:2 If they sinned before they were appointed and then they were
appointed.

3:3 Definition of the anointed high priest. Amplification of M.
3:1–3.

3:4–5 Whatever is offered more regularly than its fellow takes precedence: bullock of an anointed priest and bullock of the congregation, etc. Appendix.

The order of Scripture is to deal with unwitting sins on the
part of (1) the anointed priest, Lev. 4:3, then (2) the whole
congregation, Lev. 4:13, finally (3) the ruler, Lev. 4:22. The
Mishnah and so the Talmud revise the order and regard as
prior the unwitting sin of (2) the whole community, committed,
as we know, because of an erroneous instruction on the part of
the court; then come (1) the anointed priest and (3) the ruler;
but these are treated more or less together. What is said at I
about the sin caused by the court's error is said at II about error involving the high priest. There is a simple logic governing
I: first, the definition of culpability; second, the explanation of
the character of the court that is under discussion; and an appendix. M. 2:1–2 go over the same program. M. 2:3–4, 5–6
form an appendix to all that has gone before. The final unit
organizes relevant information but in no way advances the exposition of the topic, merely defining and clarifying terms used
earlier.

2 Yerushalmi
Horayot Chapter One

1:1

[A] [45c] [If] the court gave a decision to transgress any of all of the commandments that are stated in the Torah,

[B] and [an individual] went and acted in accord with their instruction, [so transgressing] inadvertently,

[C] [1] whether they carried out what they said and he carried out what they said right along with them,

[D] [2] or whether they carried out what they said and he carried out what they said after they did,

[E] [3] whether they did not carry out what they said, but he carried out what they said—

[F] lo, he is exempt,

[G] since he relied on the court.

[H] [If] the court gave a decision, and one of the [members of the court] knew that they had erred,

[I] or a disciple who is worthy to give instruction,

[J] and he [who knew of the error] went and carried out what they said,

[K] (1) whether they carried out what they said and he carried out what they said right along with them,

[L] (2) whether they carried out what they said and he carried out what they said after they did,

[M] (3) whether they did not carry out what they said, but he carried out what they said—

8

[N]   *lo, this one is liable,*

[O]   *since he [who knew the law] did not [in point of fact] rely upon the court.*

[P]   *This is the governing principle:*

[Q]   *He who relies on himself is liable, but he who relies on the court is exempt.*

[I.A]   ["If any one sins unwittingly in any of the things which the Lord has commanded not to be done, and does any one of them . . ." (Lev. 4:2).] If anyone sins: ". . . one sins" ". . . in doing" ". . . will sin"—lo, these [three] constitute exclusionary phrases.

[B]   [One of the afore-listed exclusionary phrases serves to exclude from punishment the one who relies on the court, so that] *he who relies on himself is liable, but he who relies on the court is exempt.*

[C]   In every context you maintain that one exclusionary phrase following another serves to encompass [within the frame of the law a category that otherwise would be omitted from it]. But here you maintain that an exclusionary clause followed by another exclusionary clause serves to exclude [from the rule someone who otherwise would be included under it].

[D]   Said R. Mattenaiah, "It is different [in the present case] for here is written an exclusionary clause after a [second] exclusionary clause after yet a [third] exclusionary clause."

[II]   [The initial discussion is this unit deals with the position of Joshua at M. Ter. 8:1, which is as follows: (1) *The wife (of a priest) who was eating heave offering, (and) they came and told her, "Your husband has died," or, "(Your husband) has divorced you" (such that the woman no longer has the right to eat heave offering); (2) and so (in the case of) a slave (of a priest) who was eating heave offering, and they came and told him, "Your master has died," or, "He sold you to an Israelite," or "He gave you (to an Israelite) as a gift," or, "He has made you a free man" (in any of which cases, the slave no longer can eat heave offering); (3) and so (in the case of) a priest who was eating heave offering, and it became known that he is the son of a divorcee, or of a halusah (and therefore cannot eat heave offering)—R. Eliezer declares (all of these individuals) liable to*

*the principal and (added) fifth (of the heave offering they unin-
tentionally had eaten as nonpriests) But R. Joshua exempts.]*

[A]   R. Haggai asked the associates, "How do we know that one
who eats [a sort of food he should not eat, e.g., an ordinary
person who ate heave offering] with the permission [of the
court] is exempt [from punishment, as in our Mishnah's law]?
What is the difference [in Joshua's view] between a case in
which someone thought that the food was unconsecrated, but it
turned out to have the status of heave-offering, in which case
he is liable, and a case in which someone assumed that he was
a priest, and he turned out to be an Israelite, in which instance
he is exempt?"

[B]   They said to him, "[The difference derives] from [the law con-
cerning] the instructions of a court, [for if the court declared
the man permitted to do so, then he is not liable, while if the
error was his own, he is liable]." [Joshua will regard the case at
M. Ter. 8:1 as analogous to one in which a person has received
incorrect instruction from a court.]

[What now follows assumes knowledge of M. Pes. 6:5,
which states: *An animal designated as a Passover offering that
one slaughtered under an improper designation on the Sabbath
that coincides with the fourteenth of Nisan—one is liable on
that account for a sin offering. And as to animals designated for
any other animal offering that one slaughtered for the sake of
Passover-sacrifice, if they are not appropriate to be offered as a
Passover-sacrifice, one is liable. But if they are appropriate
(e.g., male lambs, and so suitable to serve as a Passover-sacrifice)—R. Eliezer declares liable for a sin offering, and R.
Joshua declares him exempt.]*

[C]   He said to them, "I have yet another question requiring [your
attention]. What is the difference between a case in which one
[slaughtered a beast because he] assumed that it was an ordinary day, while it turned out to be the Sabbath, in which case
the person is liable [for violating the Sabbath], and a case in
which [on the Sabbath that coincided with the fourteenth of
Nisan, when the Passover offering was to be slaughtered] one
[carried out an act of slaughter] assuming that it was an animal
set aside as a Passover offering, but the sacrifice turned out to
have the status of a peace-offering [Levine: "presentation offering"], in which case the person is exempt [from penalty, in the
view of Joshua]?"

[D]   They said to him, "The difference is that in the latter case he carried out the act of slaughter by permission. [That is, the man assumed it was permitted to slaughter the beast as a Passover-offering, and an inadvertent error in doing a commandment is not culpable.]"

[E]   He said to them, "Yet another question do I need to raise: What is the difference between a case in which someone assumed that an act was permitted but it turned out to be forbidden, in which case one is exempt [as at M. 1:1], and a case in which one assumed that something was forbidden fat [and he ate the fat], but it turned out to be permitted fat, in which instance the person is liable?"

[F]   [Now in this case] they did not answer him at all.

[G]   He said to them, "I shall tell you how we know [the basis for the difference]: '[If any one of the common people sins unwittingly in doing any one of the things which the Lord has commanded not to be done and is guilty] when the sin which he has committed is made known to him, he shall bring . . .' " [Lev. 4:27]. [So Scripture specifies the fact of the matter. In this case, the one who sins unwittingly has no reason to recognize the sin and bring an offering (Pené Moshe).]

[H]   R. Yosé entered [the discussion]. They said to him, "Something is difficult for us."

[I]   "And why do you not answer him on the basis of the following verse: 'When the sin that he has committed is made known to him, then he shall offer . . .'?"

[J]   [45d] They said "First came Haggai, and then came another Haggai [L: QŠYTH . . . QYYMTH]!"

[III.A]   In regard to the position of R. Ishmael [spelled out below], who does not utilize the cited Scriptures for the case of those who are liable to bring sin offerings and unconditional guilt offerings [Levine: "guilt offering for a verified offense"], for whom the Day of Atonement passed [without bringing the required offerings they owed] there are no problems [in the position utilizing Lev. 4:27 as just now outlined at I.A–C].

[B]   But in regard to the position of R. ʿAqiba, who utilizes the stated verses to refer to those who are liable to sin offerings or to unconditional guilt offerings for whom the Day of Atonement passed [indicating that they retain liability to bring the offerings, there is a problem].

[C]   [The foregoing passage, A–B, refers to] that which has been taught in Tannaitic tradition:

[D]   How do we know that those who are liable to sin offerings or to unconditional guilt offerings, for whom the Day of Atonement passed [without their bringing the offerings they owed], remain liable to bring these same offerings after the Day of Atonement, [though in regard to] suspensive guilt offerings [Levine: "guilt offering for an unverified offense"], they are exempt [if they did not bring the offerings they owed and the Day of Atonement already has taken place]?

[E]   Scripture says, ". . . when the sin that he has committed is made known to him, then he shall bring [an offering]"—even after the Day of Atonement.

[F]   Note the following: "If anyone sins" ". . . one sins" ". . . in doing" ". . . will sin"—lo, these three constitute exclusionary phrases. *He who relies on himself is liable, but he who relies on the court is exempt.*

[G]   They are liable only for something that was fully known to them but then became hidden from them.

[H]   And what is the Scriptural evidence of the reason?

[I]   "And [if] a matter was hidden from knowledge of the entire congregation" (Lev. 4:13)—it was a matter that had been known to them but then was hidden from them.

[J]   Now in accord with the position of R. Ishmael, who says, "And it was hidden from him"—implying that he knew about it and he knew, lo, there are two stages of knowing.

[K]   So far as the position of R. 'Aqiba goes, who says, " 'And it was hidden from him' . . . 'and it was hidden from him,' " two times—implying that knowledge came to him at the outset and knowledge came to him at the end, but in the interim it was hidden from him,

[L]   Scripture says, "And the matter was hidden"—it was a matter that had been revealed to them, but was subsequently hidden from them.

[**IV**.A]   And [the judges of the court that gave false instruction] are liable only if they give instruction to nullify part [of the law] and
to carry out part of the law [cf. M. 1:3, below].

[B]   Samuel said, "And [the law applies in a case in which they
taught that it is permitted [to do something that in fact is pro-
hibited]. But if they gave instructions [merely] that someone is
exempt [from penalty for doing a sin], it is not in such a case
that the law applies."

[C]   They are liable only if the instruction comes from the Hewn-
Stone chamber.

[D]   Said R. Yoḥanan, "The scriptural evidence of the reason for
this Tannaitic teaching is as follows: "['Then you shall do according to what they declare to you] from that place which the
Lord will choose' (Deut. 17:11)."

[E]   Said R. Mana bar Tanḥum, "[If] a hundred judges entered the
court [decision], they are not liable unless all of them [inadver-
tently] gave [the same erroneous] instruction."

[F]   In that regard R. Zeira said, "And the law applies only if all of
them give [false] instruction on the same grounds, [unani-
mously taking the same position for the same reason]."

[G]   [Delete:] How now?

[**V**.A]   *If an individual went and carried out the law in accord with
their opinion inadvertently* [erring in accord with their opinion]
[M. 1:1B]—

[B]   Now does the issue of deliberate sin apply [that the Mishnah
must specify the sin as inadvertent]?

[C]   It is a matter of inadvertence on the part of an individual in a
context of instruction of a court. [But if there is no court instruction, the inadvertent sin of an individual, of course, is
culpable.]

[**VI**.A]   R. Immi in the name of R. Simeon b. Laqish: "The Mishnah
speaks [at M. 1:1I] of a [disciple in a case in which] someone
of the caliber of Simeon b. ʿAzzai is sitting before them."

[B]   Now how are we going to interpret the [claim that the disciple
is of Ben ʿAzzai's caliber]? If we are dealing with someone who
knows the entire Torah but does not know that particular matter [in which the court made an error], this is not someone of

the caliber of Simeon b. ʿAzzai. And if it is the case of someone who knows that matter in particular but does not know the
entire Torah, he is like Simeon b. ʿAzzai so far as that particular matter is concerned, [so it is deliberate, not inadvertent].

[C]   But thus should we interpret the matter: it deals with someone
who knows the entire Torah, and that someone [furthermore]
knows that particular matter [in which the court made its erroneous decision]. But he errs in holding the opinion that the Torah taught, "Follow them, follow them," [that is, follow the
majority, even where the majority errs].

[D]   [Now if it is a case in which someone made the error of maintaining that the Torah has said, "Follow them, follow them"],
this [too] is no Simeon b. ʿAzzai!

[E]   It is in line with the following teaching: Is it possible that, if
people should say to you that right is left and left is right, you
should listen to them? Scripture says, "To go to the right hand
or the left," meaning that [one follows the majority only if]
they declare to you that [what actually is] the right is right, and
the left, left."

[VII.A]   What is then [the correct interpretation of the Mishnah]?

[B]   R. Yosé in the name of R. Hila: "In every setting one who
does a sin in error is exempt from punishment, and one who
commits it deliberately is liable. But here, even one who commits it deliberately [also] is exempt, because he relied on the
court."

[C]   The associates in the name of Samuel: "The Mishnah deals
with a case in which an individual [M. 1:1B] completes the majority of the community. But each individual who performed
the act wrongly by himself is exempt [from a sacrifice by reason of his inadvertence]."

[D]   Said R. Yoḥanan, "Even if each individual committed the act
by himself, each one must bring a ram and a goat, [so he is not
exempt, as C has said]."

[E]   Now that ruling poses a difficulty to the opinion enunciated by
Samuel. Does it not turn out that each individual effects atonement for himself with two sin-offerings?

[F]   R. Zeira in the name of Samuel: "The status of an individual
depends [on the circumstance]. If the majority of the court ate

[that which was prohibited, they bring] a sin-offering [as specified in Lev. 4:13]. But if a minority of the court did so [and thus is not liable to a collective offering], then [there being no communal expiation] the individual brings [an offering]."

[G]   [That is to say:] In the case of any false instruction in which a court [collectively] brings a bullock, an individual need not offer a lamb and a goat. [And in the case of any improper instruction in which the court collectively does not offer a bullock, an individual does offer a lamb and a goat.]

[H]   R. Yoḥanan interpreted the cited passage to apply to a case in which a court gave instructions to remove a basic principle of the Torah. Since the court brings a bullock, an individual does not have to bring a sheep and a she-goat. If the court gave instruction to nullify part of the teaching of the Torah and to carry out part of it, since the court does not have to bring a bullock, the individual does have to bring a sheep and a goat.

[I]   Samuel explained the Mishnah: "I still maintain that if a minority of the community inadvertently did a sin, they are liable. For a court does not bring a bullock on their account. Scripture says, 'People of the land' (Lev. 4:27)—even the whole of it, even the larger part of it. [But not a minority.]"

[J]   R. Yoḥanan interpreted the Mishnah: "I still maintain, a minority of the community who inadvertently sinned not under the instructions of the court is liable, for in the case of false instruction a court does not bring a bullock."

[K]   Samuel said, "Truly they bring a sheep and a goat [as individuals]."

[L]   R. Yoḥanan said, "They do not bring a sheep and a goat [as individuals]."

[M]   So far as the position of Samuel is concerned, this is no problem, for he derives one liability from another. [That is to say, he regards the minority of the community as liable in the case of an inadvertent sin, for the court does not bring an offering on their account.]

[N]   But for the position of R. Yoḥanan, there is a problem, for does he derive the liability in a case in which one is exempt? [For the court does not bring an offering for the individual's inadvertent sin. In Yoḥanan's view the court is entirely exempt from culpability.]

[O]   The Mishnah is at variance with the position of Samuel: " 'Or when his sin which he sinned is known to him, then he will bring [an offering]'—thus excluding one who is an apostate to idolatry."

[P]   The Mishnah is at variance with the position of Samuel: "[If anyone sins] . . . one sins . . . in doing . . . will sin—lo these three constitute exclusionary phrases. *He who relies on himself is liable, but he who relies on the court is exempt.*"

[Q]   This indeed does take issue with the position of Samuel, and the position of Samuel has no visible means of support.

The discourse opens with an exegetical proof for the Mishnah's basic proposition. It is based on formal exegesis of Scripture's language, as specified at **I**.A–B. C–D then justify the procedure of exegesis. The resort to an exegetical basis for the Mishnah's law is expanded at **II**, which undertakes an important exercise. Our Mishnah-pericope treats as not culpable an act done inadvertently, while in other contexts inadvertent sins are deemed culpable. To develop this point, the Mishnah alludes to two other laws, fully cited in my text. In both instances, we have to draw a distinction between one case and the other. The solution in each case is to repeat what is essentially the position of M. Hor. 1:1. That accounts for the final question of the unit, the grounds for the basic rule, as stated in general terms at **II**.I. Here the relevant verse in Scripture is simply cited. This rather sophisticated exercise thus ends up exactly where the simple one of **I** did. The resort to the stated Scripture leads, in **III**, to a quite secondary exercise.

The relationship of **III** to **I–II** is clear, since the tie is made explicit at A–B. The formal exegesis of Scripture yields a kind of formal mathematics, in which, if an authority adduces a given verse in evidence for one proposition, he is not going to adduce the same verse in evidence for some other. That is the force of the question of A–B. C, without attribution to ʿAqiba, takes up the position imputed to him at B and spells out his reading of the stated verse. Despite the efforts of Pené Moshe, I do not see the relevance of **III**.F–L to what has gone before, nor, in this context, is it necessary to explain the materials, which are dealt with at M. Shebu. 1:1f. (volume 32 in this series). At **IV** we return to the exposition of the Mishnah. The Talmud now contributes important clarifications of the basic principle that, when the court gives false instruction, the individual is exempt from punishment for having sinned in accord with that instruction. Samuel's point is that the instruction must actually permit the act which in fact is a sin, not merely declare that the sin is not going to be punished. The other sayings are clear as given. **V** and **VI** carry forward the interpretation of the Mishnah's language. **V** is a quibble, asking why the Mishnah has had to specify what is obvious. **VI** clarifies the sort of disciple to which the Mishnah makes reference, raising the larger issue of whether or not we have a case of inadvertence at all. If someone is so knowledgeable, how can he have erred to begin with? The error is not in the law, which we must assume judges know, but in the requirement to follow the majority. The disciple assumed that one should follow the majority, even when it is in error. This is not so.

To grasp the issues addressed in the concluding discussion, **VII**, we recall that when "the whole congregation" sins, that is, from the Mishnah's reading of Lev. 4:1ff, when a *court* gives an erroneous instruction to an individual relying on the court inadvertently sins, then the congregation brings a bullock, so Lev. 4:13ff. Now if an individual sins unwittingly, he brings a female goat (Lev. 4:27–28) or a female lamb (Lev. 4:32ff). At issue here is the relationship between these two requirements. If the court brings a bullock for its sin, does an individual have also to bring a goat or a lamb for his private sin? The relevance of this question to the interpretation of the Mishnah is clear. The position that the individual must bring a goat or lamb when the court brings a bullock is difficult to square with the Mishnah's view that, when the individual relies on the court, he is exempt for what he has done. What the contrary view requires, in fact, is that the status of the court's action be shown to be susceptible to diverse interpretation. When the court acts as a majority, then indeed its bullock serves. But if only a minority of the court has given the erroneous instruction, the individual *is* liable. That is, Samuel's position at **VII**.F. We thus see the importance of the introductory statements of **VI**, that is, a set of conditions that prepares the way for the dispute enunciated at **VII**. At **VII**.F we have a complete statement of Samuel's position, making the stated distinction. O–Q conclude the matter by rejecting the position of Samuel, thus ignoring the distinction he wishes to draw, and maintaining that, under all circumstances, when the court brings a bullock for the sin of the community, the individual has no further obligation.

Thus Lev. 4:13ff is read to exclude the case of Lev. 4:27ff. There are textual problems related to G, which has to be reconstructed out of the parallel version of the matter in B; and we note that some exegetical problems remain at H–N, which deserve more protracted analysis than is required here.

1:2

[A]   *[If] the court gave a decision and realized that it had erred and then reversed itself—*

[B]   *whether [upon retraction] they had [already] brought their atonement-offering or had not brought their atonement-offering—*

[C]   *and [an individual] went and did in accord with their instruction—*

[D]   *R. Simeon declares him exempt.*

[E]   *And R. Eliezer says, "It is subject to doubt."*

[F]   *What is the doubt?*

[G]   *[If] the person had stayed home, he is liable, [for he should have known the court's decision].*

[H]   *[If] he had gone overseas, he is exempt.*

[I]   *Said R. ʿAqiba, "I concede in this case [H] that he is nigh unto being exempt from liability."*

[J]   *Said to him Ben ʿAzzai, "What is the difference between this one and one who stays home?"*

[K]   *[ʿAqiba replied:] "For the one who stays home had the possibility of hearing [that the court had erred and reversed itself], but this one did not have the possibility of hearing [what had happened]."*

[I.A]   [What follows relates to M. 1:1I and repeats 1:1 **VI.A:**] R. Immi in the name of R. Simeon b. Laqish: "The Mishnah [at M. 1:1I] speaks of [a disciple in a case in which] someone of the caliber of Simeon b. ʿAzzai was sitting before them."

[B]   Now how shall we interpret [this statement]? [If in argument] he had disproved their [the majority's] position, then their improper instruction is null. And if they had disproved his [position], then this instruction is null.

[C]   But this matter is to be interpreted as follows: This party remained firm in his reply [to the arguments of the other], and the other party remained firm in their reply [to his arguments]. Their instruction so far as he is concerned [still] is no instruction, for they did not disprove his position. But so far as other people are concerned, [their] instruction *is* valid, because [for his part] he did not disprove [their position].

[D]   Does this judgment not stand at variance with the position of R. Mana bar Tanhum? For R. Mana bar Tanhum said, "[If] a hundred [judges] entered the court, [the false instruction is not in force] until all of them will present [that same false instruction]." [The reason that this judgment does not stand at variance with that statement of Mana is that we speak of a case in which] he [who differed] in fact did not enter [the court to begin with or participate in the debate].

[E]   Now if [the fact that the dissident judge] did not enter the case [constitutes a negative factor in assessing the effect of the decision], you might as well interpret the case in accord with the position of Rabbi.

[F]   For Rabbi said, "No judge['s position constitutes a disruptive factor in issuing false instructions] except for the senior judge of a court alone."

[II.A]   Now R. Mana bar Tanhum has said, "[If] a hundred judges entered the court, [the false instruction is not in force] until all of them will present [that same false instruction]."

[B]   Does the reversal require the same unanimous decision, or is the majority of the group sufficient [to effect retraction as specified at M. 1:2A]?

[C]   It should be obvious to you that a majority of the group suffices.

[D]   Now what sort of majority [do you have in mind]? Is it the majority of those who originally gave the instruction, [or] the majority of those remaining [at the point at which the reversal comes under discussion]?

[E]   [In the context of] what concrete [case do you raise the question]?

[F]   [If] a hundred entered [the court and made a decision], and then ten of them died, if you rule that we require the majority of those who originally gave the instruction, then we require fifty-one, while if you rule that we require a majority of those remaining, we require only forty-six.

[III.A]   [If] one set aside an animal to serve as his sin-offering, [but then] was struck dumb, went insane, or apostasized, or a court instructed [that it] is permitted to eat forbidden fat [in all of which instances there no longer is an obligation to offer the animal which had been designated as a sin-offering]—

[B]   R. Yoḥanan said, "[The requirement that] he [offer a] sin offering is set aside [no matter what happens later on, e.g., if the man regained his speech or senses, returned to Judaism, or learned that the court had corrected its instruction]."

[C]   R. Simeon b. Laqish said, "The requirement that he offer a sin offering is not set aside [and the obligation is to be carried out later on, when it is possible or appropriate to do so]."

[D]   R. Yosé b. R. Bun and R. Aḥa [said]: "The tradition is to be reversed, [so that Yoḥanan takes the position assigned to Simeon b. Laqish, and vice versa]."

[E]   [This is so that] the statement assigned to R. Yoḥanan will not turn out to be at variance with another matter attributed to him.

[F]   For R. Simeon bar Ba in the name of R. Yoḥanan: "They sprinkle a cup of blood on his account [namely, one who is dying] from the blood of his sin offering and from the blood of his guilt offering." [Thus Yoḥanan says that in the case of a dying man, the sin offering *is* to be carried out, and there is no reason for him to take a contrary position here.]

[G]   The rabbis of Caesarea say [concerning] R. Ḥiyya [and R.] Ami, [that the former] reverses [the attributions] and the other said, "Thus the tradition [is to be repeated as valid, just as we have received it above]."

[H]   The one who maintains that the traditions are to be reversed is not subject to the objection [that Yoḥanan is shown to contradict himself].

[I]   In accord with the party who holds that the requirement to bring the sin offering has not been set aside—who is going to accept the animal from him [and sacrifice it, seeing that the court has given instructions that there has been no sin committed in the first place]?

[J]   [Indeed, that is correct.] Let the man wait for the time that the court will reverse itself [retracting its erroneous decision and so declaring a sin to have been committed and permitting acceptance of the offering]! [Now that answer is clearly absurd, so a different solution must be found.]

[K]   But [interpret the Mishnah to speak of a case in which] it was a priest [who had sinned, so] he carried out the sacrifice [in his own behalf] and offered the beast and effected atonement.

[L]   [Or another way in which the animal may be required and ultimately offered would be a case in which the dissenting disciple] was [of the caliber of] Simeon b. ʿAzzai.

[M]   [Nonetheless,] who is going to accept the animal from him [and sacrifice it, as above at I]?

[N]   Let the man wait for the time that the court will reverse itself, in accord with the view of him who holds that the obligation to bring a sin-offering has not been set aside.

[IV.A]   The effects produced by an erroneous instruction are tantamount to the original erroneous instruction [so that if the man ate forbidden fat, and afterward a court declared the forbidden fat permitted, the man is not obligated to bring a sin-offering. The court's bullock suffices, and the later instruction is effective even for what the man did earlier]. An erroneous instruction [yielding an improper act along] with [the result of another such erroneous instruction]—what is the law as to the two deeds being deemed to join together to constitute a single action?

[B]   What sort of case [do you have in mind]?

[C]   [For example,] if [not by court error] the community ate forbidden fat and each individual set aside his offering [on that account], [and then the court ruled that it is permitted to eat forbidden fat], if you rule that the result of an improper instruction is deemed tantamount to the original instruction, [46a] the court is liable. If you say that the results of an improper instruction are not deemed tantamount to the result of the original instruction, the court is exempt.

[D]   Now it is clear that the results of an improper instruction are tantamount to an improper instruction, [thus the court's action is valid retroactively, and its sacrifice covers the individual who earlier did what the court later declared to be valid].

[E]   [That question is obvious. The real problem is] whether an improper instruction is deemed to join together with another improper instruction.

[F]   What sort of case [do you have in mind]?

[G]   [If] the court gave instruction that the fat covering the kidney on the right is permitted, and the one on the left, which has a covering, is permitted, and then the court retracted and reversed the ruling—

[H]   a majority ate on the occasion of the first instruction, and a majority ate on the occasion of the second instruction—

[I]   now if you rule that the two distinct acts of instruction join together, they are liable for a single [bullock], but if you say that the two acts of instruction do not join together, they are liable for two bullocks, [covering the two distinct acts of false instruction to the community, for which the court bears full responsibility].

[J]   [If we have] two improper instructions dealing with a single act of transgression, what is the law as to their joining together [to be deemed a single act of improper instruction, because both dealt with the same transgression]?

[K]   What is the sort of case [you have in mind]?

[L]   [If] the majority of the court ate and slaughtered [the animal that was a sacrifice, outside of the court of the Temple],
       in accord with the opinion of R. Meir, they are liable for a single [bullock for eating a sacrifice and killing it outside the Temple],
       and in accord with the opinion of R. Simeon, they are liable for two [bullocks].

[M]   If a minority ate in the first instance and a minority ate in the second,

[N]   in accord with the opinion of R. Meir, they are liable, and in accord with the opinion of R. Simeon they are exempt.

[V.A]   Said R. Zeira, "And if there is an interval between [the action and the court's retraction]"—

[B]   R. Meir said, "They give a person an interval [of sufficient time] so he may hear [of the court's reversal of its improper ruling and so avoid following the court in its error]. [So the liability is not immediate.]"

[C]   And R. Simeon says, "They assign an interval sufficient for one to clarify the ruling, [so he is not automatically exempt, but only if he acts while he has time to clarify the court's error]."

[D]   And we have learned a Tannaitic teaching along these same lines:

[E]   [If] a court gave an improper instruction in the Upper Market and an individual was in the Lower Market,
    [or] if the court was in the house and the individual was in the upper room,
    the individual remains exempt [if he follows the improper teaching of the court and does not know about their retraction of that teaching, for whatever he may do in accord with the original, improper teaching,] during an interval long enough for him to hear in a concrete way [that the court has retracted].

[VI.A]   So far as the view of R. 'Aqiba is concerned, the matter is still subject to the doubt [of M. 1:2E].

[B]   Said R. Bun bar Ḥiyya, "That doubt derives from a case in which the individual was located between two borders, between borders of the land of Israel and those of foreign territory. [Even if the person is not yet actually abroad, he is not likely to know the court's decision.]"

[C]   R. Ami in the name of R. Simeon b Laqish, "In matters of instruction [in which an individual is abroad and has no opportunity to hear that a court has retracted its original view], they follow the status of an individual in accord with his dwelling, in the land of Israel.

[D]   "In matters of doubt involving uncleanness [if the majority is unclean, the uncleanness is null], they follow the status of the majority of those who enter into the Temple courtyard."

[E]   Now do they assess matters into terms of the status of each group [of those who come on the eve of Passover to sacrifice their lambs in the courtyard], or do they take account only of the status of the first group to enter the courtyard?

[F]   Said R. Yosé b. R. Bun, "While the group is outside, they take account of their own status."

[G]   R. Joshua b. Levi: "For bringing an appearance-offering they follow the status of those [all the way] from the entrance of Hamath to the River of Egypt [so that if a majority is unclean, the uncleanness is null]."

[H]   R. Tanḥuma in the name of R. Huna, "The Scriptural foundation for the statement of R. Joshua b. Levi is as follows: 'So Solomon held the feast at that time, and all Israel with him, a great assembly, from the entrance of Hamath to the Brook of Egypt' (1 Kings 8:65). [These boundaries thus signify 'all Israel's' location.]"

The point of the Mishnah is clear, even though its language poses problems, since there is one version to be located at A–C + D–E, and a second at A–C + G–H. This later version then is carried forward at I–K. The principle is that if one relied on the court and had no alternative but to do so (H), he is exempt for the sin, and is exculpated by the court's offering (B). The Talmud's opening unit is relevant to the Mishnah only at **I.**D, where the issue of retraction enters, and this matter is repeated and explored at **II.** The remainder of the materials is included presumably because of the discussion of the opening proposition, that is, **I.**A–C, to which Mana bar Tanḥuma's saying is pertinent. It then appears that **I–II** will have been complete before their insertion into the Talmud in their present location. **III** leaves the range of exegesis of the Mishnah and raises a question meant to broaden the discussion. The point of relevance to the Mishnah is only tangential, as is obvious at **III.**A. The matter has to do with the disposition of an animal set aside for a sin-offering, but at the moment not subject to actually being offered up because of the status or condition of the person for whose atonement the beast is designated. Since the two possible positions are represented, the only point of inquiry, which need not detain us, is the authority behind each. If our text were subjected to lower criticism, we should probably find grounds to revise or omit the repetitious materials of I–J and M–N.

IV's materials go over three problems, specified at A–C, D–I, and J–N. The questions are subtle and interesting. The one of special interest is at L and following, which introduces a distinct matter. Meir maintains that the operative criterion is the deed, the sin itself; Simeon deems the criterion to be the matter of knowledge. That is to say, in Meir's view, there has been a single action (sin), at L, and two distinct sinful acts, at M. In Simeon's view people were subject to false instruction in only one "act of knowing," and, at M, in neither instance has a majority of the court carried out the erroneous action, so there is no call for a bullock. At L, by contrast, Simeon sees two distinct erroneous pieces of instruction.

While **V** clearly carries forward the immediately preceding materials of **IV**, in fact it returns us to the matter of the Mishnah, now the idea of M. 1:2G–H that a person is exempt if he had no chance to hear the court's retraction and did the deed assuming the court's opinion was sound. Meir gives a measure of an interval long enough for the person to remain exempt if he commits an act relying on the court's opinion and ignorant of its retraction, and so does Simeon. Following Pené Moshe, I have inserted into Simeon's saying language that joins his statement here to the antecedent dispute. But the saying surely can stand by itself. D–E then go over the same matter. We come at **VI** to ʿAqiba's specification at M. 1:2 I.K. The materials of **VI** move away from the Mishnah and ask about how we assess the status of a majority, e.g., if a majority is unclean, we deem the uncleanness null. The issue is then the limits of those whose status is taken into account. None of this is important in the present context.

1:3

[A]   *[If] a court gave a decision to uproot the whole of a principle [that is, remove the entire substance of the Torah]—*

[B]   *[1] [for instance, if] they said, "[The prohibition against having intercourse with] a menstruating woman is not in the Torah [Lev. 15:19]."*

[C]   *[2] "[The prohibition of labor on] the Sabbath is not in the Torah."*

[D]   *[3] "[The prohibition against] idolatry is not in the Torah."—*

[E]   *lo, these are exempt [from the requirement of Lev. 4:14].*

[F]   *[If] they gave instruction to nullify part and to carry out part [of a rule of the Torah], lo, they are liable.*

[G]   *How so?*

[H]   *(1) [If] they said, "The principle of prohibition of sexual relationships with a menstruating woman indeed is in the Torah, but he who has sexual relations with a woman awaiting day against day is exempt."*

[I]   *(2) "The principle of not working on the Sabbath is in the Torah, but he who takes out something from private domain to public domain is exempt."*

[J]   *(3) "The principle of not worshiping idols is in the Torah but he who bows down [to an idol] is exempt."—*

[K]   *Lo, these are liable,*

[L]   *since it is said, "If something be hidden" [Lev. 4:13]—*

[M]   *something and not the whole principle.*

[I.A]   R. Hezekiah said, " 'Some thing' [Lev. 4:13] and not the whole thing [MDBR, KL DBR]."

[B]   Said R. Hila, "[And they do one of any of the commandments]—part of commandments [MMṢWT], and not whole commandments [KL MṢWT]."

[C]   And is it written thus?

[D]   It is in accord with what R. Ami said in the name of R. Yoḥanan, "They take away a letter from one word of the text and add it to another and thus interpret the entire pericope to the end [in this case, removing the M from MKL MṢWT and reading KL MMṢWT]."

[E]   R. Ḥananiah in the name of R. Jeremiah: "[And that is the case] even in the middle of a word, thus: 'And you shall put oil upon it . . . it is a cereal offering' [Lev. 2:15], meaning to encompass all meal offerings, [which require a] putting on of oil.' "

[**II**.A]   Now [in the cases of F–K], do you not [really] turn out to uproot the whole principle of the Torah [by giving the instructions specified by the Mishnah-passage]?

[B]   In the case of [the prohibition of sexual relations (M. 1:3H)]
with a woman awaiting day against day [who has had a flow on
two days, but is now counting days with no flow, to establish
her status as wholly clean], [the Mishnah refers to] a case in
which [the court] ruled, "The night is permitted [for sexual re-
lations], but the day is prohibited [that is, since Scripture refers to clean *days*, if the blood appears by day, the night is
permitted]."

[C]   And do you not turn out [at M. 1:3I] to uproot the whole principle of [on the Sabbath not] stretching something forth [that is
to say, of not standing in private domain and reaching out with
an object in one's hand and stretching that object into public
domain]?

[D]   Samuel bar Aba said, "It is a case in which [the court] ruled
that it is permitted [to stretch something forth] by a cubit, but
not by two cubits."

[E]   And [at M. 1:3J] do you not turn out to uproot the entire principle of [the prohibition of] bowing down?

[F]   [The reference is to a case] in which [the court] ruled that it is
permitted to bow down but prohibited to prostrate oneself [to
an idol].

[G]   And [at M. 1:3I] do you not turn out to uproot the entire principle of transporting an object across the line from one domain
to another?

[H]   Said Samuel bar R. Isaac, "It is a case in which [the court]
ruled that it is permitted [on the Sabbath to transport across
the line between private and public domain] a single dried fig,
but it is prohibited [to transport] two dried figs."

[I]   And the stated ruling [H] is in accord with the opinion of the
one who said that bringing something in [from public to private domain] and taking something out [from private to public
domain] are subject to a single rule.

[J]   But in accord with the opinion of the one who said that bringing something in [from public domain to private domain] and
taking something out [from private to public domain] are sub-

ject to two distinct rules, would the court not turn out to be uprooting a whole principle of the Torah concerning bringing something in [in making the ruling specified at H]?

[III.A]   Said R. Yosé, "It is not that [the court] gave instructions that it is permitted to eat prohibited fat. The court knew that [in fact] it is prohibited to eat forbidden fat. But [they thought] that the Torah had given the power to a court to give teaching [on *which* fat is forbidden and *which* is permitted, when in fact all is forbidden]."

[B]   R. Bun bar Ḥiyya asked, "[But this too would be uprooting an entire principle of the Torah, for if the court rules about] an olive's bulk [of one sort of fat] on one day [that it is permitted], and about two olive's bulks [of another sort of fat] on another day [that it too is permitted, when both sorts are prohibited, ultimately all sorts of forbidden fat will be permitted, in which case you have nothing other than an uprooting of an entire principle of the Torah, contrary to the position of Yosé]."

[C]   It is [like] a case of a prophet who incites [the people to violate the Torah, who is liable only when he incites the people to uproot a whole principle of the Torah, but if he incites them to violate part but to keep part, he is exempt]. Might one think that, in such a case, if [a false prophet] should say to you, "Do not put on *tefillin* today, but put them on tomorrow," you should pay attention to [such a prophet]? Scripture says, "To follow them" (Deut. 13:6 [?])—in all respects, and not only in some respects. Lo, you have here a case of uprooting a principle of the Torah for that entire day, and do you claim that in this instance you do not have a case of uprooting an entire principle of the Torah? Here you do indeed have a case of uprooting an entire principle of the Torah!

[D]   R. Mana heard this saying in the context of what Samuel bar Abba said [at II.D], and [he applied the same conception,] stating, "[If] it is in a case in which [the court] ruled that it is permitted [to hold something out] by a cubit but not by two cubits, lo, you have a case of uprooting a principle [of the Torah] for that entire [first] cubit [which has been declared permitted]. So will you say there is not an uprooting of an entire principle of the Torah? Here there is indeed an uprooting of an entire principle of the Torah!"

The main point of the Mishnah is in the contrast between M.
1:3 A–E and F–M. The Mishnah wishes to supply examples of
partial, as against complete, nullification of the Torah's teaching. That, in the sages' view, is the difficult task, despite the
assistance afforded by the Mishnah's examples themselves. The
proof-texts adduced at **I** complement the one of the Mishnah.
The principal topic comes at **II** and persists to the end. **II** systematically goes over the Mishnah's cases and refines them.
II.C poses difficulties, not only because (following Pené Moshe)
it requires correcting the text from SḤYTH to HWŠṬH, but
also because **II**.G goes over the same ground. The emendation
is probably in error; the whole passage presumably is to be
dropped. The rest of the materials are clear as given; J gets no
reply at all. **III** takes up the same problem from yet another
angle. Yosé's proposal allows for uprooting only part of a principle of the Torah, for the court declares only some forbidden
fat, but not all forbidden fat, to be permitted. This is given a
solid reply at B. C then goes over the same ground. The language poses some difficulty, but the gist is as stated. D then
restates the same argument as B–C have given, now to
Samuel's proposal. The result is not wholly satisfactory, since
the problem is left without a definitive solution.

1:4

[A]   *[1] [If] the court gave a decision, and one of the members of
the court realized that they had erred and said to them, "You
are in error,"*

[B]   *or [2] if the head of the court was not there,*

[C]   *or [3] if one of them was a proselyte, a "mamzer," a "Netin,"
or an elder who did not have children—*

[D]   *lo, these are exempt [from a public sin-offering under the provisions of Lev. 4:14],*

[E]   *since "Congregation" is said here (Lev. 4:13), and "Congregation" is said later on (Num. 15:24).*

[F]   *Just as "congregation" later on applies only in the case in
which all of them are suitable for making a decision,*

[G]   *so "congregation" stated here refers to a case in which all of
them are suitable for making a decision.*

[I.A]   The Mishnah-pericope follows the view of Rabbi [cited at M. 1:4B], for Rabbi says, "No judge['s position constitutes a disruptive factor in issuing false instruction] except for the senior judge of a court alone."

[B]   It is written, "Then if it was done unwittingly, without the sight of the congregation, all the congregation shall offer one young bull" (Num. 15:24)—without the sight of the one who is the eyes of the congregation [= the head of the court].

[II.A]   It is written, "[And the Lord said to Moses, Gather for me seventy men of the elders of Israel . . . and bring them to the tent of meeting,] and let them take their stand there with you" (Num. 11:16).

[B]   Just as you personally are no proselyte, *mamzer,* or *Netin* [M. 1:4C], so they are not to be proselytes, *mamzers,* or *Netins,* [let alone] slaves.

[C]   [It is] easy [enough to understand the need to include reference to a proselyte]. But does a court [ever] appoint *mamzers* [to its membership, that specification must be made that if a *mamzer* is a member of the court, the court's erroneous instruction is null]?

[D]   R. Huna said, "[The Mishnah refers to a case] in which the court transgressed and did appoint *mamzers.*"

[E]   R. Ḥananiah and R. Mana: One said, "[The Mishnah refers to a case in which there was a *mamzer* on the court,] and he was counted among the seventy." The other said, "[The Mishnah refers to a case in which there was a *mamzer* on the court,] but he was not counted among the seventy."

[F]   The one who said, "The *mamzer* was not counted among the seventy" finds no difficulty with the reference of the Mishnah. [There normally would be no *mamzer* on the court, just as we have said above, but Huna is right.]

[G]   The one who said, "The *mamzer* was counted among the seventy" [will maintain] that he is in fact not counted among the seventy. But since he was not worthy of giving instruction, he was deemed nothing more than a stone. [And the Mishnah maintains that, if he was merely present, then even after the fact his presence nullifies the instruction.]

The Talmud at **I** supplies its own proof-texts for the basic
proposition of the Mishnah. At **II** it further focuses upon the
reference to the *mamzer*, since from the Talmud's viewpoint it
is unlikely that, to begin with, such a person would be appointed to a court. Huna's solution is the simplest, and E–G
focus essentially upon the proof-text.

1:5

[A] *[If] the court gave an incorrect decision inadvertently, and the
     entire community followed their instruction [and did the sin in
     error] inadvertently,*

[B] *they [the court] bring a bullock.*

[C] *[If the court gave an incorrect decision] deliberately, but the
     community, following their instruction, did [the sin] inadver-
     tently,*

[D] *[the individuals] bring a lamb or a goat (Lev. 4:32, 27).*

[E] *[If the court gave incorrect instruction] inadvertently, and [the
     community followed their instruction and did the sin] deliber-
     ately, lo, these [individuals] are exempt [under the provisions of
     Lev. 4:4, for an offering does not atone for deliberate sin].*

[I.A] This [Mishnah-pericope] does not stand at variance with the
       position of R. Simeon b. Laqish [at M. 1:2].

[B] For R. Ammi said in the name of R. Simeon b. Laqish, "The
     Mishnah [speaks at M. 1:5C of a court on which] someone of
     the caliber of Simeon b. ʿAzzai sits, in which case [with access
     to such learning], they acted deliberately and [the people] acted
     inadvertently [in accepting wrongful instruction]." [This is the
     case of M. 1:5C–D.]

[C] And how can there be deliberation in the case of inadvertence
     with regard to an individual who acts at the instruction of a
     court? [That is, M. 1:5C has the individual bring an offering.
     So far as Simeon b. Laqish is concerned at M. 1:1, if the court
     has an authority of Ben ʿAzzai's caliber, it has acted deliber-
     ately, and an individual does not have to bring an offering.]

[D] Associates in the name of R. Simeon b. Laqish: "[This refers
     to a case] in which the majority of the community did not ac-

cept the ruling of the court [and acted inadvertently, so the individual *is* liable, for he is not able to claim to have relied on the court]."

[E]   R. Zeira in the name of R. Simeon b. Laqish: "This refers to a case in which they resisted their instruction [but carried it out], [and so have not unthinkingly relied on the court]."

[F]   What is the difference between them?

[G]   If they accepted their authority but then went and resisted it—

[H]   in the opinion of associates, since they resisted, they are exempt.

[I]   In the opinion of R. Zeira, since they accepted their authority in the first place, lo, these [individuals] are liable.

What troubles the Talmud is still the persistent problem of defining a case in which the court is liable and the people who accept the court's opinion are exempt; that is, the court brings a bullock, and individuals do not have to bring a lamb or a goat. The matter is pressed once more in terms of Simeon b. Laqish's question of how a court with a knowledgeable member ever can make a mistake, and how, further, people can be held liable for the court's error if they inadvertently do a sin because of the court's instruction. At C the question is phrased most clearly. The two answers, D and E, resort to the position that the people who did the act did not in fact rely on the court's instruction when they did it, either because they constituted a minority (D) or because they resisted the court's view—even while carrying it out(E). These are essentially technicalities.

1:6

[A]   *"[If] the court made an [erroneous] decision, and the entire community [of Israel], or the greater part of the community, carried out their decision, they bring a bullock.*

[B]   *"In the case of idolatry (Num. 14:24), they bring a bullock and a goat," the words of R. Meir.*

[C]   R. Judah says, "Twelve tribes [individually] bring twelve bullocks.

[D]   "And in the case of idolatry, they bring twelve bullocks and twelve goats."

[E]   R. Simeon says, "Thirteen bullocks, and in the case of idolatry, thirteen bullocks and thirteen goats:

[F]   "a bullock and a goat for each and every tribe, and [in addition] a bullock and a goat for the court."

[I.A]   [The following relates to M. Pes. 7:6: If the congregation was made unclean, or the greater part of it, or if the priests were unclean, while the congregation remained clean, the Passover offering is prepared in a state of uncleanness. If a minority of the congregation was made unclean, those who remain clean keep the first Passover, and those who are unclean, the second.] What Tannaitic authority taught that we require the majority [of the entire Israelite community, not just the majority of a given tribe, to invoke the stated law]? It is R. Meir.

[B]   For it has been taught in a Tannaitic tradition: Half of all of the tribes [without regard to tribal divisions] is equivalent to half of each of the [six] tribes, on condition that a majority [of the whole Israelite community carries out the instruction of the court, in which case the court brings a bullock].

[C]   R Judah says, "[The congregation may consist of] half of each tribe, on condition that there be the majority of the entire group of tribes [that is, seven,] [even if it does not add up to the majority of the Israelite population].

[D]   "A single tribe may [furthermore] draw in its wake all the tribes [if it is so numerous that half of the community has committed the sin, even if all are members of the same tribe]."

[E]   R. Meir says, "All of the tribes [together] are called a congregation."

[F]   R. Judah says, "Each [individual] tribe is called a congregation."

[G]   And R. Simeon follows the view of R. Judah. As R. Judah said, "Each tribe is called a congregation," so R. Simeon says, "Each tribe is called a congregation."

[H]   What difference is there, then, between their positions?

[I]   This matter of [a single tribe's] drawing in its wake [all of the community (D)].

[J]   R. Judah says, "A single tribe may draw in its wake all the other tribes."

[K]   R. Simeon says, "A single tribe may not draw in its wake all the other tribes."

[II.A]   And he agrees that the instruction must come forth from the Hewn Stone Chamber [for the stated bullock-offering, covering the sin of the entire community, to be called for].

[B]   Said R. Yosé, "The reason is that it is said, 'From that place which the Lord will choose' (Deut. 17:8)."

[III.A]   R. Abun in the name of R. Benjamin bar Levi: "There is a Scripture that supports the position of the one [Judah, Simeon] who says, 'Each tribe is called a congregation.'

[B]   For it is written, 'A nation and a congregation of nations will come from you' (Gen. 35:11).

[C]   "And yet [at the time that that statement was made], Benjamin had not yet been born. [So the reference to a coming *congregation* applied to a single tribe.]"

[IV.A]   Said R. Ḥiyya bar Ba, "Just as they disagree in the present setting, so they disagree about uncleanness,

[B]   "as it has been taught in a Tannaitic teaching:

[C]   **'If half of the community was clean, and half unclean, the clean ones observe the first Passover [offering], and the unclean ones observe the second' [T. Pes. 6:2C–D]."**

[D]   R. Judah [better: Simeon] says, "The clean ones do it by themselves, and the unclean ones do it by themselves."

[E]   They said to him, "The Passover is not done in halves, but [46b] either all of them do it in a state of uncleanness, or all of them do it in a state of cleanness."

[F]   Who is the Tanna who made that statement to him?

[G]   It is in accord with the position of R. Judah.

[H]   For it was taught in a Tannaitic tradition:

[I]   *If one of the loaves was made unclean, or one of the rows [of incense-dishes], R. Judah says, "Both of [the loaves or rows]*

are to go forth to the place where burning is done. For the offering of the community is not divided." And sages say, "The unclean one remains in its state of uncleanness, but the clean one may be eaten by the priests" [M. Men. 2:2].

[J] R. Yosé bar Bun in the name of R. Yoḥanan said, "Who was it who made that statement [of E] to him [Simeon, at D]? It was sages, who are in accord with the thesis of R. Judah."

The Mishnah now turns to another pericope (Num. 15:24), relevant to a case in which the public commits an error collectively. An unwitting sin done without the knowledge of the congregation is expiated with a young bull as a burnt offering and a male goat for a sin-offering. If an individual sins unwittingly, he offers a female goat (Num. 15:27). The real issue here is not the fact just stated, but the definition of the *congregation*. Meir deems only the entire community of Israel to constitute the congregation. Judah and Simeon regard each tribe as a congregation. That is why Judah and Simeon expect twelve communal sacrifices, when all twelve tribes ("congregations") have collectively sinned under the conditions of the present tractate. The important materials then are at I.C–D, E. Judah has a dual position. Half of a given tribe may constitute a congregation—large enough to require all the tribes to make the stated offerings (D). And half of each tribe has the same power, if seven tribes are involved, even if we do not have a majority of all Israel. This is in clear conflict with Meir's position, which requires a majority of the entire community of Israel, without regard to apportionment among the tribes. So the principal conflict is between C and E. The importance of D is to distinguish Judah's position from Simeon's, as is made explicit at I–K. Clearly, **II** is intruded and in fact out of place. **III** reverts to the discussion of **I**. **IV** then expands the matter by showing that the disagreement persists in other contexts, as specified.

1:7

[A] *"[If] the court gave an [erroneous] decision, and seven tribes, or the greater part of seven tribes, carried out their decision,*

[B] *"they bring a bullock.*

[C]   *"In the case of idolatry, they bring a bullock and a goat," the words of R. Meir.*

[D]   *R. Judah says, "Seven tribes who committed a sin bring seven bullocks.*

[E]   *"And the other tribes, who committed no sin, bring a bullock in their behalf,*

[F]   *"for even those who did not sin bring an offering of account of the sinners."*

[G]   *R. Simeon says, "Eight bullocks, and in the case of idolatry, eight bullocks and eight goats:*

[H]   *"a bullock and a goat for each and every tribe, and a bullock and a goat for the court."*

[I.A]   It was taught in a Tannaitic tradition: **R. Simeon b Eleazar says in his name [of Meir], "[If] six tribes sinned, and they constitute the majority [of all Israel], or seven, even though they are not the majority, lo, they are liable" [T. Hor. 1:7].**

[B]   Said R. Eleazar, "[Simeon b. Eleazar] has said only six, which constitute a majority [come under consideration]. Then, if there are five tribes, even though they constitute a majority, lo, [the court] is exempt [from bringing a bullock]."

[C]   Said R. Yosé b. R. Bun, "The Tannaitic teaching [at M. 1:6 I.B] has made the same judgment: *Half of the tribes, on condition that [they constitute] a majority* of the population."

[D]   And, [is it] similarly [the rule that we require] half of the population, on condition that it is the majority of the tribes?

[E]   R. Yosé b. R. Bun said, "This same question occurs with regard to the high priest [concerning whether, like] the instruction of the high court, the instruction of an ordinary court [also is deemed to fall under the rule of false instruction in the present regard; cf. M. 2:1]."

The Talmud goes over familiar materials, citing its discussion of M. 1:6, as indicated. C glosses the above-cited pericope.

1:8

[A]   *"[If] the court of one of the tribes gave an [erroneous] decision, and that tribe [only] carried out their decision,*

[B]   *"that tribe is liable, and all the other tribes are exempt," the words of R. Judah.*

[C]   *And sages say "[Israelites] are liable only by reason of an [erroneous] decision made by the high court alone,*

[D]   *"as it is said, 'And if the whole congregation of Israel shall err, and the matter is hidden from the sight of the congregation' (Lev. 4:13)—and not the congregation of that tribe alone."*

[I.A]   [When there is an obligation to bring a bullock, or, in the case of idolatry, a bullock and a goat, as Meir, Judah, and Simeon have maintained at M. 1:6, who bears the obligation to supply the animal for the sacrifice?] R. Meir says, "It is the obligation of the court [to supply the animal for the sacrifice]."

[B]   R. Judah says, "It is the obligation of the community [to supply the animal for the sacrifice."

[C]   Said R. Simeon, "It is both the obligation of the court and the obligation of the community [to supply the animal for the sacrifice]."

[D]   What is the reason [founded in Scripture] for the position taken by R. Meir?

[E]   It is stated here [in the setting of inadvertent commission of sins, Lev. 4:13], "from the sight," and it is stated later on [in the setting of inadvertent idolatry, Num. 15:24], "from the sight." Just as the reference to, "from the sight" stated later on speaks of the obligation of the court to bring the animals, so here too the court [is obligated].

[F]   What is the reason [founded in Scripture] for the position taken by R. Judah?

[G]   It is stated here (Lev. 4:13), "from the sight," and it is stated later on (Num. 15:24), "from the sight." Just as the reference to "from the sight" stated later on speaks of the obligation of the community, so the reference to "from the sight" in the former of the two passages speaks of the obligation of the community [to bring animals].

[H]   What is the reason [founded in Scripture] for the position
taken by R. Simeon?

[I]   It is stated here (Lev. 4:13), "from the sight," and it is stated
later on (Num. 15:24), "from the sight." Just as the reference
to "from the sight" stated later on means that the court [is obligated to bring the sacrifice], so the reference to "from the
sight" stated here means that the court [is obligated to bring
the sacrifice]. And just as "from the sight" stated later on
means that the community is obligated to bring the sacrifice, so
"from the sight" stated here means that the community [is obligated to bring the sacrifice].

[II.A]   The one who maintains that it is the obligation of the court
[will hold] that the court [supplies the animal, for there is no
alternative].

[B]   But in view of the one who maintains that it is an obligation of
the community, who will be expected actually to supply [the
funds for purchase of the sacrifice]?

[C]   [The answer is available in the following,] for it is taught:"**The
ox that is offered on account of the community's inadvertent
transgression of any and all commandments and the goats offered in atonement for idolatry to begin with are purchased
from a collection made for that purpose," the words of R.
Judah. R. Simeon says, "They derive from funds of the levy
of sheqels collected at the sheqel-chamber"** [T. Sheq. 2:6].

[III.A]   In the view of the one [Meir] who maintains that it is the obligation of the court, the court will lay hands on the sacrificial
beasts.

[B]   But in the view of the one who maintains that it is an obligation of the community, who will lay hands on the sacrificial
beasts?

[C]   [The answer is available in the following,] for it was taught in a
Tannaitic tradition: Three representatives of each tribe, with
the head of the court supervising them, lay hands on the head
of the bullock.

[IV.A]   "[And the elders of the congregation shall lay] their hands
[upon the head of the bullock]" (Lev. 4:15)—[the hands of]
each and every one of them.

[B]   "Their hands on the head of the bullock"—"the bullock requires a laying on of hands, and the goats brought on account of idolatry do not require a laying on of hands," the words of R. Judah.

[C]   R. Simeon says, "[The cited verse means that] the bullock requires a laying on of hands by the elders. The goats brought on account of idolatry do not require the laying on of hands by the elders."

[D]   For R. Simeon says, "Any sin-offering brought in behalf of the community, the blood of which is taken inside [to the inner altar], requires a laying on of hands [inclusive of the goats brought on account of idolatry]."

[E]   They reply to R. Judah [who maintains that the goats brought on account of idolatry do not require a laying on of hands], "And it is not written, 'Then the he-goats for the sin-offering were brought to the king and the assembly, and they laid their hands upon them' (2 Chron. 29:23)? [So this verse would indicate that there is a laying on of hands for the goats brought on account of idolatry, contrary to Judah's view.]"

[F]   R. Ḥiyya in the name of R. Yoḥanan: "It was an instruction required for the occasion [and not meant to provide a precedent for routine practice in the cult]."

[V.A]   R. Yoḥanan raised the question: "A congregation, one member of which dropped dead—what is the law as to bringing a sin-offering in his behalf [as part of the community obligated to make such an offering]? [Do we scruple concerning the animal set aside in his behalf?]"

[B]   They answered him, "And it is not written, 'At that time those who had come from captivity, [the returned exiles, offered burnt offerings to the God of Israel, twelve bulls for all Israel, ninety-six rams, seventy-seven lambs, and as a sin-offering twelve he-goats; all this was a burnt offering to the Lord (Ez. 8:35)'?

[C]   ("It obviously is not possible that a sin-offering was a burnt offering. Therefore we must derive the lesson that, just as a burnt offering is not eaten, so a sin-offering is not eaten.")

[D]   R. Judah says, "It was on account of idolatry that they brought them, [so the goats indeed are offered in behalf of those who have died before the sin-offering was completed]."

[E]   R. Hezekiah, R. Jeremiah, R. Ḥiyya in the name of R.
       Yoḥanan: "It was an instruction required for the occasion."

[VI.A]   R. Jeremiah taught likewise [with regard to Simeon's saying]
          that the bullock requires a laying on of hands, but the goats
          brought on account of idolatry do not require the laying on of
          hands by the elders. But by whom [are hands then laid on]?

[B]   R. Jeremiah gave thought to ruling that it was by Aaron and
       his sons [= the priests].

[C]   Said to him R. Yosé, "And has it not been taught as Tannaitic
       teaching of R. Ḥiyya: 'And *he* will lay on hands' [is not stated,
       but] 'And *they* will lay on hands' (Lev. 4:15)—to encompass the
       goats brought on account of idolatry [where no laying on of
       hands is specified] within the rule of laying on of hands?"—

[D]   but *not* the laying on of hands by elders.

[E]   R. Yosé taught likewise, "For it is written, 'He shall present
       the live goat, and Aaron shall lay both his hands upon the head
       of the live goat and confess over him all the iniquities of the
       people of Israel' (Lev. 16:20–21)]. Thus the living goat requires
       the laying on of hands by Aaron. The goats brought on account
       of idolatry do not require the laying on of hands by Aaron.

[F]   "And so it is written, 'He shall present the live goat, and
       Aaron shall lay both his hands upon the head of the live goat'
       (Lev. 16:20–21). Thus the living goat requires the laying on of
       hands by Aaron, and the goats brought on account of idolatry
       do not require the laying on of hands by Aaron."

[G]   And how does R. Jeremiah deal with the cited verse [which ap-
       pears to yield an exegesis contrary to his position that Aaron
       and his sons do lay hands on the goats brought on account of
       idolatry]?

[H]   He interprets [the matter that the laying on of hands in the
       case of the goat offerings brought on account of idolarty is by]
       an ordinary priest, [not by a *high* priest, like Aaron].

[VII.A]   R. Zeira in the name of R. Hamnuna [in the following is] in
           accord with the position of R. Meir.

[B]   We have learned in a Tannaitic teaching as follows: [If] the
       court gave an erroneous instruction, and the congregation car-
       ried out the instruction, [if] then a member of the court died,
       [the court] is exempt [from bringing an offering]. If one of the

members of the community died, [the court] remains liable to bring an offering. [For, following Meir, the obligation rests on the court, not the community. If a member of the court dies, then we have a situation parallel to a case in which one of the partners in a sin-offering dies. The offering is no longer made.]

[VIII.A]   [At this point the reader should reverse the order of the Talmud's materials, consulting the *baraita* below, at C, on which Meir comments, then Meir's comment that follows:] Said to them R. Meir, "Now if the bullock renders others exempt, should it not all the more so render the court itself exempt?"

[B]   They said to him, "It well serves to exempt others, who have that on which to depend [as Scripture says], but let it not exempt the court itself, which has nothing on which to depend."

[C]   R. Zeira in the name of R. Ḥisdai: "We have learned there, 'If the court gave an erroneous instruction and [the people] carried it out (and they knew).' [So the *instruction* depends on the court, and the *deed* on the people. Now A and B follow.]

[D]   "What is the meaning of 'gave an instruction'? They erred.

[E]   "What is the meaning of 'gave an instruction'? They erred inadvertently.

[F]   "What is the meaning of 'gave an instruction?' One might say that they should be liable. Scripture therefore says 'And the sin becomes known' (Lev. 4:14, 28)—and not that the sinners should be informed [without knowing just what sin they have committed. So if they do not know what sin the court has caused, they are exempt]."

[G]   [To understand the following, we must have in hand two Mishnah-pericopes. First is M. Ker. 3:2B: *If one ate forbidden fat and blood and remnant and refuse of an offering in a single spell of inadvertence, he is liable for each one of them.* The point is that there is a liability on the distinct count for each bit of forbidden food. Second is M. Ker. 4:2G–H, M–N: *If forbidden fat and remnant are before him, and a person ate one of them but is not certain which one of them he ate, R. Eliezer declares him liable to a sin-offering, and R. Joshua exempts him.* Now at F we are told that the court must be informed that they have sinned by giving false instruction, and they also must know what sin they have caused. To that position, the Talmud now asks:] Now do you want [concrete knowledge of]

the forbidden fat['s having been eaten, as at F? What difference does it make whether they ate forbidden fat or remnant,
since on either count they are guilty, as specified at M. Ker.
3:2! Why should the court be exempt?]

[H]   [The reply is that the position taken at F] is in accord with the
teaching of R. Joshua [at M. Ker. 4:2G–N].

[I]   [What we have is a case] in which the court gave instruction,
but then lost sight of what instruction they had given, whether
it dealt with [an erroneous teaching concerning] idolatry or [an
error regarding] any of the other commandments.

[J]   But if it had concerned idolatry, [then would the sin be ex-
piated] with a bullock, and if it had to do with other commandments, would it have to be expiated with a goat? [What
difference would it make, so that the court is exempt from an
offering anyhow?]

[K]   What we have here is a matter of doubt concerning whether a
bullock or a goat is required. And since there is a possibility of
changing an offering [for a beast which is not required], and
since we do not know what sin has been committed by the
court in this case, the court is exempt. [That is the meaning of
the exegesis given above at F.]

M. 1:8 clarifies the position of Judah. Now we have only a single tribe that has committed a sin in line with Lev. 4:14. Only
that tribe is liable. Judah does not require the other tribes to
bring an offering too. The sages disagree with all of the views
just now outlined at M. 1:5–8, since, as far as they are concerned, *no* tribal court has the status of the high court. The erroneous decision of none of them is going to be punished in the
way specified by Scripture. Still, this is congruent to Meir's
principle, if not to his position.

To the Mishnah-pericope at hand the Talmud is essentially
irrelevant. The principal focus here is the question at M. 1:5 as
to who bears responsibility for paying for the offerings owing
when the court and community inadvertently err, as specified at
Leviticus 4 and Numbers 15. The opening unit states the basic
issue and further engages in the familiar exercise of linking the
several positions to an exegetical base, forthwith ignored. The
next two units, **II** and **III**, simply carry forward the basic dispute. **II** deals with the source of funds, and **III** the matter of

the laying on of hands. The introduction of that issue then governs the outline of the remainder of the Talmud. The first of the secondary developments of the matter of laying hands on the sacrificial beast comes at **IV**. At issue, as is clear, is the dispute on whether the goats brought on account of idolatry are treated as is the bullock brought on account of all other sins. Simeon takes the affirmative, Judah the negative, and the relevant Scriptural verses are interpreted in accord with the position assigned to each. The reason for the interpolation of **V**, which hardly belongs, obviously is to be found in the presence of **V**.E = **IV**.F. (Clearly, **V**.C is out of context and does not belong.) At **VI** the discourse of **IV** resumes. The issues are laid out clearly, and the point of it all is to explore the exegetical basis for the position of Simeon.

Sections **VII** and **VIII** pose special problems, because their materials are in a peculiar order. First we have a comment on a Tannaitic teaching, and only then are we given the teaching itself. That this is intentional is indicated by the repetition of the pattern twice, first at **VII**.A, which comments on B and is incomprehensible without B, and then at **VIII**.C, A–B.

Let us deal with the two components. **VII** poses no problems. It cites a teaching that assumes that the obligation of bringing the offering devolves upon the court, not the community, just as Meir has said. The relevance to the opening discourse is self-evident. **VIII** has Meir take the position that the bullock offered by the court for the sin committed by the community at the instruction of the court serves to expiate both the sin of the community and also the sin of the court itself. This notion is expressed in the discourse to be reconstructed by reading C, then A–B. The court teaches; the people do. Now, Meir argues (A), if Scripture declares the bullock sufficient expiation for the sin of the deed of the community, it surely should serve to expiate the sin of the instruction of the court. The reply at B is that which is at M. 1:1: the community has relied upon the court, so the court is culpable and must expiate the sin of the community. But this expiation does not serve the court itself. Once the exegesis of the cited passage is undertaken (C), it is carried forward at D, E, and F, a second and separate unit of exegesis. The materials require no comment beyond what is supplied in the translation itself.

2:1

[A] *[46c] [If] an anointed [high] priest made a decision for himself [in violation of any of the commandments of the Torah], doing so inadvertently, and carrying out [his decision] inadvertently,*

[B] *he brings a bullock [Lev. 4:3].*

[C] *[If] he [made an erroneous decision] inadvertently, and deliberately carried it out,*

[D] *deliberately [made an erroneous decision] and inadvertently carried it out,*

[E] *he is exempt.*

[F] *For [as to A–B] an [erroneous] decision of an anointed [high priest] for himself is tantamount to an [erroneous] decision of a court for the entire community.*

[I.A] ["If any one sins unwittingly in any of the things which the Lord has commanded not to be done and does any one of them, if it is the anointed priest who sins, thus bringing guilt on the people, then let him offer for the sin which he has committed a young bull" (Lev. 4:2–3).] "Anyone . . . ," "if it is the high·priest . . . ,"—lo, [the Scripture would seem to imply that] the high priest is tantamount to an individual [and not, vs. M. 2:1F, to an embodiment of the community and thus not subject to a bullock-offering].

[B] [In this case, Scripture's purpose is to say:] Just as an individual, if he ate [something prohibited] at the instruction of a court is exempt, so this one [subject to court authority], if he ate something at the instruction of the court, is exempt.

[C]   Just as an individual, if he ate [something prohibited] without the instruction of a court is liable, so this one, if he ate something not at the instruction of a court, is liable.

[D]   [To encounter that possible interpretation] Scripture states, "Thus bringing guilt on the people," [meaning] lo, [the high anointed priest's] guilt is tantamount to the guilt of the entire people [just as M. 2:1F states].

[E]   Just as the people are not guilty unless they gave instruction [Lev. 4:13], so this one is not guilty unless he gave instruction.

[F]   There is a Tannaitic tradition that interprets [the matter with reference to] the people [and] the court:

[G]   Just as [if] the people gave instruction and other people did [what the people] said, [the people] are liable, so this one, [if] he gave [erroneous] instruction and others did [what he said], should be liable.

[H]   [It is to encounter that possible interpretation that] Scripture states, "[If it is the high priest] who sins," [meaning] for the sin that this one himself committed he brings [a bullock], but he does not have to bring a bullock on account of what other people do [inadvertently sinning because of his instruction].

[I]   There is a Tannaitic tradition that interprets the [matter with reference to] the people [and] the community:

[J]   Just as in the case of the people, if others gave erroneous instruction and they [inadvertently] committed a sin, they are liable, so in the case of this one, [if] others gave erroneous instruction and he carried it out [and so sinned], he should be liable.

[K]   [To counter that possible, wrong interpretation,] Scripture states, "[If it is the high priest] who sins," [meaning] for the sin that this one committed, he brings [a bullock], but he does not have to bring a bullock on account of what other people do [inadvertently sinning because of their instruction].

[II.A]   R. Jacob in the name of R. Eleazar: "[The rule stated by the Scripture and Mishnah, treating the anointed priest as equivalent to the people or court] applies in a case of an anointed priest who knows how to participate in the give and take of the law.

[B]   "For if that is not the case, then shall we have to say, 'And do idiots give instruction?' "

[III.A]   An anointed high priest who ate [forbidden food] at the instruction of a court [thus inadvertently sinning] is exempt.

[B]   [If he did so] at the instruction of another anointed high priest [and inadvertently sinned], he is liable.

[C]   [If he did so] at the instruction of a court, he is exempt [from bringing a bullock, but covered by the bullock they will bring], because the instruction of others as compared to the instruction of [a court] is null.

[D]   [If he did so] at the instruction of another anointed high priest, he is liable.

[E]   But that is the case [only if the anointed high priest himself] gave out exactly the same instructions [as he did, at which point we invoke the stated law].

While the principal exercise of M. 2:1ff. is to invoke with regard to the anointed priest the rules already stated for the court's erroneous instruction, the Talmud has a more original interest. It wants to know the relationship of an anointed priest to a court, that is, the reciprocal authority of autonomous institutions. Scripture has specified several autonomous persons and institutions or groups that atone with a bullock for erroneous actions committed inadvertently. That is why the Talmud now raises the interesting question of the rule that applies when one of these autonomous bodies follows instructions given by another. The opening unit explores this question, first establishing that the anointed priest is equivalent to the community, just as Scripture states, and drawing the consequence of that fact. Then comes the important point that the anointed priest is autonomous of the community. He atones for what he does, but is not subject to atonement by, or in behalf of, others. **III** qualifies this matter, placing the anointed priest into the jurisdiction of the court. So the upshot is that, in the present context, he is within the court's, but not the people's jurisdiction. The interpolated item at **II** is a familiar point.

2:2

[A]   *[If] he made an [erroneous] decision by himself and carried it out by himself,*

[B]   *he effects atonement for himself by himself.*

[C]   *[If] he made [an erroneous] decision with the community and carried it out with the community,*

[D]   *he effects atonement for himself with the community.*

[E]   *[For] a court is liable only if it gives an erroneous decision to nullify part and to carry out part [of the teachings of the Torah], and so is the rule for an anointed high priest [= M. 1:3].*

[F]   *And [likewise they] are [liable] in the case of idolatry [subject to an erroneous decision] only if they give a decision to nullify in part and to sustain in part [the requirements of the Torah = M. 1:3].*

[I.A] [If] a court gave [erroneous] instruction [concerning part of a commandment, e.g., declaring that some forbidden fat in fact is permitted], and [the anointed priest] gave instruction after them [concerning another part of the same commandment, e.g., declaring that other forbidden fat in fact is permitted, so in consequence nullifying the entire commandment concerning forbidden fat], and reversed [their decision, so what he permitted they forbade and vice versa],

it is self-evident that the matter so far as he is concerned is turned into a case of uprooting a fundamental principle of the Torah [and, because he has permitted what they forbade, while what they permitted remains so, the ruling is null and not subject to a bullock-offering, as stated at M. 2:2E].

[B]   But if he gave [erroneous] instruction first [e.g., declaring that some forbidden fat in fact is permitted], and they [the court] only afterward gave instruction, and reversed his decision [and so completed the matter, for the court confirmed what he permitted and permitted what he forbade, so now declaring all forbidden fat to be permitted, then covering the entire commandment against eating forbidden fat, do we rule that] even in this instance, so far as he is concerned, the matter is turned into a case of uprooting a fundamental principle of the Torah [so that he has to bring a bullock]?

[C] [Or do we maintain that] since he gave instructions first and [his instruction] was set aside, his instruction is tantamount to their [the court's] instruction, and the matter is therefore not turned into a case of uprooting a fundamental principle of the Torah?

[The matter is left unresolved.]

[II.A] [If] the court gave instruction, and he gave instruction after them [and he carried out the deed, so that the issue is whether in fact he has carried out his own instructions or the instructions of the court], it is self-evident that he has eaten [the forbidden fat] on account of the instructions of the court [and so is exempt from bringing a bullock, being covered by theirs].

[B] [But if] he ate [forbidden fat] after the court had retracted their original ruling [and so he did so solely on the basis of his own original erroneous instruction], he is liable.

[C] Said R. Yosé, "Now does not the Mishnah make the same statement on its own: *If he made an erroneous decision by himself and carried it out by himself, he effects atonement for himself by himself* [M. 2:2A–B]."

[D] That is because he made an erroneous decision by himself and carried it out by himself.

[E] But *if he made an erroneous decision with the community and carried it out with the community, he effects atonement for himself with the community* [M. 2:2C–D], it is because he made an erroneous decision with the community and carried it out with the community.

[F] But if he gave instruction by himself, he effects atonement by himself. [The cited case of B is not covered by the statement of the Mishnah because B speaks of a case in which the court retracted, and it has to be dealt with separately from the Mishnah. The version here is faulty in not linking E–F to the antecedent materials, but what has to be stated is obvious.]

Both units are interesting. In the former we raise a subtle question. The court nullifies part of a commandment, e.g., declaring some forbidden fat to be permitted. The anointed priest nullifies another part, e.g., declaring other forbidden fat to be permitted. In consequence of this decision *all* forbidden fat is permitted—thus uprooting a principle of the Torah. The

anointed priest is not obligated to bring a bullock; we do not
invoke the law, for the reason given by the Mishnah. But what
if the high priest rules first, permitting some fat, and then the
court rules that what he had declared forbidden was permitted,
while what he had permitted remains permitted? How do we
rule? Is this too a case of uprooting an entire principle? As B–C
spell out, there are two possible scenarios, and it is that of C
which is the more original. The second unit raises the equally
subtle question of a case in which the anointed priest, subject
as he is to court instruction, gives a false rule, then the court
gives the same rule. He is not liable to the bullock. (But compare M. 2:1 I.A–E!) The court's suffices, because he is subject
to their authority. But what if the court retracts? Since the
anointed priest is an autonomous authority, subject to the same
basic requirement as the court, we maintain that the anointed
priest's original ruling now stands, and he therefore is subject
to the requirement to bring a bullock. So we see once more
that the purpose of the Talmud is systematically to investigate
the interplay among the several autonomous figures of the
scriptural account, high priest, court, and people.

2:3

[A]   *They are liable only on account of "something's being hidden"*
       (Lev. 4:13) along with an act [of transgression] that is per-
       formed inadvertently,

[B]   *and so in the case of the anointed [high priest].*

[C]   *And [they are] not [liable] in the case of idolatry except in the*
       case of "something's being hidden" along with an act [of
       transgression] that is performed inadvertently.

[I.A] R. Zeira in the name of R. Jeremiah: "Does this Mishnah state
       the view of R. Meir [who maintains that the bullock is the obli-
       gation of the court, as may be claimed to be the implication of
       the pericope], or is it a teaching distinct from R. Meir's[, so we
       should not assume the implication is that the bullock is the ob-
       ligation of the court]?"

[B]   Said R. Yosé, "It is R. Meir, who said [that] it is the obligation
       of the court."

[C]   Said R. Mana, "It is in accord with R. Meir [in the teaching
       that now follows]."

[D]   It has been taught there [see above, 1:8 **VII**.A–C]: [If] the court gave an erroneous decision and the community carried out the decision [as at M. 2:3A], [if] one of the members of the court died, they are exempt [from bringing the bullock]. [If] one of the members of the community died, they remain liable to bring the bullock. [It follows that the obligation for the sin offering pertains to the court, not to the community.]

[E]   Said R. Meir to them [to Simeon], "Now if the bullock renders others exempt, should it not all the more so render the court itself exempt [so it must follow that the community is not liable to the bullock, and only the court is liable]?"

[F]   They said to him, "It well serves to exempt others, who have that on which to depend, but let it not exempt the court itself, which has nothing on which to depend."

[**II**.A]   [With regard to M. 2:3C,] R. Jeremiah asked in session before R. Zeira, "What [is the reason that M. 2:3C omits reference to the case of the anointed high priest, as at A–B? The issue is whether the omission is in accord with the position of Judah the Patriarch, who maintains that the rule about inadvertently giving out false instruction does not apply to the anointed high priest. In the case of idolatry, in Rabbi's view, the matter need not be "hidden" from the anointed high priest. That is to say, if there is an inadvertent comission of the sin of idolatry, without erroneous instruction, liability to the offering is incurred. The rule of C simply does not apply to the high priest, which is why there is no allusion at C to the matter stated at M. 2:3A–B].

   "[If it is] in accord with the view of Rabbi, the anointed priest *is* [delete: not] subject to culpability for transgression [of idolatry] performed inadvertently [without prior, erroneous instruction].

   "[If it is] in accord with the view of the rabbis, it *is* subject to the consideration of *something's being hidden* [that is to say, prior erroneous instruction]."

[B]   Said R. Huna, "In regard to the position of the rabbis it is required [to state matters as the Mishnah does], so that you will not maintain that the Mishnah follows the view of Rabbi in the following dispute:

[C]   "As regards the anointed high priest in a case of inadvertent instruction regarding idolatry,

[D]   "Rabbi said, '[If there is only] inadvertent carrying out of the deed [without the high priest's instruction as well], there [nonetheless] is a requirement of a bullock.'

[E]   "And rabbis said, 'It also is a matter of *something's being hidden* [that is, inadvertent error in instruction as well as in action is required if the high priest is to be liable to the bullock, just as in the case of the other commandments, subject to the rule of M. 2:3A–B].' "

[F]   He [R. Huna] said to him [R. Jeremiah], "Now what is the problem? Is it because we do not find in the Mishnah a clear reference to the anointed priest [at M. 2:3C]? Now, lo, in the earlier pericope, there also is no clear reference to the anointed priest in the Mishnah, and yet the anointed priest is included under the [earlier] rule. Here, too, even though there is no clear reference in the Mishnah to the anointed priest, the anointed priest is included under the rule."

M. 2:3A makes the simple point that there are two elements in the matter of a public sin done inadvertently and expiated through a bullock-offering. First, the court makes an erroneous decision, that is, gives false instruction, e.g., that prohibited fat is permitted. This is expressed in the language of *something's being hidden*. Second, the majority of the community accepts this decision or instruction and, therefore, by inadvertence carries out the sin, e.g., of actually eating that prohibited fat. In the case of the anointed high priest, he must inadvertently both make the erroneous decision and also carry it out, thus M. 2:3A–B. The first of the Talmud's two units chooses for its inquiry a continuing issue, in no way relevant to the Mishnah-pericope before us. Not only so, but I.D–F are repeated from M. 1:8 **VII.**A–C and hardly contribute to answering the question raised at I.A. In all, it is not a felicitous discussion. **II**, by contrast, does raise an important and relevant question. Since the rule of M. 2:3A is followed by an explicit application of that rule to the anointed priest (B), and since the rule at M. 2:3C does not carry in its wake a parallel statement, we must ask why. There are two possibilities. First, the omission of a parallel to B is because the formulator of the Mishnah, that is, Judah the Patriarch, does not deem the anointed high priest to fall under the rule of C at all. Second, the Mishnah's formulator deems it obvious that C does pertain to the anointed high priest and regards it as unnecessary to say so. This is the force of the question at **II**.A. Once the question is understood, the rest of the discussion is clear. Huna states matters clearly (B–E), and at F the argument from the style of the Mishnah is dismissed.

2:4

[A]   *[The court] is liable only [if they will give an erroneous decision] in a matter, the deliberate commission of which is punishable by extirpation, and the inadvertent commission of which is punishable by a sin-offering,*

[B]   *and so in the case of the anointed [high priest],*

[C]   *and [they are] not [liable] in the case of idolatry, except in the case [in which they gave instruction] in a matter the deliberate commission of which is punishable by extirpation, and the inadvertent commission of which is punishable by a sin-offering.*

[I.A]   "[If anyone sins unwittingly in any of] the things which the Lord has commanded [not to be done]" (Lev. 4:2)—

[B]   I might have said, Also those who eat abominations and creeping things are included in consideration [so that even if a court gave instruction concerning one of the commandments, the deliberate commission of which is *not* punishable by extirpation, the court would be liable for the bullock].

[C]   Here ["And the thing is hidden] from the eyes [of the assembly"] is stated, and [with regard to idolatry, Num. 15:24.] later on, ". . . from the eyes . . ." is stated. Just as "from the eyes" stated later refers to a matter, the deliberate commission of which is punishable by extirpation and the inadvertent commission of which is punishable by a sin-offering, so the reference to "from the eyes" in the present context means to refer to a matter, the deliberate commission of which is punishable by extirpation and the inadvertent commission of which is punishable by a sin-offering.

[D]   Or perhaps just as "from the eyes" mentioned later refers to a matter that is subject to the death penalty inflicted by the court [if there are witnesses and admonition], so "from the eyes" stated here refers to a matter that is subject to the death penalty administered by the court?

[E]   [The following is to be deleted: Said R. Yosé bar Hanina, "In
the context in which all of the prohibited relationships are
listed and stated to be subject to extirpation, e.g., a marriage
between close relatives, the father's wife explicitly listed
(though it did not have to be), to give evidence concerning the
mamzer." In place of the above, the following is to be supplied.
Num. 15:24ff., assumed to deal with idolatry, is clear that the
penalty is the sacrifice of the bullock. The penalty of death is
specified for idolatry, but not in this context. That is the meaning of the following statement, following the text given by Pené
Moshe and demanded by **II**.C:]

Said R. Yosé b. R. Hanina, "In the context in which
idolatry is discussed, dealing with those who are liable to extirpation, the sole penalty therein specified concerns extirpation.
The matter of the death penalty derives from another place [in
Scripture]."

[**II**.A]   Rabbi says, "'LYH . . . 'LYH . . . : Here it is said, '[If the
whole congregation of Israel commits a sin unwittingly and the
thing is hidden from the eyes of the assembly . . . , when the
sin] which ('LYH) [they have committed becomes known . . .]'
(Lev. 4:13–14), and there it is said '[And you shall not take a
woman as a rival wife to her sister, uncovering her nakedness]
while ('LYH) [her sister is yet alive]' (Lev. 18:18).

"Just as 'LHY which is stated later on [Lev. 18:18] refers to
a matter, the deliberate commission of which is punishable by
extirpation and the inadvertent commission of which is punishable by a sin-offering, so 'LYH stated here [Lev. 4:13–14] refers to a matter, the deliberate commission of which is
punishable by extirpation and the inadvertent commission of
which is punishable by a sin-offering."

[B]   Now why did Rabbi not accomplish the same exegetical purpose by deriving the desired lesson from the congruence of
"from the sight . . . ," "from the sight . . ."?

[C]   Said R. Yosé, "Now if Rabbi should have accomplished the desired exegesis through reference to 'from the sight . . . ,' 'from
the sight . . . ,' he might have drawn the conclusion that, just
as 'from the sight' stated later on [with reference to idolatry,
Num. 15:24] refers to a matter that may be subject to punishment of the death penalty administered by the human court
[**I**.D], so 'from the sight . . .' referred to here [Lev. 4:13–14]
speaks of a matter that is subject to punishment inflicted by a

human court. It was on this account that Rabbi did not accomplish the desired exegesis by reference to the confluence of "from the sight . . . ,' 'from the sight. . . .'

[D]   "But in the end, will Rabbi not have to resort to the exegesis based upon the confluence of 'from the eyes . . . ,' 'from the eyes . . .'?

[E]   "For if he does not [do so], how will he know the law concerning the individual, the prince, and the anointed priest? Is it not from the confluence of 'from the sight . . . ,' 'from the sight . . .'?

[F]   "And if he does not do so, how will he know that the erroneous instruction of a high court [is comparable to the erroneous decision of] an ordinary court? Is it not from the confluence of 'from the sight. . . . ,' 'from the sight . . .'?"

[G]   Said R. Ḥananiah in session before R. Mana, "[The fact that the bullock offeirng is not required] unless [the court] gives an erroneous decision to nullify part of the law and to affirm part of the law—is that not derived by exegesis from the confluence of 'from the sight . . . ,' 'from the sight . . .'?

[H]   "And [if you do] not [maintain that] same position, how does [Rabbi] know that the erroneous instruction given by an ordinary court [is punishable by the bullock-offering]? Is it not from the confluence of 'from the sight' 'from the sight'?"

[I]   Said R. Ḥananiah in session before R. Mana, "But in the end, will Rabbi not have to resort to the exegesis based on the confluence of 'from the eyes . . . ,' 'from the eyes. . . .'?"

[J]   He said to him, "Now just what do you demand of Rabbi?

[K]   "Rabbi is consistent with his position held elsewhere, for Rabbi said, 'The anointed priest is subject to the rule only of an act of transgression which is performed inadvertently' [M. 2:3A–B].

[L]   " 'And the matter of deliberate instruction in error of a sin along with inadvertent commission of that sin is written not with reference to an individual [such as the anointed priest] but only with reference to a court.' "

[III.A]   "[And the anointed priest shall take some of the blood of the bull and bring] it [to the tent of meeting]" (Lev. 4:5).

The explicit reference to *it* [that is, to the blood of the bull] serves as an exclusionary clause, to exclude his offering for the violation of the special commandment [idolatry], indicating that the blood should not enter inside [and be tossed on the gold altar].

[B]   Is this teaching not in accord with the position of Rabbi?

[C]   For Rabbi [46d] said, "The anointed priest is culpable in the case of a deed done inadvertently."

[D]   And it is not in accord with the position of rabbis, who maintain that the anointed priest [also] is subject to the bullock-offering in the case of *something's being hidden* [that is, giving an erroneous decision] [cf. 2:3 **II**].

[E]   Said R. Huna, "It is required also for the position of the rabbis, so that you may not rule, 'Since he is subject to extirpation, let the blood of his offering enter into the inner sanctuary.'

[F]   "On this account it was necessary to state explicitly, *It*, excluding his offering for violating the special commandment [of idolatry], to specify that in such a case, the blood of his offering should not be taken inside."

Since the provisions of Leviticus 4 lead to the offering of a bullock, described specifically as a sin-offering, the Mishnah now makes explicit the obvious fact that the court and anointed priest are liable for the sin-offering of a bullock in the case of their giving an erroneous decision in a matter for which, to begin with, a sin-offering is called for. This is precisely that sort of deed which, done deliberately, is punished by extirpation. M. Ker. 1:1–2:2 lists those transgressions in the Torah subject to extirpation if people do them deliberately, and subject to the bringing of a sin-offering if people do them inadvertently. Thirty-six in all are listed at M. Ker. 1:1 (*Holy Things* 5, pp. 7ff.). The Talmud here simply wishes to discover the source of that rule and to explore the implications of the verses adduced in proof of it. The opening unit, **I**, goes over the ground. E poses a major problem, which Pené Moshe solves, as I have indicated, by providing a completely different text for Yosé bar Ḥanina's saying. The position of Rabbi on the exegetical foundations of the Mishnah's rule is the focus of interest (**II**), and

the reason he rejects the exegetical proof given at **I** is specified
(**II**.H). A better text for **I**.D–E may be constructed out of the
materials of **II**.A–C. The textual problems run on through **II**
itself, since there is an obvious repetition of F at H, not to
mention of G at I. The gist of the matter is that the scriptural
origins of critical propositions derive from the very exegesis rejected by Rabbi. Mana's answer (K) at the surface pertains to
E. Rabbi indeed does not deem the anointed priest to be subject to provisions of the law providing for a bullock-sacrifice in
the case of incorrect instruction by a court and consequent
commission of a sin by the community. In Rabbi's view, M.
2:3A–B apply to the court, not to the high priest. So far as
Rabbi is concerned, for an individual, culpability is for inadvertent sin, not for inadvertent error in issuing a decision. For
who cares what decisions individuals issue? This is very com-
monsensical. Underneath, Mana holds, all the objections of
D–I, therefore, are null. Rabbi rejects the very propositions, to
maintain which he is supposed to require the stated exegesis.
The relevance of **III** to **II** is located at **III**.D. Rabbis link the
laws governing "the special commandment," namely, idolatry,
to those governing the violation, through inadvertent decision
and action, of all the other commandments. This is on the basis of the confluence of the two usages of "from the eyes. . . ."
Rabbi rejects all the consequences of that view, as Mana has
just implied, so he also does not deem the anointed priest to be
subject to the law of idolatry should he merely give erroneous
instruction, that is, just as we saw above (2:3). So **III** supplements interest of **II** in Rabbi's position on the role of the
anointed priest, and his position is that the priest is culpable
for deed, not decision. We may also observe that when the
anointed priest brings the offering on his own account, he
brings the blood to the altar in front of the tent of meeting's
veil (Lev. 4:5), so he puts the blood on the horns of the altar at
the door of the tent of meeting. But when he brings the blood
for the court's offering (Lev. 4:13ff.), he puts it on the horns of
the altar that is *in* the tent of meeting (Lev. 4:18). Now, A
points out, that specification means the blood of the offering of
the anointed priest is not brought *into* the inner altar. Why not?
My guess is that, because, in line with Rabbi's thinking, while
the anointed priest is culpable in case of an inadvertent sin, he
is not culpable in case of erroneous instruction. So he atones
for a sin different from that for which the court of Lev. 4:13ff.
atones. In consequence, the blood of the one is put on an altar

different from the blood of another. That is the theory of B–D, which, as we see, really serve to link 2:4 **II** to 2:3. Huna replies that that is not the case, for the rabbis concur that the anointed priest's offering's blood is not taken into the inner altar (E–F), in the case of violating the law against idolatry. Num. 15:24ff. is not clear on this point, and a proof is required so that the effect of linking Lev. 4:1ff. to Num. 15:24ff. ("from the eyes . . .") will not yield a false proposition. So the exegesis cited at **III**.A need not accord only with Rabbi, who excluded the anointed priest from culpability to a bullock-offering in the case of idolatry inadvertently carried out. It also accords with the rabbis' view and is necessitated by their position.

2:5

[A]   *They are not liable on account of [a decision inadvertently violating] a positive commandment or a negative commandment concerning the sanctuary.*

[B]   *And they do not bring a guilt-offering for an unverified offense on account of [violation of] a positive commandment or a negative commandment concerning the sanctuary.*

[C]   *But they are liable for [violating] a positive commandment or a negative commandment involving a menstruating woman.*

[D]   *And they do bring a suspensive guilt-offering on account of [violation of] a positive commandment or a negative commandment concerning a menstruating woman.*

[E]   *What is a positive commandment concerning a menstruating woman? To keep separate from a menstruating woman.*

[F]   *And what is a negative commandment? Not to have sexual relations with a menstruating woman.*

[I.A] [The reason that they do not bring a guilt-offering for an unverified offense on account of violation of a positive or negative commandment concerning the sanctuary, M. 2:5B,] Kahana said, [is that] it is not possible that there will have been knowledge at the outset and at the end [of violation of the laws of cleanness of the sanctuary], with an interval of inattention in the middle. [So there is no solid moment of doubt, on account of which a guilt-offering for an unverified offense would be required.]

[B]   Responded R. Samuel bar Abdimi in session before R. Mana, "And let it be so [that a guilt-offering is required] in the case of those who give an erroneous instruction, [so causing uncleanness for the sanctuary and its Holy Things]."

[C]   He said to him, "We require [the reason that] those who enter [the sanctuary in a state of uncleanness themselves do not bring a suspensive guilt-offering = M. 2:5B], and now are you bringing us the case of those who give erroneous instruction [about the uncleanness of the sanctuary and its Holy Things]?!"

[D]   What is the upshot of the matter?

[E]   Said R. Samuel bar R. Isaac, "['If any one sins unwittingly in any of] the commandments [which the Lord has commanded not to be done,'] (Lev. 4:2) . . . ['If any one sins, doing any one of the] commandments [which the Lord has commanded not to be done, though he does not know it, yet he is guilty and shall bear his iniquity' (Lev. 5:17)].

[F]   "Just as 'commandments' stated below involves an offering the value of which is fixed, so 'commandments' stated here involves an offering the value of which is fixed [excluding the possibility of a suspensive guilt-offering, which is of variable, not fixed, value. The offering of variable value is called for at Leviticus 5 for contamination of the sanctuary].

[II.A]   And are they not liable on account of [violation of] any positive commandment that is in the Torah [and not only for the menstrual taboo, M. 2:5C–F]?

[B]   Said R. Mattenaiah, "We come to repeat the tradition only with regard to matters similar to one another."

[C]   What would be an exemplary case [in which uncleanness of the sanctuary and of menstrual taboo would be comparable]?

[D]   [If] someone entered the sanctuary while unclean, he is liable.

[E]   [If] he was clean when he entered and [while in the Temple] was made unclean, if he then came along [outside] through the longer route, he is liable. [If he exited] through the shorter route, he is exempt.

[F]   And along these same lines, if one was having sexual relations with an unclean woman, he is unclean.

[G]   [If] he was having sexual relations with one who was clean, and she said to him, "I have just become unclean," if he then exited through the longer route, he is liable.

[H]   If he exited through the shorter route, he is exempt.

[I]   What is his shorter route?

[J]   That he [refrained from withdrawing until] he became limp.

[III.A]   *What is a positive commandment concerning a menstruating woman [M. 2:5E]?*

[B]   Said R. Abin, " 'Thus you shall keep the people of Israel separate from their uncleanness [lest they die in their uncleanness by defiling my tabernacle that is in their midst]' (Lev. 15:31)."

[C]   R. Yoḥanan sent to ask R. Simeon b. R. Yosé bar Laqonia, "Where do we find a warning [against violating the law] for the one who has sexual relations with an unclean woman?"

[D]   And he wanted to throw a heap of stones at him! He said, "Something which every child can tell you in school any day of the week is what you're asking me! [The relevant verse is,] 'You shall not approach a woman to uncover her nakedness while she is in her menstrual uncleanness'!"

[E]   He said to him, "But that is not what I needed to know. This is what I needed:

[F]   "If one was having sexual relations with one who was unclean, he is liable. If he was having sexual relations with one who was clean, and she said to him, 'I have become unclean,' if he then withdrew forthwith, what is the law as to his being liable?"

[G]   He said to him, "Both you and I need to know the answer to that question. Let's go out and learn it."

[H]   They went out and heard the voice of a repeater of traditions who was teaching the following tradition in the name of Ḥezekiah:

[I]   " 'And if any man lies with her, [and her impurity is on him, he shall be unclean seven days]' (Lev. 15:24).

[J]   "I know only that he who has sexual relations with an unclean woman is liable. If one was having sexual relations with a clean woman, and she said to him, 'I just became unclean,' if he separated forthwith, what is the law as to his being liable?

[K]   "Scripture says, 'And her impurity is on him'—and even if he separated from her, her uncleanness is on him."

[L]   What should he do?

[M]   R. Hoshaiah, R. Judah in the name of Samuel, "[Let him not withdraw until] he grows limp."

[N]   [If he] did not grow limp?

[O]   Said R. Yosé, "I recite concerning him the scriptural verse, 'Do not draw near,' meaning, 'Do not withdraw' [until he may do so without deriving sexual enjoyment]."

[P]   Drawing near is the same as withdrawing?

[Q]   R. Huna in the name of R. Abba, "Indeed, so, in accord with the following verse: '. . . who say, Keep to yourself, do not keep near me, for I am set apart from you' (Is. 65:5)."

[R]   Said R. Zeira, "Let him regard the sword as if it is cutting into his flesh and his whole body with it[, and he will cool off]."

[S]   R. Zeira, R. Tanhuma in the name of R. Huna, "Let him dig his fingers into the wall, and he will cool off."

[IV.A]   It is written [concerning Joseph before Potiphar's wife], "Yet his bow remained unmoved" (Gen. 49:24).

[B]   R. Samuel bar Nahman: "The bow became tense and returned [and turned limp]."

[C]   Said R. Abun, "His semen became diffused and spit forth from his finger nails."

[D]   "His arms were made agile" (Gen. 49:24).

[E]   R. Huna in the name of R. Mattenaiah, "He closed his eyes and saw the visage of [Jacob,] our father. Forthwith he cooled off."

[F]   "By the hands of the Mighty One of Jacob" (Gen. 49:24).

[G]   Said R. Abin, "Even the visage of Rachel did he see: 'By the name of the Shepherd, the Rock of Israel' (Gen. 49:24)."

The sin-offering serves, as we now know, to expiate those matters subject to the erroneous instruction and unwitting sin by
priest, ruler, and people of Leviticus 4. What the Mishnah now
points out is that, if an offering different from a sin-offering is
involved as a penalty for a sin, then the issue of erroneous instruction and unwitting sin—that is, the matter of Leviticus
4—is not raised at all. What is excluded, then, is the sort of sin
for which a guilt-offering, not a sin-offering, is required. Specifically, the sins listed at Leviticus 5 (1) hearing a public adjuration to testify and refraining from doing so, (2) imparting
uncleanness to the Temple and its Holy Things, (3) taking a
rash oath and the like, for which expiation through a guilt-offering is prescribed, are not going to fall within the framework
of the bullock brought in behalf of an unwitting sin committed
by the community, e.g., because of the erroneous decision or
instruction of a public official. That is the point of M. 2:5A–B,
and it also requires the qualification of M. 2:5C–F. What is a
specified type of sin expiated through a sin offering, representa-
tive of those for which the matter of improper decision and unwitting sin do form a consideration? The Talmud's treatment of
the matter provides an exegesis of the Mishnah's two principal
points, first, its opening assertion, second, its curious allusion
to only one commandment, the menstrual taboo. The former
discussion presents no problems. The latter provides the excel-
lent solution that there is an analogy to be drawn between contaminating the sanctuary and violating the menstrual taboo,
since there are parallel circumstances, which are specified at **II**.
III then provides the expected secondary amplification of **II**,
and **IV** tacks on a thematic complement to **III**.

2:6

[A] *They are not liable because of inadvertent violation of the law
concerning hearing "the voice of adjuration" [Lev. 5:1], a rash
oath [Lev. 5:4], or imparting uncleanness to the sanctuary and
to its holy things [Lev. 5:3]—*

[B] *"and the ruler follows suit," the words of R. Yosé the Galilean.*

[C] *R. ʿAqiba says, "The ruler is liable in the case of all of them,*

[D] *"except in the case of 'hearing the voice of adjuration.'*

[E] *"For: 'The king does not judge and others do not judge him,*

[F]   " 'does not give testimony, and others do not give testimony
concerning him' [= M. San. 2:2]."

[I.A]   Said R. Yoḥanan, "The scriptural basis for the position of R.
Yosé the Galilean [excluding the ruler from liability to the offering of variable value required by the rules of Lev. 5:1ff. is to
be found at Lev. 5:7]: 'But if he cannot afford a lamb' (Lev.
5:7). [Scripture speaks] of one who can fall into poverty, thus
excluding the anointed priest [better: *ruler*] who cannot fall into
poverty."

[B]   Simeon b. Levi said, "[Proof for the same proposition derives
from a different verse, namely, Lev. 5:5], 'When a man is
guilty in any of these. . . .' One who is liable to all of them is
liable to some of them, and one who is not liable to all of them
is not liable to some of them. [The king will not be poor, so is
excluded.]"

[C]   R. Isaac asked, "If so, he should not be subject to becoming
unclean through ṣaraʿat, for he is not suitable to fall into poverty [cf. Lev. 14:21: 'But if he is poor and cannot afford so
much']. And so is the rule for poverty, and so for the most
poverty-stricken."

[D]   R. Hoshaiah asked, "If so, a woman should not be liable for
entering the sanctuary [in a state of uncleanness, for she is not
liable to the voice of adjuration, not being able to testify, so she
is not subject to all the rules]!"

[E]   But does not a woman bring an offering?! [Obviously she does
if she contaminates the sanctuary.]

[F]   R. Yosé in the name of R. Yoḥanan, "The basis for the ruling
of R. ʿAqiba [who excludes the anointed priest] is as follows:

[G]   " 'This is the portion of Aaron and of his sons [from the offerings made by fire to the Lord]' (Lev. 7:35).—This he brings,
and he does not bring any other tenth of an *ephah* [as specified
at Lev. 5:7]."

[H]   R. Zeira asked in session before R. Yasa, "And does he not
bring a freewill offering?"

[I]   He said to him, "Of course. An offering brought as an obligation he will not bring. A freewill offering he most certainly will
bring."

[**II**.A]   And what the Mishnah itself teaches [which is relevant to M. 2:6D is]: A king does not give testimony, and others do not give testimony concerning him [M. San. 2:2, so he will not be subject to the oath or an offering for violating it].

The Mishnah goes back over the rule of M. 2:5, with two fresh exclusions, and forms a transition to the matter of the ruler, Lev. 4:22. C–D are explained by F. As I explained just now, the point is that if a court, high priest, or ruler inadvertently gave and carried out an erroneous decision on a matter of an oath of testimony (M. Sheb. 4:2–3), a rash oath (M. Sheb. 3:7), or cultic contamination (M. Sheb. 1:1, 2–4), there is no bullock-offering. The several exclusions make sense when we consider that the violation of the oath of testimony (Lev. 5:1ff.) is punishable by an offering of variable value. In that very same context is reference to becoming unclean (Lev. 5:3) and the rash oath (Lev. 5:4). When a person is guilty of any of these three sins, he brings a sin-offering, a female from the flock, a lamb, or a goat for a sin-offering (Lev. 5:7). If he cannot afford the birds, he brings a tenth of an *ephah* of fine flour (Lev. 5:11). Scripture is clear that these offerings of variable value apply specifically to the three sins listed at A. The Talmud concentrates on supplying an explanation for Yosé the Galilean's view (I.A, B). At C and D, this reasoning is challenged, but the discussion stops before a full reply is provided. G–I then go on to treat ʿAqiba's position, and at **II**, the Talmud specifies that portion of the cited Mishnah-pericope which accounts for ʿAqiba's position, a minor clarification.

2:7   [In Leiden MS and *editio princeps*: 2:8]

[A]   *In the case of all the commandments in the Torah, on account of which they are liable for deliberate violation to extirpation, and on account of inadvertent violation to a sin-offering,*

[B]   *an individual brings a female lamb or a female goat [Lev. 4:28, 32];*

[C]   *a ruler [brings] a male goat [Lev. 4:23];*

[D]   *and an anointed [high priest] and a court bring a bullock [M. 1:5, 2:1].*

[E]   *But in the case of idolatry, the individual, ruler, and anointed*
       [high priest] bring a female goat [Num. 15:27].

[F]   *And the court brings a bullock and a goat [M. 1:5],*

[G]   *a bullock for a whole offering and a goat for a sin-offering.*

[H]   *As to a guilt-offering for an unverified offense, an individual*
       and a ruler may become liable,

[I]   *but the anointed [high priest] and court do not become liable.*

[J]   *As to guilt-offering for a verified offense, an individual, a ruler,*
       and an anointed [high priest] may become liable, but a court is
       exempt.

[K]   *On account of "hearing the voice of adjuration," a rash oath,*
       and imparting uncleanness to the sanctuary and its Holy
       Things, a court is exempt, but an individual, a ruler, and an
       anointed [high priest] are liable.

[L]   *"But a high priest is not liable for imparting uncleanness to the*
       sanctuary and its Holy Things," the words of R. Simeon.

[M]   *And what do they bring? An offering of variable value.*

[N]   *R. Eliezer says, "The ruler brings a he-goat."*

[I.A] "[If] anyone [sins doing any one of the things which the Lord
       has commanded not to be done, though he does not know it,
       yet he is guilty]" (Lev. 5:17). [The reference to] anyone [is
       meant to encompass] the ruler[, that he is liable to a suspensive
       guilt-offering under the stated circumstance, as at M. 2:7H].

[B]   And let [the law] also encompass the anointed priest?

[C]   "[And the priest shall make atonement for him] for the error
       which he committed unwittingly [and he shall be forgiven]"
       (Lev. 5:18). One who is subject to the rule of unwitting com-
       mission of a sin is subject to the suspensive guilt-offering, ex-
       cluding the anointed priest, who is not subject to a bullock-
       offering in the case of unwitting commission of a sin [M. 2:7I].

[D]   And in accord with Rabbi, who maintained that an anointed
       priest indeed is subject to bringing a bullock for unwitting
       commission of a sin, [one may state matters as well]: He who is
       liable [to a bullock-offering for unwitting commission of a sin]
       under all circumstances [falls under the stated rule], excluding

the anointed priest, who is not subject [to a bullock] for unwitting commission of a sin under all circumstances.

[E]   "[If] anyone [commits a breach of faith and sins unwittingly in any of the holy things of the Lord, he shall bring as a guilt offering to the Lord a ram without blemish out of the flock . . . it is a guilt offering]" (Lev. 5:15)—to encompass both the ruler and the anointed priest.

[F]   Here [at A] you state that ["anyone"] is meant to include the ruler, while there [at E] you maintain that it is meant to encompass the anointed priest [as well]?

[G]   [The rule for] the sin-offering is comparable [to the rule for] the guilt-offering.

[H]   Just as the sin-offering effects expiation and effects forgiveness, so the guilt-offering effects both expiation and forgiveness.

[I]   Thus excluded is the suspensive guilt-offering, which effects expiation but leaves over [the attainment of forgiveness], [since a sin-offering may yet be required].

[That is to say, one subject to a sin-offering may be subject to a guilt-offering of an unconditional character. The two are wholly comparable. The reason is that there is no further offering to be required. But the one subject to a suspensive guilt-offering may yet have to bring a sin-offering. So there is no link to be drawn to the suspensive guilt-offering, A–B. The anointed priest is excluded, because he is not subject to it, as at H–I.]

[**II**.A]   Thus one must repeat the Mishnah-pericope [at L, K]:

[B]   *"But the high priest is not liable for imparting uncleanness to the sanctuary and its Holy Things"*—the words of all authorities.

[C]   "And the ruler [is not liable] on account of hearing the voice of adjuration," the words of R. Simeon.

[D]   [Explaining why all parties concur at B,] said R. Yohanan, " 'Neither shall [the high priest] go out of the sanctuary or profane the sanctuary of his God' (Lev. 21:12)—lo, if he should go out [and become unclean], he has not profaned [the sanctuary of his God, anyhow]."

[E]   R. Asiyan, R. Yonah, R. Bun bar Kahana, raise the following question: "And lo, it is written, 'A widow, divorcee, woman who has been defiled, or a harlot—these he shall not marry [but he shall take to wife a virgin of his own people that he may not profane his children among his people]' (Lev. 21:14)—lo, [by the same reasoning we should conclude] if he should take such a woman as his wife, he does *not* profane [his children]! [This is clearly absurd.]"

[F]   So why [is the high priest not liable for the contamination of the sanctuary and its Holy Things]?

[G]   Said Ḥezekiah, " '[But the man who is unclean and does not cleanse himself,] that person shall be cut off from the midst of the assembly, [since he has defiled the sanctuary of the Lord]' (Num. 19:20).

[H]   "[The verse thus refers] to one whose offering [of atonement] is the same as that of the community [in general], excluding the anointed priest, whose offering [of expiation] is not the same as that brought by the congregation[, for he brings a bullock, while ordinary folk bring a lamb or goat]."

[I]   They answered [this attempted proof]: "Now lo, there is the ruler, and his offering is not the same as that of the community[, for he too brings a bullock, yet he is subject to the rule against imparting uncleanness to the sanctuary and its Holy Things, while the high priest is not subject to that rule]!"

[J]   But the offering of the ruler *is* equivalent to that of the community on the Day of Atonement.

[K]   And lo, there are the brethren of the high priest, the other priests[, whose offering is different from that of the community, so they too should not be subject to penalty for imparting uncleanness to the sanctuary and its Holy Things]?

[L]   Theirs is not the same as his on the Day of Atonement.

[M]   But their offering is the same as his on the other days of the year.

[III.A]   Said R. Yudan bar Shalom, "The [offerings of ruler and community] are the same in that blood of their offerings [in both cases] is put on the outer altar" [which explains M. 2:7H–I].

[B]   Said R. Yoḥanan, "R. Eliezer gave his ruling only in the regard to the matters of extirpation. [That is, Eliezer has the ruler bring a he-goat only in the case of his imparting uncleanness to the sanctuary and its Holy Things, for this is a case in which, in the case of deliberate transgression, there is the penalty of extirpation, and in the case of inadvertent transgression, a sin offering of fixed value. The law is the same in this case as in others of the same character of transgression.]"

[C]   R. Hoshaiah raised the question: "If so, let [Eliezer have] him make atonement even with an offering of fixed value [at M. 2:7E, with a he-goat, as is the offering in other matters involving extirpation]."

[D]   Said R. Yonah, "Was R. Hoshaiah offering the theory that the ruler was removed from liability in regard to the entire pericope? No, [R. Eliezer] treated him as equivalent to an ordinary person who was rich [and so excluded from the rule governing a poverty-stricken person, that is, from the offering of variable value. This then would remove the ruler from the law of M. 2:7L]."

[E]   Said R. Mana, "If R. Eliezer treated him as equivalent to an ordinary person who was rich [and so excluded him from the rule governing a poverty-stricken person, as above], then even on account of *hearing the voice of adjuration*, and a rash oath he should have excluded him [and the dispute of M. 2:7M–N should occur at M. 2:7K].

[F]   "For it was taught, 'R. Eliezer and sages did not differ concerning penalties for *hearing the voice of adjuration* and a rash oath, that he brings not a he-goat but a she-goat.' Concerning what did they differ? Concerning imparting uncleanness to the sanctuary and its Holy Things [alone].

[G]   "And in this case, R. Eliezer says, 'Since he is subject to extirpation, is that why he brings not a he-goat but a she-goat?' "

[H]   They answered [R. Eliezer], "Lo, there is the anointed priest in the setting of idolatry, and lo, he brings not a he-goat but a she-goat. [Why should he not bring a bullock? It is simply Scripture's decree, and we cannot compare one rule with another.]"

The suspensive guilt-offering is required (M. 2:6H–N) when there is a case of doubt of having committed a sin for which, on account of the certain commission thereof, one is obligated for a sin-offering of fixed value. If an individual or a ruler erred or gave an erroneous ruling (in the context of our tractate), and the error is subject to doubt, a suspensive guilt-offering is required. But an anointed high priest and a court are not liable for a suspensive guilt-offering. An unconditional guilt offering will come for five sorts of causes from an individual, ruler, or anointed high priest, as specified at M. Zeb. 5:5. Here the anointed high priest is included. The court is excluded, for the court becomes liable only in the case in which one would be subject to extirpation on account of a deliberate commission of a sin, as stated at M. 2:3. To complete the triplet, K goes over familiar ground of M. 2:4, 2:5. Simeon rejects this view. M glosses K. Eliezer rejects the concept that the ruler may bring an offering of variable value, because, as we have noted, the ruler is not ever deemed to be in a state of poverty in which such an offering is acceptable. He brings the goat-offering.

The Talmud's interest in explaining the Mishnah-pericope focuses upon the scriptural basis for the laws before us. The exegesis of the Mishnah centers upon why one or another category is excluded, e.g., the anointed priest and court at M. 2:7H–I, the court at J, the high priest at L. The Talmud's opening unit, I, explains why the ruler is included but the anointed priest is excluded (M. 2:7H–I). The exegesis of verses provides ample basis for the ruling. I.E then goes on to contrast the inclusion of the ruler and anointed priest at one point and the exclusion of the anointed priest at another. How can the same exegetical technique accomplish contradictory purposes? I.G–I effect the necessary differentiation. II proceeds to revise the sense of the Mishnah by making all parties agree on the position, M. 2:7L, which the Mishnah as we know it gives only to Simeon. The piece of text criticism in no way elicits comment. In fact, by analogy to III, II is to be assigned to Yohanan. At D, Yohanan provides a reason for the attempted revision, which he endorses. But Yohanan's position is rejected at E–F, supported at G–H, and further criticized at I–M. The attempted distinctions in the end do not work. Yohanan's position does not emerge without flaw. In fact, the Talmud's clear intent is to reject the position explained by Yohanan. The final unit, III, takes up the position of Eliezer, and here, too, it is Yohanan's interpretation of the matter that is the center of interest. Yohanan interprets the position of Eliezer (III.B), and

his position again is rejected (C). The remainder of the pericope continues to focus upon Eliezer's views. The Talmud as a
whole therefore works its way through the important or difficult points of the Mishnah, following the order of the Mishnah
and systematically taking up its problems.

4 Yerushalmi
Horayot Chapter Three

3:1   [In Leiden MS and *editio princeps*: 3:2]

[A]   *[47a] An anointed [high] priest who sinned and afterward passed from his office as anointed high priest,*

[B]   *and so a ruler who sinned and afterward passed from his position of greatness—*

[C]   *the anointed high priest brings a bullock,*

[D]   *and the ruler brings a goat [M. 2:6].*

[E]   *An anointed high priest who passed from his office as anointed high priest and then sinned,*

[F]   *and so a ruler who passed from his position of greatness and then sinned—*

[G]   *a high priest brings a bullock.*

[H]   *But a ruler is like any ordinary person.*

[I.A]   [L here cites M. 3:1E.] Said R. Eleazar, "A high priest who sinned—they administer lashes to him, but they do not remove him from his high office."

[B]   Said R. Mana, "It is written, 'For the consecration of the anointing oil of his God is upon him: I am the Lord' (Lev. 21:12).

[C]   "That is as if to say: 'Just as I [stand firm] in my high office, so Aaron [stands firm] in his high office.' "

[D]   Said R. Abun, " 'He shall be holy to you [for I the Lord who sanctify you am holy]' (Lev. 21:8).

70

[E]   "That is as if to say: 'Just as I [stand firm] in my consecration, so Aaron [stands firm] in his consecration.' "

[F]   R. Haninah Ketobah, R. Aha in the name of R. Simeon b. Laqish: "An anointed priest who sinned—they administer lashes to him by the judgment of a court of three judges.

[G]   "If you rule that it is by the decision of a court of twenty-three judges [that the lashes are administered], it turns out that his ascension [to high office] is descent [to public humiliation, since if he sins, he is publicly humiliated by a sizable court]."

[II.A]   R. Simeon b. Laqish said, "A ruler who sinned—they administer lashes to him by the decision of a court of three judges."

[B]   What is the law as to restoring him to office?

[C]   Said R. Haggai, "By Moses! If we put him back into office, he will kill us!"

[D]   R. Judah the Patriarch heard this ruling [of Simeon b. Laqish's] and was outraged. He sent a troop of Goths to arrest R. Simeon b. Laqish. [R. Simeon b. Laqish] fled to the Tower, and some say, it was to Kefar Hittayya.

[E]   The next day R. Yohanan went up to the meeting house, and R. Judah the Patriarch went up to the meeting house. He said to him, "Why does my master not state a teaching of Light [Torah]?"

[F]   [Yohanan] began to clap with one hand [only].

[G]   [Judah the Patriarch] said to him, "Now do people clap with only one hand?"

[H]   He said to him, "No, nor is Ben Laqish here [and just as one cannot clap with one hand only, so I cannot teach Torah if my colleague, Simeon b. Laqish, is absent]."

[I]   [Judah] said to him, "Then where is he hidden?"

[J]   He said to him, "In the Tower."

[K]   He said to him, "You and I shall go out to greet him."

[L]   R. Yohanan sent word to R. Simeon b. Laqish, "Get a teaching of Light [Torah] ready, because the patriarch is coming over to see you."

[M]   [Simeon b. Laqish] came forth to receive them and said, "The example that you [Judah] set is to be compared to the paradigm of your Creator. For when the All-Merciful came forth to redeem Israel from Egypt, he did not send a messenger or an angel, but the Holy One, blessed be he, himself came forth, as it is said, 'For I will pass through the land of Egypt that night' (Ex. 12:12)—and not only so, but he and his entire retinue.

[N]   "[What other people on earth is like thy people Israel, whom God went to redeem to be his people (2 Sam. 7:23).] 'Whom God went' [sing.] is not written here, but 'Whom God went' [plural—meaning, he and all his retinue]."

[O]   [Judah the Patriarch] said to him, "Now why in the world did you see fit to teach this particular statement [that a ruler who sinned is subject to lashes]?"

[P]   He said to him, "Now did you really think that because I was afraid of you, I would hold back the teaching of the All-Merciful? [And lo, citing 1 Sam. 2:23F.,] R. Samuel b. R. Isaac said, '[Why do you do such things? For I hear of your evil dealings from all the people.] No, my sons, it is no good report that I hear the people of the Lord spreading abroad. [If a man sins against a man, God will mediate for him; but if a man sins against the Lord, who can intercede for him? But they would not listen to the voice of their father, for it was the will of the Lord to slay them' (1 Sam. 2:23–25).] [When] the people of the Lord spread about [an evil report about a man], they remove him [even though he is the patriarch]."

Since the main point of M. 3:1E–H is that the high priest retains his consecrated status for all time, the Talmud's first question is the source for that ruling. Unit I provides ample exegetical proof. The second unit is devoted to the case of the punishment of a ruler. I have followed the version of the story as it appears at Y. San. 2:1.

3:2   [In Leiden MS and *editio princeps*: 3:3

[A]   [*If*] *they sinned before they were appointed, and then they were appointed,*

[B] lo, [so far as expiating the sin done prior to appointment] they have the status of any ordinary person.

[C] R. Simeon says, "If [their sin] became known to them before they were appointed, they are liable.

[D] "But if it was after they were appointed, they are exempt."

[E] And who is a ruler? This is the king, as it is said, "And does any one of all the things which the Lord his God has commanded not to be done" (Lev. 4:22)—

[F] a ruler who has none above him except the Lord his God.

[G] Who is the anointed [high priest]? It is the one who is anointed with the anointing oil [in the First Temple], not the one who is dedicated by many garments [in the Second Temple].

[H] There is no difference between the high priest who is anointed with anointing oil and the one who is dedicated with many garments, except for [the latter's obligation to bring] the bullock which is brought because of the [violation] of any of the commandments.

[I] There is no difference between a [high] priest presently in service and a priest who served in the past except for the bringing of the bullock of the Day of Atonement and the tenth of an ephah.

[J] This one and that one are equivalent in regard to the service on the Day of Atonement.

[K] And they are subject to the commandment concerning [marrying] a virgin.
And they are forbidden [to marry] a widow.

[L] And they are not to contract corpse-uncleanness on account of the death of their close relatives.

[M] Nor [as a sign of mourning] do they mess up their hair.

[N] Nor do they tear their clothes [on the occasion of a death in the family].

[O] And [on account of their death] they bring back a manslayer.

[I.A] Associates state the reason of R. Simeon [that if the sin becomes known after appointment, the priest or ruler is exempt from having to bring a sin-offering], because the rise to a position of power effects atonement for sin.

[B]   Said R. Yosé, "[The reason of R. Simeon is] that a man's [obligation to bring an offering on the occasion of] the sin and on that of knowledge of the sin are not equivalent to each other, [for when he sinned, he was an ordinary person, and liable for a she-lamb or she-goat, but the knowledge coming after appointment means that the sin is atoned for by a different sort of animal sacrifice. If the man had now committed the sin, the one appointed ruler would have to bring a he-goat and the anointed priest would have to bring a bullock]."

[C]   Now what is the practical difference between the two explanations just now given?

[D]   [The difference is whether R. Simeon differs also concerning] the opening unit of the chapter:

[E]   *An anointed priest who sinned and afterward passed from his office as anointed priest, and so a ruler who sinned and afterward passed from his position of greatness—the anointed priest brings a bullock, and the ruler brings a goat* [M. 3:1A–D]. [If the criterion is that reaching a position of greatness atones for sin, that does not apply, and Simeon will not differ. If the criterion is Yosé's, then Simeon will differ also at M. 3:1.]

[F]   [If] the sin of the man was subject to doubt [before he was appointed to high office, and afterward it became known that he indeed had committed the sin], in accord with the view of the one who holds that the rise to a position of high office effects atonement, just as it effects atonement in the case of a sin that one knows certainly has been committed, so it effects atonement in the case of a sin that is subject to doubt.

[G]   In accord with the view of the one who holds that [Simeon's reason is] that the man's [obligation to bring an offering on the occasion of] the sin and on that of knowledge of the sin are not equivalent to each other, here too the obligation to bring an offering on the occasion of the sin and the obligation to bring an offering at the moment of the knowledge of the sin are not equivalent to each other, [so the same consideration applies].

[H]   [If the high priest and ruler] sinned before they were appointed [and also sinned]after they were appointed [and then] they left their high office [and sinned yet a third time],

[I]   the one who maintains the position that the rise to a position of power effects atonement for sin [will hold] that the position of high office has effected atonement for the first of the two sins, but the man is liable for a sin-offering on account of the second and the third.

[J]   The one who maintains that [the man's obligation to bring an offering on the occasion of] the sin and on that of knowledge of the sin are not equivalent to each other[, will maintain the same position].

[K]   [A further point of difference may be shown in a case in which] they sinned in regard to *hearing the voice of adjuration*, a rash oath, or imparting uncleanness to the Sanctuary and its Holy Things.

[L]   The one who maintains the position that the rise to a position of greatness is the operative factor will rule here that even in this case rise to a position of power effects atonement. [The one who holds that the criterion is the difference in sacrifices required in the differing circumstances here will hold that the man now owes the offerings, since the same sacrificial animal is required both of an ordinary person and of the holder of high office.]

[M]   Said R. Mattenaiah, "Under no circumstances does rise to high office effect atonement for sin, unless [the fact that the person has attained the high office] is made known to the person [himself so that it may not be subject to doubt whether the sin took place before he was appointed or afterward]."

[II.A]   [If a person] ate half an olive's bulk [of forbidden fat] before he was appointed to high office and half an olive's bulk afterward [thus completing the minimum volume of an olive's bulk to become culpable], even in a single spell of inadvertence, he is exempt [from obligation to bring an offering. The half-olive's bulk eaten while the person was an ordinary man does not join together with the half-olive's bulk he ate after he rose to high office, since the offering required for the commission of such a sin differs in accord with the change in the person's status].

[B]   [If it is] a matter of doubt whether a person ate a half-olive's bulk [of forbidden fat] before he was appointed to high office, and it is a matter of doubt whether he ate a half-olive's bulk [of forbidden fat] after he was appointed to high office, he brings a suspensive guilt-offering.

[C]   Now do we really find a case in which a principal matter does
       not produce liability [for an offering, so that if we knew for
       sure that the man had done the deed as described above, he
       would be exempt, as at A], while when the matter is subject to
       doubt, he is liable?

[D]   Do we find no such case? [To the contrary:] If one [in a single
       spell of inadvertence] ate two olive's bulks of fat [and we do
       not know whether the pieces were forbidden or permitted fat],
       and you found out for certain [that the fat was the forbidden
       kind], the status of the second piece of fat remains subject to
       doubt [since we have no solid evidence that it too was forbid-
       den fat].

       [In this case the man's original obligation to bring a suspen-
       sive guilt-offering—an obligation that applies when we do not
       know about the status of either piece of fat—remains in place,
       on account of the second piece of fat. So here is an example in
       which a matter subject to doubt continues to impose liability. If
       later on the man discovers that the second piece of fat also was
       forbidden, he has to bring another offering. He then does not
       effect atonement through the offering that he had set aside on
       account of the first piece of fat.]

[E]   [Now it was on this case that] R. Jacob, the southerner, asked
       in the presence of R. Yosé; "[Now why should he not carry out
       his obligation through a single offering?] What do you want?
       [For] the fat that he ate he has effected atonement. [Since he
       ate both pieces of fat in a single spell of inadvertence, the offer-
       ing he brought on account of the first piece should cover all the
       fat he ate.]"

[F]   [Then] said R. Yosé, "[The fact that he ate both pieces of fat
       in a single spell of inadvertence makes no difference.] In regard
       to any matter that subjects a person [47b] to bring a suspensive
       guilt-offering, certain knowledge of a matter formerly subject
       to doubt imposes on the man the firm obligation to bring a sin-
       offering. [These are two distinct pieces of fat. If the matter
       subject to doubt is resolved, a sin-offering is required, and this
       is the case even for the second piece of fat.]"

[G]   Thus we have found a case in which an actual matter does not
       produce liability for an offering, while when the matter is sub-
       ject to doubt, there indeed is liability for an offering. [If the
       man had certain knowledge that both pieces of fat, eaten in a
       single spell of inadvertence, were forbidden, he would have

brought a single sin-offering, covering both. But since the status of the second piece is subject to doubt, it is separated from the first and imposes liability for an offering on its own.]

[H]   So here is a case in which the principal matter does not produce liability for an offering, while when the matter is subject to doubt, there indeed is liability for an offering.

[**III**.A]   [If a man] ate an olive's bulk of forbidden fat before he was appointed to high office, and an olive's bulk of forbidden fat after he was appointed to high office, in a single spell of inadvertence, he is liable only for a single [sin-offering, in line with I.A].

[B]   [If] it is a matter of doubt whether he ate an olive's bulk before he was appointed, and a matter of doubt whether he ate an olive's bulk after he was appointed, in a single spell of inadvertence, he is liable for only a single suspensive guilt-offering.

[C]   [If he did so] in two distinct spells of inadvertence, he is liable for two suspensive guilt-offerings.

[D]   [If] one ate three olive's bulks of forbidden fat, but thought that they were two, [that is, he became aware that two pieces were forbidden,] and he separated an animal for a sin-offering [and then discovered that the third piece of fat also was forbidden],

[E]   in accord with the position of R. Yoḥanan, [he has atoned,] for R. Yoḥanan maintains, "If one has effected atonement for part of a sin, he has effected atonement for the whole of it [so there is no need for another sacrifice]."

[F]   R. Simeon b. Laqish said, "If one has effected atonement for part of a sin, he has not effected atonement for the whole of it."

[G]   [If] one has eaten five olive's bulks [of fat, in a single spell of inadvertence], and he was informed about a matter of doubt concerning each one of them [individually], and afterward he was informed as a matter of certainty, after eating them all, [that they were forbidden fat],

[H]   R. Simeon b. Laqish said, "Mere knowledge of doubt imposes on him an obligation to bring a sin-offering. [The fact that a matter of doubt has arisen concerning each piece of fat, in sequence, divides the several acts of eating. Thus the man is lia-

ble to five sin-offerings when he discovers that he has eaten five
pieces of forbidden fat. 'Doubt divides the deed,' so to speak.]"

[I]   R. Yoḥanan said, "Mere knowledge of doubt does not impose
on him an obligation to bring a sin-offering."

[J]   R. Yosé b. R. Bun in the name of R. Samuel b. R. Isaac: "R.
Simeon b. Laqish concedes in the case of an anointed priest,
that mere knowledge of doubt does not impose on him an obligation to bring a sin-offering. [Doubt does not divide the
deed.]"

[K]   Now what is the scriptural basis for this position? [It is found
in the following verse:] "The guilt offering is like the sin offering[; there is one law for them]" (Lev. 7:7).

[L]   In the case of that deed for which one brings a suspensive
guilt-offering [in a case of doubt], knowledge that what had
been subject to doubt in fact was a sin imposes the obligation
to bring a sin-offering, and in the case of that deed for which
one does not bring a suspensive guilt-offering [in a case of
doubt], knowledge that what had been subject to doubt in fact
was a sin does not impose the obligation to bring a sin-offering.
[In the case of the sequence of actions, broken by doubt, the
man has to bring a suspensive guilt-offering for each piece of
fat. He likewise has to bring a sin-offering for each one, when
he learns that each piece of fat was, in fact, forbidden.]

[M]   The position attributed to R. Simeon b. Laqish has been
switched about. There [in the present instance], he maintains
that mere knowledge of doubt [= clarification of what had
been in doubt] imposes an obligation to bring a sin-offering[,
for the imposition of doubt breaks up a single, continuing act
of sinfulness into its components, each one subject to doubt on
its own, as we have just seen]. But here [in connection with M.
Shebu. 2:5], Simeon b. Laqish does not maintain that mere
knowledge of doubt imposes said obligation], that is, the position that knowledge subject to doubt is tantamount to certain
knowledge, so that it has the effect of distinguishing among
elements of a single sinful action; doubt does not break up a
single continuing act of sinfulness into its components].

[N]   There [in the present case] the reason of Simeon b. Laqish [is
that] the fact that he has to bring a suspensive guilt-offering
establishes the obligation [if what was subject to doubt becomes
certain knowledge that the man has sinned, he must bring a

sin-offering, since the requirement to bring a suspensive guilt-offering is transformed into the requirement to bring a sin-offering when one finds out he has sinned]. But here [in regard to M. Shebu. 2:5], what choice do you have? [The suspensive guilt-offering does not apply to imparting uncleanness to the sanctuary and its Holy Things, which is the case discussed here, for it is an offering of variable value, and we have already demonstrated that an offering of variable value is not brought in that regard. It must follow that there is sound reason to distinguish Simeon b. Laqish's two positions.]

[O]   The position imputed to R. Yoḥanan appears to be switched about. There [here] he has said that if part of a sin has been subject to atonement, the whole of it has been expiated, while he here has said the opposite. [The supposition is that Yoḥanan's reasoning is as follows. At the outset the man thought he had eaten two pieces of fat, but he was in doubt as to the third. Then, when he found out later on that he had eaten a third, we do not take account of what at the end he learned as a matter of certainty. We maintain that, since at the outset he was subject to doubt about the third, the sin-offering that he has offered assuming that he had eaten two pieces in some measure covers the third. But in the case that will now be cited, where we have five olive's bulks, he takes the position that clarification of what had been subject to doubt does *not* impose the obligation to bring a sin-offering. We follow the situation that prevails at the end, at which position the man had certain knowledge concerning all five pieces of fat.]

[P]   R. Yoḥanan made the statement only concerning the clarification that came at the end of the process, on which occasion there is no offering at all. [Yoḥanan's stated position applies to the case in which there is no offering, because part of the sin already has been expiated at that point at which the man made his offering for the two pieces of fat he ate at the outset. Yoḥanan's reasoning is not that clarification of what had been subject to doubt in regard to the third piece of fat constitutes a valid clarification. In his view clarification of the doubt is null. Now in the case of five pieces of fat, since the matter of doubt and its clarification does not serve to divide the act and to impose the requirement in the case of each of the five pieces for a suspensive guilt-offering in the case of doubt, and a sin-offering when the doubt is clarified, the act of clarification that comes at the end covers the entire case. The prior actions are deemed a single protracted case, and the clarification at the end thus covers all of them. That is why a single sacrifice suffices.]

[Q]   All concur that if the animal designated at the outset is yet available. [Yoḥanan maintains that it is not necessary to bring another offering on account of the third olive's bulk of forbidden fat, unless the man already has effected atonement for that which was clarified at the outset. Here he maintains that, if part of the sin has been expiated, the whole of it, subject to a single spell of inadvertence, has been covered. But if the animal has not been offered, he concedes that after the matter of the third olive's bulk of forbidden fat has been clarified, the man must separate another sin-offering to effect atonement for all three pieces. The one set aside at the outset is dismissed.]

[R]   What should he do with [the first animal designated as a sin-offering and now set aside]?

[S]   R. Yosé said, "It is held in anticipation of atonement. [It is put out to pasture until it is disfigured and sold, and with the proceeds one brings another animal for use for atonement.]"

[T]   Said R. Zeira, "In the case of any beast that is not fitting [for use for atonement], neither the beast nor the money received for the sale of the beast may be used. It is put to death forthwith [as is a beast set aside for a sin-offering, the owner of which has attained atonement through use of another beast and no longer requires this one. Since a sin-offering must be made for a particular sinful act, it cannot be used to cover some other sinful act]."

[IV.A]   [If] one has eaten five olive's bulks [of fat, before being appointed to office], and a matter of doubt concerning each one of the pieces of fat became known to the man once he had been appointed to office, and after he had left office [the matter of doubt was resolved into] certainty [that indeed the fat had been forbidden fat]—

[B]   in accord with the thesis of R. Simeon b. Laqish, he is exempt [from having to bring an offering], [for he maintains that a matter of doubt as to the status of what one has eaten is tantamount to knowledge that one has eaten forbidden fat. That is, doubt about what one has done distinguishes each act of eating from the others and imposes the requirement of bringing a suspensive guilt-offering when there is doubt, and a sin-offering

when the doubt is clarified. So what was subject to doubt before the man reached high office is clarified after he has
reached high office. So far as Simeon is concerned, the man is
exempt. The offering required at the point of the sin and the
offering required at the point of the clarification that the sin
has been committed are not the same offering.]

[C]   In accord with the thesis of R. Yoḥanan, he is liable [to bring
an offering, for we follow the man's status only when the matter is fully clarified. We do not take account of the status earlier. A matter of doubt is not deemed equivalent to a matter of
clarification of doubt. The prevailing situation at the end is de-
terminative. Now when the man is informed, after he has left
office, that he had sinned earlier, he is an ordinary person. So
the prevailing condition at the time of the sin (he was an ordinary person) and the prevailing condition at the time of the
clarification (*after* he has left office) are the same. There is no
reason that the man should not bring an offering. It is the same
sort of beast in both cases].

[D]   Now did R. Simeon b. Laqish rule to exempt the man and not
to impose liability on him? [Did Simeon b. Laqish take the position that a matter of doubt has the same effect as certain
knowledge so that the person would be *exempt* from an offering? Was his intention not solely so that we could *impose liability* for an offering on him? Even though the man has not got
certain knowledge of what he has done at the moment between
eating each piece of forbidden fat, but only knows of the possibility that he has sinned, still here we impose the requirement
of five sin-offerings. True, the doubt suffices to divide the protracted act of sinfulness into its component parts. But when the
result of making such a distinction is to free the man from having to bring a sin-offering, as in the case of the attempted
interpretation of the Mishnah-pericope, he would not take such
a position. So this reading of Simeon b. Laqish's position on
the Mishnah-pericope, in interpretation of the Mishnah's
Simeon's rule, is false.]

[E]   But thus the matter should be interpreted [to see how Simeon
b. Laqish would interpret the position outlined in the Mish-
nah-pericope]:

[F]   [If] one ate five pieces of fat the size of an olive's bulk, and
then the doubt concerning the status of this fat was made
known to the man before he was appointed to high office, and

[the man received] certainty about the forbidden status of the fat after he was appointed to high office,

[G]   in accord with the position of R. Simeon b. Laqish, who maintains that knowledge of the doubt concerning what he has done [divides the sequence of actions into their components and so] imposes on the man the obligation to bring a sin-offering, the man is liable [for five sin-offerings]. [Just as Simeon b. Laqish imposes a strict ruling in the case of the matter of doubt's dividing the action into its components, so he imposes a strict ruling in the case involving the Mishnah's R. Simeon where the man ate the forbidden fat before he was appointed to high office, and the matter of doubt was brought to his attention before his appointment, and after he was appointed the certainty that he had sinned became known. Here we maintain that a matter of doubt and a matter of certain knowledge have that same effect of dividing the sinful action into its components. So we have a case in which the offering required at the moment of sin and the offering required at the moment of clarification that sin has been committed are one and the same sort.]

[H]   In accord with the position of R. Yohanan, who maintains that knowledge of the doubt concerning what the man has done [does not impose distinctions among the several actions in eating the forbidden fat and so] imposes the obligation to bring a sin-offering, he is exempt. [Recognition of the possibility of doubt is not tantamount to certain knowledge that one has sinned. We follow the status of the man at the end of the process only. The man knew that he had sinned only after he was appointed to high office. The offering required for the sin is different from the one required at the moment that the sin became known. The man is exempt, in Yohanan's view of the Mishnah's R. Simeon.]

[I]   All concur that if the animal designated at the outset is yet available, it is set aside.

[J]   What should he do with [the first animal, designated as a sin-offering and now set aside]?

[K]   R. Yosé said, "It is held in suspense for atonement. [It is set out to pasture until it is disfigured and then it is sold, and with the proceeds one brings another animal for use for atonement]."

[L]   Said R. Zeira, "In the case of any beast that is not fitting [for use for atonement], neither the beast nor the money received for the sale of the beast may be used. It is put to death forthwith [for the reasons stated at **III**.T]."

[**V**.A]   [If] someone ate a half-olive's bulk of [forbidden] fat before he was appointed to high office, a half-olive's bulk of fat after he was appointed, and a half-olive's bulk of fat after he left office, [in a single spell of inadvertence, what is the law]?

[B]   Since the obligation to bring an offering [other than that brought for the first and third pieces] has applied in the meanwhile, do they [first and third] join together [so that an offering covering the two half-olive bulks of prohibited fat is required]? [The middle piece of fat does not join together with the first piece the man ate, when he was an ordinary person. All parties will concur on this point. But if he ate yet a third half-olive's bulk, then we have a problem. Do the two halves eaten while the man was an ordinary person join together? Or perhaps, since the half-olive's bulk eaten in the middle, while the man is in power, does not join together either with the first or with the third, it constitutes an interruption. The answer is as given at the outset: the first and third do join together to form the requisite bulk of forbidden fat to impose the obligation to bring a sin-offering.]

[C]   Let us infer the correct rule from the following case:

[D]   [If] there were three pieces of fat before a man, and he ate the first, and did not know that it was prohibited fat, [then he ate the] second during the same spell of inadvertence as had pertained to the first, but he then discovered concerning the first [that it was forbidden fat], but he was then not informed as to the status of the second,

[and then he ate] the third piece of fat during the spell of inadvertence governing the second piece of fat, and afterward he was informed about the condition of all of them [that all three were prohibited fat]—

[E]   R. Yoḥanan said, "He is liable on account of the first and second, but exempt on account of the third. [Since he learned of the inadvertent sin of the first during the spell of inadvertence covering the second, he is liable on account of the first by itself. There is no connection to the second. Knowledge concerning the first sin separates the protracted act of sinning, and the

second is a sin unto itself, even though it was originally committed in a single spell of inadvertence with the first. The same
is to be said of the second in regard to the third. But since the
third piece of fat was eaten during that same period of inadvertence governing the second, it is deemed part of the sin committed when the man ate the second piece of fat. Consequently
there is no further requirement to bring a sin-offering covering
the third piece of fat that the man inadvertently ate.]"

[F]   Said R. Yosé, "As to the second, the matter depends on the
man's own opinion. If he wanted, the matter of the second is
atoned for along with the first, and if he wanted, the matter of
the second is atoned for along with the third [piece of fat that
the man ate. The second piece of fat belongs with the first,
having been subject to the same spell of inadvertence. Still, it
may be assigned to the third, for the same reason. Consequently, the man may bring two offerings, one governing the
first, one governing the third, and the matter of the second is
assigned to expiation achieved by one or the other of the two
offerings. But of course the first and the third pieces of fat are
totally unrelated, since they were not eaten within a single span
of inadvertence]."

[G]   The associates compare the matter to [a case of one's having
eaten] four half-olive's bulks of forbidden fat. If one is smart,
he brings a single offering for all [four, that is, two complete
minimum volumes], and if not, he brings two offerings[, one
for each set of two half-olive's bulks].

What would be a concrete instance [of being stupid]? He
brings one offering for the first and second, and another offering for the third and fourth. [But if he is smart], he should
bring one offering for the two in the middle, [and] he then is
exempt from having to bring an offering for the first and for
the fourth half-olive's bulks [which are distinct and too small to
matter].

[H]   R. Yosé compares the matter to a case of eating whole olive's
bulks of forbidden fat[, each one of requisite volume to impose
liability]. If he was smart, he brings two offerings, and if not,
he brings three offerings.

What would be a concrete instance? He brings one offering
for the first and for the second, and one for the third and
fourth. If he should bring a single offering for the two in the
middle, however, then he is liable for an animal-sacrifice as a

sin-offering on account of the first piece of forbidden fat that he ate, by itself, and he also is liable for a separate animal-offering as a sin-offering for the fourth, by itself. [In Yosé's view the second animal belongs with the first, the fourth with the third, because there has been a single spell of inadvertence covering each pair. Consequently, if he decides to atone for numbers 1 and 2 together, he will suffice with two beasts, whereas if he decides to atone for numbers 2 and 3 together, he will have to bring three, one for number 1, one for number 4, and one for numbers 2–3. So the man has a choice, and will do well to make it as indicated.]

[I]   R. Isaac asked, "Is the rule also the same when it comes to [joining together the intervals required for] eating half-loaves of bread?" [We maintain that if one eats one olive's bulk of forbidden fat within the spell of inadvertence governing the one before it, the second is deemed to join together with the first to be subject to a single offering. Do we hold the same rule to apply to eating a sequence of half-loaves of bread? That is to say, the specified interval for a spell of inadvertence to apply is the time required to eat a half-loaf of bread. Isaac's question now is whether one such spell joins together with the distinct spells of time sufficient to eat a half-loaf, to form a very long, single, and protracted period of a single sin. So what Isaac wishes to know is whether a spell of inadvertence can run longer than the time it takes to eat a half-loaf.]

[J]   Said R. Yosé, "This entire matter of the question of R. Isaac is worthless! Now does the matter depend upon the interval for eating a half-loaf of bread at all? [That is, if we should conceive that the matter of an interval is measured by the joining together of the stated interval, then the interval—eating a half-loaf of bread—is meaningless. It suffices merely to specify a single spell of inadvertence, however long that spell may take. But in point of fact the two half-olive's bulks of forbidden fat join together if they are eaten within a single spell of inadvertence, which can be no longer, under any circumstances, than the time required for eating a half-loaf of bread. The entire conception stated by Isaac thus is based on a false conception. Yosé proceeds along these same lines as follows:]

[K]   "Now if the man had eaten a half-olive's bulk of forbidden fat during one interval of time sufficient for eating a half-loaf of bread, and another half-olive's bulk of forbidden fat during another interval sufficient for eating a half-loaf of bread, what difference would it make?

[L] "If he ate a number of olive's bulks of forbidden fat and a number of half-loaves of bread in a single spell of inadvertence, he is liable for only a single sin-offering."

[M] [What follows depends upon a dispute involving R. Yosé, parallel to the one we have just now considered. The materials not given in the Talmud's present unit are as follows: If on the Sabbath one has taken out a half of a dried fig from private to public domain and went back and took out another half of a fig, in a single spell of inadvertence, he is liable, since the volume necessary to impose liability for carrying an object from one domain to the other is a whole dried fig. But if he did so in two distinct spells of inadvertence, he is exempt. R. Yosé says, "If he did so in a single spell of inadvertence in the case of a single domain, he is liable. If he did so in a single spell of inadvertence but in regard to two different domains, or if he did so in two spells of inadvertence in regard to a single domain, he is exempt." So R. Yosé compares the matter of domains to the matter of eating a half-loaf of bread. If he ate a half-olive's bulk of forbidden fat in the interval of time sufficient for eating a half-loaf of bread, and another half-olive's bulk in another such interval, is he going to be liable? Yosé maintains that two distinct domains do not join together with each other, even if the person has taken out the requisite volume from the two of them, respectively, during a single spell of inadvertence. Likewise, the two pieces of fat should not join together. It is in this context that the following is stated:] The rabbis of Caesarea say, "Instead of comparing the matter to the eating of forbidden fat, let us compare it to the matter of the Sabbath.

[N] "[If] one has woven a single thread into one garment, and a single thread into some other garment, does this matter? [Certainly not. Liability for weaving on the Sabbath depends on weaving two threads. But it is only in a single garment that that measure applies. Threads woven into two different garments are not deemed to join together to impose the liability for a sin-offering.] If one has woven a number of threads into a number of garments in a single spell of inadvertence [moreover], he is liable for only a single sin-offering."

[O] [This case now permits us to return to the matter left off above (A), concerning eating a half-olive's bulk of fat before being appointed to high office, half while in office, and half after leaving office in a single spell of inadvertence. This brings us to the dispute of Yoḥanan and Yosé (E, F).] Now here is a case in which there is liability for an offering in the interval between the two other acts of sinfulness, and you rule that they do indeed join together, [so long as the spell of inadvertence is not broken. Similarly, the half-olive's bulk the man ate before he was appointed and the one he ate after he left office, in which case the same offering will be required of both incidents, do indeed join together, and are not split up by the imposition of a sin-offering for what he has done in the meantime.]

[P]   Said R. Abun, "There you have a case of the obligation to bring a single kind of offering, while here there is a requirement of a different sort of offering. [The cases are not parallel. Granted, there is an obligation to bring an offering. But the offering is the same for what he did in the interval, and for what he did before and afterward. Here there is a different offering for an ordinary person and for one in office.]"

[VI.A]   [If] one ate an olive's bulk of forbidden fat before he was appointed to office, and an olive's bulk of forbidden fat after he was appointed to office, and a third olive's bulk of forbidden fat after he left office [all in a single span of inadvertence],

[B]   in the opinion of Associates, who maintain that the rise to high office effects atonement, his rise to high office effects atonement on account of the first piece of fat he ate, but he remains liable on account of the second and the third pieces of fat he ate.

[C]   In the opinion of R. Yosé, who maintains that [the reason for Simeon's opinion at M. is that] the offering required at the time that he sinned and the one required at the time that he gained knowledge of having sinned [and so became liable for the offering] are not one and the same sort of animal, he is liable for the sin-offering to cover the first piece of fat he ate, and so too is he liable for a sin-offering on account of the second piece of fat he ate, but he is exempt from a sin-offering on account of the third piece of fat he ate.

[D]   [If] he ate an olive's bulk of forbidden fat, but it is a matter of doubt whether he did so before he was appointed to high office, or after he was appointed to high office,

[E]   or if it is a matter of doubt whether one did so before he converted to Judaism or after he had converted to Judaism,

[F]   or if it is a matter of doubt whether he did so before he produced two pubic hairs [and so became liable for his sins], or after he had produced two pubic hairs,

[G]   he brings a suspensive guilt-offering.

[H]   [If] he ate prohibited fat but it was a matter of doubt whether it was an olive's bulk, and it is not known whether he ate it on the Day of Atonement or whether he did so before the Day of Atonement,

[I]   in a matter of doubt involving atonement, [the Day of Atonement is assumed to have] effected atonement for him.

[J]   [If it is a matter of doubt] whether he ate it on the Day of Atonement or whether he ate it after the Day of Atonement,

[K]   the Associates rule, "In a matter of doubt involving atonement, [even part of the Day of Atonement is assumed to have] effected atonement for him."

[L]   Said R. Mattenaiah, "Under no circumstances in a matter of doubt involving atonement [is the Day of Atonement assumed to have] effected atonement, except in a case involving diverse kinds of blood [and we do not know the status of the blood a woman has produced]."

[M]   The following Mishnah-pericope supports the position of the Associates:

[N]   **In the case of the Sabbath that coincided with the Day of Atonement, if one has performed an act of labor at twilight [and does not know whether the act was performed on the Sabbath that coincided with the Day of Atonement, or whether it was performed on the prior day, which was not a holy day at all] [T. Ker. 2:16A]—**

[O]   now [from the viewpoint of Associates] how do you want to decide on the matter? [If] it was the Day of Atonement, that [part of the day that remained] effected atonement for him, and if it was an ordinary day, it was permitted to do the act of labor in any event [so the position of Associates, that in a matter of doubt involving atonement, the Day of Atonement is assumed to effect atonement, is valid in this case].

[P]   And lo, it is taught, ". . . and he ate" [that is, the case before us involves a doubt concerning whether it was an olive's bulk, and a doubt concerning when the man ate the fat to begin with].

[Q]   Said R. Yosé b. R. Bun, "[The dispute of Associates and Mattenaiah concerns] eating permitted food, [but doing so at twilight]." [Mattenaiah's position is that the Day of Atonement does not effect atonement for a matter of doubt concerning what the man has eaten; the twilight under discussion is the one at the end of the Day of Atonement. The Day of Atonement effects atonement only for a matter subject to doubt involving diverse kinds of blood, on account of doubts concerning which the man has to achieve atonement for an event that took place prior to the Day of Atonement. Sages maintain that the man is exempt from a suspensive guilt-offering, because if the event took place on the Day of Atonement, the remaining part of the Day of Atonement has effected atonement, and if it was afterward, then there is no reason to atone at all.]

[VII.A]   [If] one has eaten five olive's bulks of forbidden fat [in a single spell of inadvertence], and one was informed of a doubt concerning their character before he was appointed to high office, and then he was appointed to high office and thereafter learned that he certainly had eaten forbidden fat,

[B]   in accord with the opinion of R. Simeon b. Laqish, he is liable.

[C]   In accord with the opinion of R. Yohanan, he is exempt.

[D]   Now did R. Simeon b. Laqish rule to exempt the man and not to impose liability on him? [As above, IV.D.]

[E]   But thus the matter should be interpreted:

[F]   If one ate five pieces of fat the size of an olive's bulk, and the doubt concerning the status of this fat was made known to the man [47C] after he was appointed to high office, and [the man received information creating] certainty about the forbidden status of the fat after he had left his high office [cf. IV.E–F],

[G]   in accord with the opinion of R. Simeon b. Laqish, who maintains that if one has achieved atonement for part of a sin, he has not achieved atonement for the whole of it, the man is exempt.

[H]   In accord with the opinion of R. Yoḥanan, who maintains that if a man has attained atonement for part of a sin, he has attained atonement for the whole of it, he is liable.

[I]   All concur that if the animal designated to atone for the first sin is yet available, that it is set aside.

[J]   What should one do with [the first animal, designated as a sin-offering, now set aside]?

[K]   R. Yosé said, "It is held in suspense for atonement. [It is put out to pasture until it is disfigured and sold, and with the proceeds one brings another animal for use for atonement.]"

[L]   Said R. Zeira, "In the case of any beast that is not fitting [for use for atonement], neither the beast nor the money received for the sale of the beast may be used. It is put to death forthwith."

[M]   R. Yoḥanan concurs that, if the beast set aside for expiation of the first sin is available, it is put aside.

[N]   What should one do with it?

[O]   R. Yosé said, "It is held in suspense for atonement."

[P]   [Said R. Zeira, "In the case of any beast that is not fitting for use for atonement, neither the beast nor the money received for the beast may be used. It is put to death forthwith."]

[VIII.A]   On the following account, R. Yosé b. R. Bun raised a question.

[B]   [If] one ate five olive's bulks of forbidden fat [not knowing that it was forbidden], and he learned the true character of the first piece of fat he had eaten, and he designated an offering,

[C]   [and he learned the character of] the second [piece of fat he had eaten], and he designated an offering,

[D]   [and he learned the character of] the third [piece of fat he had eaten], and he designated an offering,

[E]   [and he learned the character of] the fourth [piece of fat he had eaten], and he designated an offering,

[F]   [and he learned the character of] the fifth [piece of fat he had eaten], and he designated an offering,

[G]   R. Yoḥanan said, "He achieves expiation for himself through the first animal [that he set aside and offered], for it comes before the act of eating of all of the other pieces of fat."

[H]   "And as to the disposition of the other animals, they are to fall to use for a freewill offering."

[I]   R. Simeon b. Laqish said, "He achieves atonement for himself through the last animal that he has set aside, for it is in regard to the end of eating of all the pieces of fat."

[J]   "And the other animals he has set aside are to be put away."

[IX.A]   R. Ḥisda and R. Hamnuna,—

[B]   R. Ḥisda takes up the position of R. Yoḥanan, and R. Hamnuna takes the position of R. Simeon b. Laqish.

[C]   R. Ḥisda objected to R. Hamnuna, "And lo, the Mishnah supports your position and is at variance with my position:

[D]   *"Just as if one ate forbidden fat and again ate forbidden fat in a single spell of inadvertence, he is liable for only a single sin-offering, so in connection with a situation of uncertainty involving [two bits of forbidden fat], he is liable to bring only a single guilt-offering. If there was a clarification in the meantime, just as he brings a single sin-offering for each and every transgression, so he brings a suspensive guilt-offering for each and every [possible transgression]* [M. Ker. 4:2].

[E]   "Now if the Mishnah-pericope had spoken only of a single guilt-offering, it would have been well [for my position. But here the Mishnah-pericope is explicit that Hamnuna's and Simeon b. Laqish's position is valid]."

[F]   Said R. Ḥinena [in response to the position of Ḥisda and Yoḥanan that a case of doubt does not divide a deed into its constituent parts], "Even so, the rule applies even for the cases before and after the interval in the middle. And so you find stated in Scripture, '. . . when a ruler sins' (Lev. 4:22) [—and not *if* a ruler commits a sin, as is the usage in other parts of the same pericope. This shift in the language of Scripture, from *if* the entire community shall sin, or *if* the anointed priest, and the like, indicates a shift in the law]."

[X.A]   ["When ('ŠR) a ruler sins".] Said Rabban Yoḥanan ben Zakkai, "Happy ('ŠRY) is he whose ruler brings a sin-offering."

[B]   For [the ruler's] sin committed inadvertently he brings [a sin-offering].

[C]   How much the more so will he bring an offering for the sin he commits deliberately!

[D]   If one's ruler brings a sin-offering, how much the more will an ordinary person [do so].

[E]   ["When] a ruler [sins"]. Might one suppose that Scripture refers to a ruler of one of the tribes, like Naḥshon?

[F]   Scripture [here] states, ". . . doing unwittingly any one of the things which the Lord his God has commanded not to be done" (Lev. 4:22). And elsewhere it states, ". . . so that [the king on the throne, who writes a copy of the Torah for himself] may learn to fear the Lord his God" (Deut. 17:19).

[G]   The use of "his God" in both contexts serves to establish the meaning through analogy. Just as in the latter context, the reference is to a ruler who is subject to no one but God, so in the former context, the reference is to a ruler who is subject to no one but God [cf. M. 3:2E–F].

[H]   "[There is a vanity that takes place on earth,] that there are ('ŠR) righteous men to whom it happens according to the deeds of the wicked, and there are wicked men to whom it happens according to the deeds of the righteous" (Qoh. 8:14). Happy ('ŠRY) are "the righteous, to whom it happens according to the deeds of the wicked" in this world [so they enjoy the world to come], and woe to the wicked "to whom it happens according to the deeds of the righteous" in this world [so they get what is coming to them in the next world].

[I]   As to the king of Israel and the king of Judah, the two of them are equals. This one is no greater than that, nor is that one greater than this one.

[J]   Now what is the scriptural basis for the preceding statement? It is to be found at the following: "Now the king of Israel and Jehoshaphat the king of Judah were sitting on their thrones, arrayed in their robes, at the threshing floor at the entrance of the gate of Samaria" (1 Kings 22:10)—[not on the floor but] at the threshing floor, as if [at an equal plane] on the threshing floor.

[K]   Said R. Yosé b. R. Bun, "And that is so, in particular, until
the time of Jehu son of Nimshi [from which time they were not
regarded as legitimate]. What is the scriptural basis? "[And the
Lord said to Jehu, 'Because you have done well in carrying out
what is right in my eyes and have done to the house of Ahab
according to all that was in my heart,] your sons of the fourth
generation shall sit on the throne of Israel' " (2 Kings 10:20).
But from that time onward, they seized [the throne] by thug-
gery."

[L]   *Who is the anointed priest? It is the one who is anointed with
the anointing oil, not the one who is dedicated by many garments* [M. 3:2G].

[M]   Said R. Huna, "For all those six months during which David
was on the run from Absalom, it was through a she-goat that
he would attain atonement for himself, like any ordinary person."

[N]   It was taught in a Tannaitic tradition: R. Judah b. R. Ilai says,
"As to the anointing oil that Moses prepared on the mountain,
miracles were done with it from beginning to end.

[O]   "For at the beginning it was only twelve *logs*, as it is said,
'And a *hin* [= twelve *logs*] of olive oil' (Ex. 30:24).

[P]   "If it was merely to anoint the *logs* of wood, there would not
have been enough. How much the more so [would this small
volume be lacking], since the fire fed on it, the kettle fed on it,
the wood fed on it. From it the tabernacle and all its utensils
were anointed, 'the altar and all its utensils, the candelabrum
and all its utensils, the laver and its base' (Ex. 30:27). From it
were anointed Aaron the high priest and his sons all seventy
days of consecration. From it were anointed high priests and
kings."

[Q]   A king at the outset requires anointing. A king who is son of a
king does not require anointing,

[R]   for it is said, ["And the Lord said to him,] Arise, anoint him,
for this is he" (1 Sam. 16:12)—this one requires anointing, but
his descendants do not require anointing.

[S]   But a high priest, son of a high priest, even in the tenth generation, requires anointing.

[T] "And yet all of [that original oil, used for so many purposes] remains for the age to come, as it is said, 'This shall be my holy anointing oil throughout your generations' (Ex. 30:31)."

[U] They anoint kings only by a spring, as it is said, ". . . and cause Solomon my son to ride on my own mule and bring him down to Gihon, and let Zadok the priest and Nathan the prophet there anoint him king of Israel" (1 Kings 1:33–34).

[V] They anoint kings only on account of strife. On what account was Solomon anointed? Because of the strife raised by Adonijah, and Joash, because of Athaliah, and Jehu, because of Joram.

[W] Now has it not been written as follows: "Arise, anoint him, for this is he," meaning, this one requires anointing, but the kings of Israel do not require anointing?

[X] And did not Josiah hide it away?

[Y] It was said that they were anointed by balsam oil.

[Z] Joahaz [was anointed] on account of Jehoiakim his brother, who was two years older than he.

[AA] They anoint kings only from a horn. Saul and Jehu, who were anointed from a curse, had a transient reign. David and Solomon, who were anointed from a horn, had an enduring reign.

[BB] They do not anoint priests as kings.

[CC] R. Judah of Ein-Todros: "This is on account of the verse that states, 'The scepter shall not depart from Judah' (Gen. 49:10)."

[DD] Said R. Ḥiyya b. Ba, " '[That he may not turn aside from the commandment . . . ,] so that he may continue long in his kingdom, he and his children, in Israel' (Deut. 17:20). What is written thereafter? 'The Levitical priests, that is, all the tribe of Levi, shall have no portion or inheritance with Israel' (Deut. 18:1)."

[EE] And is it not written, "The sons of Josiah, Johanan the first born" (1 Chron. 3:15)—first born to rule?

[FF] And is it not written, "The second Jehoiakim, the third Zedekiah, the fourth Shallum"? Zedekiah was third for the throne, and fourth in order of birth.

[GG]   He was called Zedekiah, because he accepted the righteousness of the harsh decree.

[HH]   Shallum was so called for in his time the household of David fulfilled its time.

[II]   His name was not really Shallum, nor was it Zedekiah, but it was Mattenaiah,

[JJ]   as it is written, "And the king of Babylonia made Mattenaiah, Jehoiachin's uncle, king in his stead, and changed his name to Zedekiah" (2 Kings 24:17).

[KK]   The priest was consecrated with anointing oil in the former [first] building [of the Temple], and was dedicated by many garments in the [time of] the latter building.

[LL]   And this view is in accord with that which R. Ina said in the name of R. Aḥa, "In five respects was the latter building of the sanctuary less than the former building of the sanctuary."

[MM]   What is the scriptural basis for this statement? "Go up to the hills and bring wood and build the house, that I may take pleasure in it and that I may appear in my glory, says the Lord" (Hag. 1:7–8).

[NN]   "These are the five things in which the latter house of the sanctuary was less than the former one, and these are they: fire, ark, Urim, Thummim, and holy anointing oil [none of which was available in the Second Temple]."

[**XI**.A]   It has been taught in Tannaitic tradition [cf. T. Hor. 2:3]: An anointed priest brings a bullock [in the case of issuing an erroneous decision], but a high priest consecrated by many garments does not bring a bullock [under the stated circumstances] [= M. 3:2G].

[B]   And this teaching is not in accord with R. Meir [cf. T. Hor. 3:1B: **"But the one who is dedicated by many garments has to bring a bullock if he inadvertently gives an erroneous decision,"** the words of R. Meir].

[C]   What is the scriptural basis for R. Meir's position? Scripture stated, "[If it is the] anointed [priest who sins]" (Lev. 4:3). Now why [in addition to anointed] does Scripture also state "priest"? It is to encompass the priest [who is not anointed but dedicated by] many garments.

[D]   What is the scriptural basis for the position of the rabbis [who hold that the law applies only to an anointed priest]? Scripture states "anointed." Is it possible that the law applies to the king [who also is anointed]? [To prevent that false conclusion, Scripture must state] "priest" as well. [Add: Is it possible that the law applies to the priest dedicated by many garments? Scripture says "anointed."]

[E]   Now here you [who hold the position of the rabbis] interpret the passage to exclude the priest dedicated by many garments, but there you interpret the passage to make provision for the priest dedicated by many garments [who must bring the tenth ephah of fine flour specified at Lev. 6:10].

[F]   Said R. Hila, "Each exegesis serves its purpose [and is therefore required and in order].

[G]   "Now if 'anointed' had been stated, but 'priest' had not been stated, I should have concluded that on account of an inadvertent, erroneous ruling he brings a bullock, but on account of an inadvertent deed [of sin] he brings a he-goat. So there was need to make an explicit reference to the priest.

[H]   "And if it had said 'priest' but had not said 'anointed,' I should have reached the false conclusion that this passage refers to the king.

[I]   "If you should state, 'But the pericope concerning the king indeed has been spelled out [at Lev. 4:22–26],' I should then say to you, it was necessary to refer explicitly to the priest.

[J]   "Now if it had referred to 'priest' but not to 'anointed,' I should have concluded, For an erroneous instruction [47d] he brings a bullock, but for an erroneous deed [of sin] he brings a he-goat. Thus there was need to refer explicitly to anointed, and there was need to refer explicitly to priest."

[XII.A]   Said R. Yoḥanan, "[If an anointed priest] left office and then brought the tenth of an ephah of fine flour he was owing, it is valid" [M. 3:2I–J].

[B]   They arrange another priest to take his place lest a cause of invalidation [of the high priest who is to officiate on the Day of Atonement] should occur [M. Yoma 1:1B–C].

[C]   Now do they designate another priest along with him?

[D]   Said R. Haggai, "By Moses! If they designate another priest alongside, he may kill him."

[E]   "[This is the offering which Aaron and his sons shall offer to the Lord on the day when he is anointed: A tenth of an ephah of fine flour as a regular cereal offering. . . . The priest from among Aaron's sons who is anointed to succeed] him [shall offer it to the Lord . . .]" (Lev. 6:19–22)—one do they anoint, and they do not anoint two[, so the substitute is not anointed at all].

[F]   R. Yoḥanan said, "On account of hatred did this one pass from office, and that one served in his place.

[G]   "As to the former, all of the sanctity of the high priesthood pertains to him. The second [substitute] in no way is valid either to serve as high priest or to serve as an ordinary priest."

[H]   Said R. Yoḥanan, "If he [the first] passed from office and [nonetheless] performed an act of sacrificial service [on the Day of Atonement], his act of sacrificial service is invalid."

[I]   The act of sacrificial service of which one [is under discussion by Yoḥanan]?

[J]   Let us infer the answer to that question from the following:

[K]   (MꜤSH B) Ben Elem of Sepphoris: The high priest was affected by a seminal emission on the Day of Atonement [which rendered him invalid for service], and Ben Elem entered and served in his place.

[L]   He came out and said to the king, "The bullock and ram that are offered this day—from whose animals are they offered, mine or the high priest's?"

[M]   Now the king knew full well what he was really asking[, which was to stay in office and provide the animals himself]. He said to him, "It is not enough for you that you served for one moment before Him who spoke and brought the world into being."

[N]   Then Ben Elem understood that he had been separated from the high priesthood.

[O]   MꜤSH B: Simeon b. Qimḥit went out to take a walk with a king on the eve of the Day of Atonement at twilight, and a spurt of spit [from the king's mouth] splattered on [the priest's] garment and so rendered him unclean. Judah his brother went in and served in his stead. On that day, their mother [Qimhit] had the pleasure of seeing two sons in the office of the high priest.

[P]   Seven sons did Qimhit have, and all of them served in the high priesthood. They sent and said to Qimhit, "Now what kinds of good deeds [did you do to merit such glory]?"

[Q]   She replied to them, "May [a terrible thing] happen to me, if [even] the beams of my house ever once gazed upon the hair of my head or the thread of my chemise in my entire life [because of my modesty]."

[R]   They said, "All meal [QMH] is fine, but the meal of Qimhit is the finest of fine flour."

[S]   They recited in her regard the following verse: "The princess is decked in her chamber with gold-woven robes" (Ps. 45:13).

[XIII.A]   Is it possible that the priest anointed for war brings the tenth of an ephah from his own property?

[B]   Scripture says, "[The priest who is appointed from among Aaron's] sons, who is anointed to succeed him, [shall offer it to the Lord]" (Lev. 6:22).

[C]   The one who has a son ready to succeed him shall bring the tenth of an ephah, and the one who has no son ready to succeed him does not bring a tenth of an ephah.

[D]   And how do we know in regard to the anointed for war that his son is not standing ready to succeed him?

[E]   Scripture says, "The son who is priest in his place shall wear them seven days when he comes into the tent of meeting to minister in the holy place" (Ex. 29:30)—as to the one who comes into the tent of meeting for service in the holy place, his son is ready to succeed him, and, as to the one who does not come into the tent of meeting for service in the sanctuary, his son does not succeed him.

[F]   And how do we know that [a priest anointed for war] may be designated for service as high priest?

[G]   "And Phineas son of Eleazar was the ruler over them in time past; the Lord was with him" (1 Chron. 9:20) [and he served as both anointed for war and high priest].

[H]   (When R. Yosé wanted to speak critically to R. Eleazar b. R. Yosé, he would say to him, " 'He *used* to be with him.' In the time of Zimri he opposed [evil], and in the time of the concubine of Gibeah, he did not oppose [evil].")

[I]   And how do you know that [the anointed for war] would serve in eight garments?

[J]   R. Ba bar Ḥiyya in the name of R. Yoḥanan: " 'The holy garments of Aaron shall be for his sons after him, to be anointed in them and ordained in them' (Ex. 29:29). What does Scripture mean in saying 'after him'? They shall follow him in order of high position."

[K]   And how do we know that [the anointed for war] receives inquiries while wearing the eight garments [e.g., before the battle]?

[L]   R. Jeremiah, R. Imi in the name of R. Yoḥanan: " 'The holy garments of Aaron shall be for his sons after him.' Why does Scripture say 'after him'? In succession to sanctification that is after him."

[M]   And how many garments does he wear when he performs an act of sacrificial service?

[N]   R. Hoshaiah introduced the Mishnah-tradition of Bar Qappara of the South and taught the following Tannaitic tradition: "He does not serve in the four garments of an ordinary priest or in the eight of a high priest."

[O]   Said R. Ba, "In logic the law should have been that he performs his act of service wearing four garments. And why does he not serve [in four]? So that people should not say, 'You know, we saw an ordinary priest who sometimes served in the eight garments of the high priest!' "

[P]   Said R. Jonah, "But does he not carry out the act of service at the inner altar [where people will not see him anyhow]?"

[Q]   But does he not receive inquiries outside [where people will see him]?

[R]   So people will [not] err by assuming that what he wore outside he also wore inside.

[S]   For did not R. Ṭarfon, the rabbi of all Israel, err in mistaking the shofar-sounding of the community for the shofar-sounding on the occasion of an offering?

[T]   For it is written, "And the sons of Aaron, the priests, shall blow the trumpets" (Num. 10:8)—

[U]   "when they are unblemished, and not if they bear blemishes," the words of R. ʿAqiba.

[V]   Said to him R. Ṭarfon, "May I bury my sons, if I personally did not see Simeon, my mother's brother, who was lame in one of his legs, and yet he was standing in the courtyard with his trumpet in his hand, and he was sounding it!"

[W]   Said to him R. ʿAqiba, "Now is it possible that you saw him only at the time of the communal sounding of the trumpet?

"But I was stating the rule as it applies in the time of an offering [at which point the priests who blow the trumpet must be unblemished]."

[X]   Said to him R. Ṭarfon, "May I bury my sons if you have [not] erred, either to the right hand or to the left. I was the one who heard the tradition but could not explain it. But you explained the tradition and made it match the tradition [of what was actually done]. Lo, whoever leaves you leaves his own life."

[Y]   "And the priest who is anointed [and consecrated as priest in his father's place] shall make atonement[, wearing the holy linen garments]" (Lev. 16:32).—

[Z]   Why does Scripture say so?

[AA]   For the entire pericope is stated with regard to Aaron. I know only that the Scripture thus speaks of a priest anointed with anointing oil. How do I know that the priest dedicated by many garments [also carries on the same rite]? Scripture for that reason finds it necessary to specify ". . . consecrated as priest in his father's place. . . ."

[BB]   And how do I know that the law applies to another who may be appointed [who was not the sonof the preceding high priest]?

[CC]   Scripture states, "And the priest shall make atonement.

[DD]   With what is he [who was not the son] appointed?

[EE]   The rabbis of Caesarea in the name of R. Ḥiyya bar Joseph, "By a word of mouth [with no other rite but verbal appointment]."

[FF]   Said R. Zeira, "Thus does the tradition state, that they appoint elders by word of mouth."

[GG]   Said R. Ḥiyya bar Ada, "The Mishnah tradition itself has made the same point, when [at M. Ed. 2:7 sages say to ʿAqabiah b. Mehallel,] 'Retract [merely verbally] four teachings of yours, and we shall [verbally] make you head of the court of Israel.' "

[XIV.A] Now *he* [who marries only a virgin, Lev. 21:14] is neither king nor Nazir [cf. M. 3:2K].

[B]   And when Scripture says "*he*," it is to encompass also the priest anointed for war [who marries only a virgin].

[C]   "He shall take to wife a virgin of his own people" (Lev. 21:14).

[D]   This excludes a mature girl, in whom the signs of the virginity have disappeared.

[E]   R. Eleazar and R. Simeon declare valid [a priest's marrying] a mature girl.

[F]   R. Isaac asked [with regard to M. Ter. 8:1: "If a priest was standing and sacrificing at the altar, and it became known that he was the son of a divorcee or of a woman who had performed the rite of removing the shoe (Deut. 25:10), R. Eliezer says, 'All the offerings he had offered on the altar are invalid.' R. Joshua declares them valid"]: "Is the rule the same for other matters?"

[G]   [Yes. Thus if he is doing another sort of rite, he completes it, e.g.,] he takes a handful of meal offering and burns it up; he collects the blood and tosses it; he burns the cow and sprinkles [the ashes of the cow mixed with water].

[H]   R. Jacob bar Idi in the name of R. Isaac: "They treated the case as a purification offering [a red cow] that had been stolen, but about which people in general did not know. [This is deemed an acceptable offering.]"

[I]   Thus has it been said, "He takes a handful and burns it up; he receives the blood and he sprinkles it on the altar; he burns [the red cow] and sprinkles [the ashes and water]."

[J]   R. Berekiah, R. Jacob bar Idi, R. Isaac asked, "If he was
      standing and making an offering at the altar, and it became
      known that he was the son of a divorcee or the son of a woman
      who had undergone the rite of removing the shoe [and thus
      was equivalent to a divorcee], what does one do? [That is, if
      such a person was performing a rite, and turned out during the
      rite to be found not valid, and then died, do we deem the
      death to be that of a valid high priest, such that a murderer in
      a city of refuge is permitted to return home? Since the rite is
      deemed valid, do we then conclude that, for other purposes,
      the priest's status was valid for a time, including the purpose of
      allowing the murderer to leave the city of refuge?]

[K]   "[Do we rule that] if he dies, the murderer returns from the
      place of refuge to his home?

[L]   "Or should [the murderer] be treated as one whose trial was
      completed and sentence laid down while there was no high
      priest at all, and let him not go forth from his place of refuge
      forever?" [The question is not answered.]

The focus of interest at the outset is Simeon's position, M.
3:2A–D, and his reasoning. Unit I presents two possible bases
for Simeon's distinction between the status of the man before
and after the rise to a position of greatness, and this opens the
way to a most interesting and protracted inquiry, as we see.
The opening thesis (I.A, B) is that the reasoning of Simeon is
based on the effect of the rise to power. Since, after all, the one
in power is subject to different laws from the ordinary person,
the rise to power should have an impact as well. Yosé maintains
that the criterion is that the offering required from an ordinary
person is different from the one required from an anointed
priest or ruler. At this point several concrete instances in which
the differing reasons yield conflicting judgments on diverse
cases are offered (I.D–G, H–J, and K–M). These are fully
spelled out in the materials given in square brackets. From this
point forth the Talmud goes its own way, developing a secondary expansion of materials originally introduced for the sake of
explaining the Mishnah-pericope. The connection of unit II to
the closing materials of unit I is obvious. The issue then is the
shift in the person's status and its effect upon a single, continuous act of sinfulness. The case involves a person who has inadvertently eaten part of the minimum volume of forbidden fat

before appointment, part afterward (**II**.A), and, we know, the shift in his status means the two partial quantities of fat are not deemed to join together to constitute the whole minimum volume of what is forbidden. The real point of interest is at **II**.B, when we have a matter of doubt about the person's status during the commission of the sin. C points out the paradox yielded by A–B, and the remainder of the unit spells out the possibility that we may indeed find such a paradoxical situation.

As tightly joined to **II** as **II** is to **I**, unit **III** begins with a restatement of the basic problem analyzed in the preceding unit. But it quickly states its own interests, which lie in the positions of Yohanan and Simeon b. Laqish on a number of distinct but related matters. **III**.A–B open discourse with the case in which the man ate the requisite volume of forbidden fat both before and after appointment to high office. In line with the position of the Associates, there is a completed sin, namely, that committed after the man entered high office, so too at B. These two statements serve only as a prologue to introduce the case that presents the first dispute between Yohanan and Resh Laqish. In fact, they are nothing more than a literary device, joining the opening two units to the massive discourse that will follow. **III**.D–F are clear as stated. G–I then develop a second dispute. At this subtle dispute the effect of the rise of doubt *upon* a sequence of forbidden actions is discussed. Simeon b. Laqish takes the position that, if one is eating pieces of fat, thinking they are permitted, and between eating one and the next he becomes aware of the possibility that the piece he has eaten was forbidden, that fact distinguishes one act of eating from the next—the former, known to be forbidden, from the latter, still supposed permitted. If then he later on discovers that indeed all of the fat was of the forbidden kind, each act of eating imposes the requirement of a sin-offering, that is, is deemed a distinct act. So "doubt imposes division" on a single spell of inadvertence. This is a fairly reasonable position, in that it deems the spell of inadvertence to be brought to a close at that point at which there is a possibility of one's having done the wrong thing. Now Yohanan rejects this reasonable, if subtle, view. So the two points at issue are closely related. One is the power of a single act of sacrifice retrospectively to *join together* a number of sins, under the conditions expressed at **III**.D. The other is the power of the development of a matter of doubt to *distinguish* a protracted sequence of sins into individual actions. So if we want to know whether at the outset, the act of sin, or at the end, the act of atonement is decisive, we admit the possibility of differentiation or fusion. What is interesting here is that there is a shift in positions (E–F, H–I). Yet a second look shows that each authority is consistent in taking the basic position that one differentiates or does not differentiate. That is, Yoḥanan treats the group of sins as subject to a single offering (D) and he also treats a sequence of actions as a single protracted deed, subject to a single sin-offering, at **I**. And the same is to be said for Simeon b. Laqish, who at both points imposes distinctions among actions done in a single spell of inadvertence (H) and also distinguishes among the sins for which a single offering is supposed to atone (F). The positions of both authorities then are subjected to the test of consistency with what each one says in a related context. Ample language is inserted so that further comment here is superfluous.

IV carries forward the inquiry into the positions of Simeon b. Laqish and Yoḥanan. The main issue now is whether we deem one's knowing that there is a possibility he has sinned as tantamount to knowing that he indeed has sinned. If there is a protracted sequence of actions, and one knows for sure that he has sinned in doing one of them, then each action in the sequence is deemed distinct from the others. The issue is whether or not we maintain that knowledge of the possibility of having sinned ("doubt") is equivalent. If it is, then the "doubt divides the deed." That is, knowledge that one may have sinned at one point in a sequence of actions divides the sequence into its parts, each of them distinguished by that moment of doubt concerning its predecessor. This is the position of Simeon b. Laqish. Yoḥanan maintains that we take account only of the situation prevailing at the moment of complete clarification (**IV.**C). Once this matter of the positions of each authority is laid forth, we then clarify that of Simeon b. Laqish (**IV.**D). The relevance of the whole to the Mishnah is made explicit at **IV.**F. **IV.**I–L should surely be dropped; they add nothing to what has been said.

Unit **V** raises subtle and difficult questions. Its principal interest is in exploring the matter of combining two distinct actions. The matter is worked out in terms of the case before us. If one has eaten only part of the requisite volume to become liable for a sin-offering, then changes in status, eats another part, then changes in status once more and returns to his original status, we want to know whether the two bits of fat he ate when he had the same status (numbers 1, 3) join together to form a sufficient volume to impose an obligation to bring a sin-offering. This is the question raised at **V.A, B.** The mode of answering the question is to seek cases parallel in principle (D–F). Here, however, the cases deal with the power of a single spell of inadvertence to join distinct actions into a single span of culpability. The inserted language at D and E explains the case. Then the unit proceeds to move in its own direction (F–H). What we have now is the matter of offerings involved in the cases spelled out at D–E. G and H present no difficulties. Isaac (I) then raises yet another, rather difficult question. We have thus far treated the spell of inadvertence as the criterion for uniting discrete actions. That is, if a person does a number of acts but is never aware that he is sinning, all are deemed culpable as one action. Yet, Isaac points out, we also know that, in addition to the individual's protracted inadvertence, there is a separate and distinct criterion, which is the actual time-span in which a person does the act. This fact, for instance, means that if one ate a number of bits of forbidden fat in a single specified time-span—enough time to eat a half-loaf of bread—all of the bits of fat form a single unit and impose only one sin-offeirng. So what Isaac asks is whether the one criterion limits the other. At J–L, the question is answered negatively. To understand M we have to take up a quite separate matter, but the relevance is clear once we understand that the issue raised by Isaac is phrased in a different way in the parallel materials. O–P then bring us back to the point at which we started this difficult but truly magnificent exercise of analysis.

Unit **VI** begins by going over familiar ground (A–C). It proceeds to present problems of doubt (D–G). Then its problem shifts to whether a part of the Day of Atonement effects atonement (H and following). Associates hold that a part of the Day of Atonement effects atonement in cases of doubt, such as those before us. The matter is restated at Q. **VII** again goes over familiar ground, and by this point requires little comment. I see nothing in unit **VII** that does not duplicate familiar materials.

VIII is fresh. The case is a familiar one, in which in a single spell of inadvertence the man has eaten five pieces of forbidden fat. Then, successively, he discovers what he has done, piece by piece. So he sets aside animals to atone for his sin, one by one. He therefore has five beasts designated as sin-offerings. Yoḥanan says he makes use of the first animal he has desig-

nated. The spell was interrupted, and so the animal to be sacri-
ficed as a sin-offering for the first piece of fat is the one that
covers all the rest. Simeon b. Laqish sees the last animal set
aside as the principal one. This one was set aside in full knowledge that the man indeed had eaten all five pieces of forbidden
fat, so it covers all of them. Since there is this dispute, Yosé b.
R. Bun challenges the assertion of **VII.I**, that all parties concur
on setting aside the animal. Here one party says we sell the animal and make use of the proceeds for freewill offering.

At **IX** we return to the issue of whether information on the
possibility that the fat is prohibited, received between eating
one piece and the next, divides the act of eating a number of
pieces of forbidden fat into a number of distinct actions, each
one liable to a suspensive guilt-offering, just as information that
one surely has committed a sin does distinguish one act of eating forbidden fat from another and imposes distinct sin-offerings. Ḥisda takes the view of Yoḥanan, that knowledge of a
possible sin (and consequent suspensive guilt-offering) does not
break up an act of eating a number of pieces of forbidden fat
into several distinct actions. Hamnuna concurs with Simeon b.
Laqish that information on the probably forbidden status of the
fat is tantamount to information that the fat is definitely forbidden. The cited pericope, M. Ker. 4:2, surely conforms to the
position of Hamnuna and Simeon b. Laqish, so E. (Pené
Moshe explains E as Ḥisda's reply to the Mishnah-pericope adduced in evidence.) I am not clear on the meaning of F.

Unit **X** starts by presenting a pastiche of plays on the word
'ŠR, beginning in a relevant way, then proceeding in its own
direction. The citation of the Mishnah at L is out of place and
should be set after M, but even here it is simply to introduce a
theme, not to preface an analysis. N–P are interrupted by Q–S
and then resume at T. U then reverts to the theme of Q. U, V,
AA, BB then present four rules on anointed kings, originally a
single set, but not heavily glossed. CC and DD present two
reasons for the idea of BB. I do not understand why EE–JJ are
included. KK–NN do revert to the problem of the Mishnah-
pericope. How MM proves the view of LL I do not see. In all,
the unit is constructed in a reasonably coherent way, though
not all of its materials are entirely clear to me.

After the sizable unit of theological and exegetical materials,
the Talmud returns to its exposition of the Mishnah, now to
M. 3:2G. From here to the end of this sizable Talmud passage
the status and duties of the anointed priest come under analy-

sis. The first and most important point of **XI** is that there is an
alternative view to that of the Mishnah, which would apply the
rules of Leviticus 4 to the high priest of the Second temple.
even though he was consecrated by being given eight garments,
not by the application of anointing oil. The Mishnah's contrary
position is now shown to differ from that view, assigned to
Meir. **XI**.C–J provide an exegetical foundation for both opinions. I have followed Pené Moshe in revising our Talmud's version somewhat, but have not gone the whole route of simply
inserting what is found in the parallel versions of the same discussion. What happens at **XII** is not surprising. Once a topic is
introduced, a whole passage tangentially relevant to that topic,
borrowed from a more appropriate location, is simply dropped
in without significant variation. In the present context, it is M.
Yoma 1:1B–C, the rule that, prior to the Day of Atonement, a
substitute high priest is made ready, in case the one who is to
perform the rites should be found invalid. What triggers this
vast interpolation is M. 3:2I–J, the comparison of the anointed
priest in office and the one who has left office. Yoḥanan's contribution, which *is* relevant, is that the rule of the Mishnah
does not preclude a *post facto* rite of the tenth of an ephah of
meal. Then, since the Mishnah also has made reference to the
Day of Atonement, the rest follows. The theory of editing is
not without reason; the operative reason derives from the notion that what is required is an anthology of generally relevant
materials, not an analysis of pertinent ones. The succession of
analyses and stories is clear as given. **XIII** returns to the exposition of M. 3:2I, the tenth of an ephah of fine flour to be offered by the anointed priest. The issue now is whether the
same requirement pertains to priests anointed for special purposes, e.g., the one anointed to serve on the battlefield. The
bulk of units **XIII** and **XIV** moves far from the exposition of
the Mishnah and simply amasses materials whose proper location is elsewhere.

3:3   [In Leiden MS and *editio princeps*: 3:6]

[A]   *A high priest tears his garment [on the death of a close relative]*
       below [at the bottom hem], and an ordinary one, above [at the
       hem of his garment hearest his shoulder].

[B]   *A high priest makes an offering while he has the status of one who has yet to bury his dead, but he may not eat [the priestly portion].*

[C]   *And an ordinary priest neither makes the offering nor eats [the priestly portion].*

[I.A]   [The reference to tearing above in M. 3:3A is at issue.] R. Eleazar in the name of Kahana: " 'Above' means above the binding, and 'below' means below the binding."

[B]   R. Yoḥanan said, " 'Below' means what it says, literally [near the ground]."

[C]   R. Yoḥanan went up to visit R. Ḥanina. When he was yet on the road, he heard that he had died. He sent word and said to send to him his best Sabbath garments, and he went and tore them [on account of this news]. [Thus he holds that one tears a garment at the demise of someone who is not a close relative.]

[D]   R. Yoḥanan differs from R. Yudan in two matters. [First, that he maintains one has to tear the garment as a sign of mourning for any master who has died, not merely for the one from whom one learned most; second, that one does the tear above the binding.]

[E]   The teaching of R. Eleazar in the name of Kahana is in accord with R. Judah [who does not distinguish among relationships to the deceased].

[F]   And if he is in accord with R. Judah, [the high priest] should not perform the act of tearing at all except for his father and his mother.

[G]   It is in accord with the view of R. Meir, for it has been taught in a Tannaitic teaching:

[H]   "For no dead does one undo the binding, except for his father and his mother," the words of R. Meir.

[I]   R. Judah says, "Any tear that does not separate the binding, lo, this is a worthless act of tearing."

[J]   What is the rule [for the high priest]?

[K]   It is a more strict ruling in the case of the high priest, that he should not undo the binding [but he rips through the fabric].

[**II**.A] *"A high priest makes an offering while he has the status of one who has yet to bury a close relative, but he does not eat* [the priestly portion]." **the words of R. Meir** [M. Hor. 3:3B; T. Zeb. 11:3].

[B] **R. Judah says, "That entire day."**

[C] **R. Simeon says, [48a] "He completes all the act of sacrifice that is his responsibility and then he goes along [and leaves the altar]."**

[D] The difference between the view of R. Meir and R. Simeon is one point[, specifically: in Simeon's view, when the priest hears the news while he is performing the rite, that a close relative has died, he completes the entire rite for which he is responsible. But if he has not begun the rite, he should not do so. And after he has completed the rite, he should not begin another. In Meir's view, he may carry on an act of service, without condition.]

[E] The difference between the view of R. Judah and R. Simeon is one point[, specifically: in Judah's view, the priest makes offerings that entire day, while in Simeon's, once he has completed the rite in which he is involved, he leaves the altar].

[F] The difference between the views of R. Meir and R. Judah is [whether or not the priest who has not yet buried his close relative] enters [the Temple at all. Meir maintains that if he has not gone out of the sanctuary, he is permitted to make an offering. But if he has gone out, he does not enter the sanctuary. Judah maintains that that entire day the priest is permitted even to enter the sanctuary and to undertake offerings].

[G] R. Jacob bar Disai [says, "Whether or not the priest at the altar] interrupts [his act of service] is what is at issue between [Meir and Simeon]."

[H] R. Meir says, "[If when the priest heard the news,] he was inside, he would go out [of the sanctuary]. [If] he was outside [the sanctuary], he would [not] go back in."

[I] R. Judah says, "[If when he heard the news, the priest] was inside, he would go in [and, for the entire day on which he heard, carry out an act of service, as is his right], but if he was outside, he would not go in [to perform an act of service]."

[J]   **R. Simeon says, "He completes all the act of service that is his responsibility and then he goes along."**

[III.A]   R. Yosé b. R. Bun in the name of R. Huna: "The following Mishnah saying [belongs] to R. Simeon: " 'And from the sanctuary he will not go forth' (Lev. 21:12)—with [the bearers of the bier] he does not go forth, but he does go forth after them."

[B]   *"When [the bearers of the bier] are not visible, he is visible, when they are visible, he is not. And he goes with them to the city gate," the words of R. Meir.*

[C]   *R. Judah says, "He never leaves the sanctuary, since it says, 'Nor shall he go out of the sanctuary' (Lev. 21:12)"* [M. San. 2:1G–J].

[D]   If he did go out, he should not come back.

[E]   R. Abbahu in the name of R. Eleazar: "The word 'mourning' applies only to the corpse alone, as it is written, 'And her gates shall lament and mourn' (Is. 3:26)."

[F]   Ḥiyya bar Abba replied, "And is it not written, 'The fishermen shall mourn and lament' (Is. 19:8)?"

[IV.A]   Said R. Ḥanina, "[So does] thes45Mishnah [teach, that] the consideration of uncleanness by reason of mourning applies only on account of the corpse [and not on account of hearing of the death. The day of the death, along with the night, imposes the status of the one who has yet to bury his close relative]."

[B]   It has been taught in a Tannaitic tradition: At what point does the status of the one who has yet to bury his close relative apply?

[C]   "It applies from the moment of death to the moment of burial," the words of Rabbi.

[D]   And sages say, "It applies for that entire day [on which the deceased dies]."

[E]   You may then discern both a lenient and a strict side to the ruling of Rabbi, and a lenient and a strict side to the ruling of rabbis.

[F]   What is the difference between their two positions [for strict and lenient rulings]?

[G]   If one dies and is buried at the proper time—

[H]   in accord with the position of the rabbis the mourner [in such a case] is subject to prohibitions applying to mourning for that entire day. In accord with the position of Rabbi the mourner is subject to prohibitions only in the period of the day down to that hour [of burial] alone.

[I]   If one dies and is buried three days later—

[J]   in accord with the opinion of rabbis, the prohibitions applying to the mourner are valid throughout that entire day [but not for the next two].

[K]   In accord with the position of Rabbi, the prohibitions applying to the mourners pertain for all three days.

[L]   R. Abba came [to teach] in the name of R. Yoḥanan, [and] R. Ḥisda—both of them teach: "Rabbi concurs with sages [in the case of O] that the prohibition applies only to that day alone." [The dispute concerns only M–N.]

[M]   That is in accord with the following teaching on Tannaitic authority:

Rabbi says, "You should know that the status of mourning by the authority of the Torah does not apply to the night, for lo, they have said, 'A mourner may immerse and eat his Passover-offering in the evening [of the fifteenth of Nisan, having suffered a bereavement on the fourteenth].' "

[N]   And lo, they have said that the laws of mourning do apply by the authority of the Torah!

[O]   R. Yosé b. R. Bun in the name of R. Huna, "You may solve the contradiction by referring [Rabbi's ruling, M] to the case in which the [death was at dawn and] burial took place in the last rays of sunlight [and Rabbi (M) holds that to that following night the status of mourning does not apply by the authority of the Torah]."

Unit I is relevant to M. 3:3A only at its opening lines. From that point the interest is in the relationship of the opinions of Yoḥanan and those of the Tanna, Judah. Unit II takes up M. 3:3B and brings the Mishnah's position into relationship with a richer account of the same matter supplied by the Tosefta. The exegesis then is of the Tosefta's version. Unit III serves M.

San. 2:1, which is cited verbatim. Unit **IV**'s interest, in the point at which the prohibitions applicable to one who has suffered a bereavement but has yet to bury his dead, is relevant to M. 3:3B. So, in all, the Talmud draws upon materials generally but not specifically relevant to the Mishnah-pericope before us.

3:4   [In Leiden MS and *editio princeps*: 3:7]

[A] *Whatever is offered more regularly than its fellow takes precedence over its fellow, and whatever is at a higher level of sanctification than its fellow takes precedence over its fellow [= M. Zeb. 10:1A].*

[B] *[If] a bullock of an anointed priest and a bullock of the congregation [M. 1:5] are standing [awaiting sacrifice]—*

[C] *the bullock of the anointed [high priest] takes precedence over the bullock of the congregation in all rites pertaining to it.*

[D] *The man takes precedence over the woman in the matter of the saving of life and of returning lost property [M. B.M. 2:11].*

[E] *But a woman takes precedence over a man in the matter of [providing] clothing and redemption from captivity.*

[F] *When both of them are standing in danger of [sexual] defilement, [in effecting rescue,] the man takes precedence over the woman.*

[I.A] **[The reason of M. 3:4B–C is] that the anointed [high priest] effects atonement, while for the congregation, it is required that atonement be effected.**

[B] **It is best that that which effects atonement should take precedence over that for which atonement must be effected,**

[C] **as it is said, "And it will atone for him, for his house, and for all the congregation of Israel" (Lev. 16:17) [T. Hor. 2:4C–E].**

[D] As to the freewill offering of the anointed priest and the freewill offering of the ruler, the freewill offering of the anointed priest takes precedence.

[E] As to the freewill offering of the community and the freewill offering of the ruler, the freewill offering of the ruler takes precedence.

[F]   As to the freewill offering of the anointed priest and the free-will offering of the community, which one takes precrdence?

[G]   Let us infer the rule from the following: As to the freewill of-fering of the anointed priest and the goats brought on account of idolatry that are standing [and awaiting sacrifice], the goats brought on account of idolatry take precedence, because their blood is taken inside [and tossed on the inner altar].

[H]   This statement has ruled only that [the operative criterion is that] their blood is taken inside. Lo, [in the absence of that consideration] the rule should be that [if] the freewill offering of the anointed priest and the freewill offering of the commu-nity [are awaiting preparation], the freewill offering of the anointed priest takes precedence.

[I]   [If] there was the bullock brought on account of idolatry, the goats that are brought with it, and another sin-offering, the bullock takes precedence over the goats, the goats take prece-dence over the other sin-offering, and the other sin-offering takes precedence over the bullock.

[J]   What would be a case [illustrative of the foregoing rule]?

[K]   Said R. Yosé, "Since the goat is second in time to the bullock [which is mentioned first in Scripture (M)], it is like one over which the bullock has taken precedence."

[L]   And another sin-offering takes precedence over the bullock.

[M]   A bullock brought on account of idolatry takes precedence over the goat that is brought with it, because it is mentioned first in Scripture [Num. 15:24].

[N]   R. Samuel, brother of R. Berekiah, asked, "On the basis of the same reasoning, the one brought on account of the new moon should take precedence over the goat that is brought with it, because [Scripture mentioned it] first [Num.29:11, 15]."

[O]   Said R. Ba, "My lord, you cannot [interpret matters thus. For the spelling of 'sin-offering' at the specified verse is] lacking [since it is written ḤṬṬ, not ḤṬ'Ṭ, and this is taken to mean that it does not enjoy precedence, despite its position in the rel-evant verses of Scripture. That is, one cannot draw an analogy from this ḤṬṬ to other references to ḤṬ'Ṭ].

[P]   " 'And also one male goat for a sin-offering to the Lord [on the occasion of the new moon]; it shall be offered besides the con-

tinual burnt-offering and its drink-offering' (Num. 28:15),
Scripture has set it next to the continual offering. [This indicates that the specified offering follows the continual offering,
before the bullocks of the additional offering.]"

[**II**.A]   As to the offering of a man and the offering of a woman, the
offering of a man takes precedence [cf. M. 3:4D].

[B]   That rule which has been stated applies to a case in which the
two [offerings] are of equivalent character.

[C]   But if this one [belonging to a woman] was a bullock and that
one [belonging to a man], a lamb, in such a case [the woman's
will take precedence].

[D]   That is in accord with that which R. Pinḥas said in the name
of R. Hoshaiah: "And if a slave brings a bullock, while his
master brings a he-goat, the bullock of the slave takes precedence to that of his master.

[E]   "For we have learned the tradition:

[F]   *"If the bullock of the anointed priest and the bullock of the
congregation are standing [and awaiting preparation], the bullock of the anointed priest takes precedence over the bullock of
the congregation for all aspects of its preparation"* [M. 3:4B–C].
[In this case the animals are alike. But if they were not alike,
the rule is different.]

[**III**.A]   MᶜSH B: R. Eliezer, R. Joshua, and R. ᶜAqiba went up to
Ḥolat Antokhiya in a connection with collecting funds for
sages.

[B]   Now there was a certain man there, by the name of Abba Judah. He would fulfill the commandment [of supporting the
sages] in a liberal spirit. One time he lost all his money, and he
saw our rabbis and despaired [of helping them]. He went
home, and his face was filled with suffering.

[C]   His wife said to him, "Why is your face filled with suffering?"

[D]   He said to her, "Our rabbis are here, and I simply do not
know what I can do for them."

[E]   His wife, who was even more righteous than he, said to him,
"You have a single field left. Go and sell half of it and give the
proceeds to them."

[F]   He went and did just that. He came to our rabbis, and he gave
       them the proceeds.

[G]   Our rabbis prayed in his behalf. They said to him, "Abba Ju-
       dah, may the Holy One, blessed be He, make up all the things
       you lack."

[H]   When they went their way, he went down to plough the half-
       field that remained in his possession. Now while he was
       ploughing in the half-field that remained to him, his cow fell
       and broke a leg. He went down to bring her up, and the Holy
       One, blessed be He, opened his eyes, and he found a jewel. He
       said, "It was for my own good that my cow broke its leg."

[I]   Now when our rabbis returned, they asked about him. They
       said, "How are things with Abba Judah?"

[J]   People replied, "Who can [even] gaze upon the face of Abba
       Judah—Abba Judah of the oxen! Abba Judah of the camels!
       Abba Judah of the asses!" So Abba Judah had returned to his
       former wealth.

[K]   Now he came to our rabbis and asked after their welfare.

[L]   They said to him, "How is Abba Judah doing?"

[M]   He said to them, "Your prayer in my behalf has yielded fruit
       and more fruit." They said to him, "Even though to begin with
       other people gave more than you did, you were the one whom
       we wrote down at the top of the register."

[N]   They took and seated him with themselves, and they pro-
       nounced upon him the following scriptural verse: "A man's gift
       makes room for him and brings him before great men" (Prov.
       18:16).

[O]   R. Ḥiyya bar Ba made a pledge in support of the house of
       learning of Tiberias. Now there was there one of the household
       of Silni, and he pledged a liter of gold. R. Ḥiyya the Great
       took him and seated him next to himself and pronounced con-
       cerning him the following scriptural verse: "A man's gift makes
       room for him and brings him before great men."

[P]   Simeon b. Laqish went up to Boṣrah. Now there was there a
       head of a band of "deceivers." It was not that the man was ac-
       tually a deceiver, but he would practice deceit in regard to
       [generous practice of] commandments. When he saw how
       much the community had pledged, he pledged to accept on

himself [a pledge in the same amount]. R. Simeon b. Laqish took him and seated him next to himself and he pronounced him the following scriptural verse: "A man's gift makes room for him and brings him before great men."

[**IV**.A]   *The man takes precedence over the woman.*

[B]   Now that is the rule if *one had this one to save and that one to save, this one to clothe and that one to clothe [M. Hor. 3:4D, E].* [That is, when all things are equal, the man takes precedence in the one instance, the one in the other.]

[C]   Lo, if one had this one to restore to life and that one to clothe, [what is the rule]?

[D]   Let us infer the rule from that which R. Joshua b. Levi said in the name of R. Antigonos: "[If there is a choice of] providing a garment for the wife of an associate, and saving the life of an ordinary person, the garment for the wife of the associate takes precedence over saving the life of the ordinary person, on account of the honor owing to the associate."

[E]   Now the rule has been stated only with regard to providing a garment for the wife of an associate in the lifetime of the associate. But if it was a case of saving this one [48b] and clothing that one, saving the live takes precedence.

[F]   *[If one has the choice of retrieving] that which he has lost and that which his father has lost, his own takes precedence. [If he has a choice of retrieving] that which he has lost and that which his master has lost, his own takes precedence. [If he has a choice of retrieving] that which his father has lost and that which his master has lost, that of his master takes precedence [over that of his father]. For his father has brought him into this world, but his master, who taught him wisdom, has brought him into the life of the world to come [M. B.M. 2:11A–H].*

[G]   [Now under discussion is] his master who taught him the Mishnah, not his master who taught him Scripture.

[H]   Now if his father was the equal of his master, his father takes precedence.

[I]   What is the difference favoring [the father]?

[J]   "It is a case in which," said R. Yosé b. R. Bun, "half of his learning came from this one, and half of his learning came from that one[, so the father's having brought him into the world now registers]."

[K]   [If it is a choice of retrieving] that which his father, from whom he had acquired half of his learning, has lost, and that which his mother, whom his father has divorced, has lost, who takes precedence?

[L]   Is it the father who takes precedence?

[M]   Or [do we give the father precedence] only when the whole of the man's learning has derived from the father?

[N]   [If there is a choice of retrieving] that which his master has lost, from whom the man has derived half of his learning, and the object that his mother, the divorced wife of his father, has lost, which one takes precedence?

[O]   Is it his master who takes precedence, or [do we say that that is the case] only when all of his learning has come from the master?

[P]   [If it is a choice of retrieving] that which he has lost, that which his mother has lost, that which his father has lost, and that which his master has lost, that which he has lost takes precedence over that which his father has lost, that which his father has lost takes precedence over that which his mother has lost, and that which his mother has lost takes precedence over that which his master has lost.

[Q]   Now is this teaching not made explicit in the Mishnah:

[R]   *The man takes precedence over the woman in the matter of the saving of life and in the matter of returning lost property [M. B.M. 2:11 = M. Hor. 3:4D]?*

[S]   They had in mind to rule that that is the case when his master is not present at all. So this teaching [Q] comes along to tell you that the rule applies even when his master is present.

[T]   **He, his mother, his master, his father are standing in captivity [and awaiting ransom]:**

[U]   **he takes precedence over his mother, and his mother over his master, and his master takes precedence over his father. [So ransoming] his mother takes precedence over all other people [T. Hor. 2:5A–C].**

[V]   Now does not the Mishnah say this explicitly: *A woman takes precedence over a man in the matter of providing clothing and redemption from captivity [M. Hor. 3:4E]?*

[W]   One might consider ruling that the Mishnah speaks of a case in which his master is not present. So the Mishnah comes to tell you that that is the rule even if his master is present.

[X]   **Who is one's master?**

[Y]   **"It is the one who has taught him wisdom [and not the master who has taught him a trade].**

[Z]   **"It is anyone who started him off first,"** the words of R. Meir.

[AA]   **R. Judah says, "It is anyone from whom he has gained the greater part of his learning."**

[BB]   **R. Yosé says, "It is anyone who has enlightened his eyes in his repetition of traditions" [T. Hor. 2:5C–H].**

[CC]   R. Abbahu came [and taught] in the name of R. Yoḥanan: "The law is in accord with the position of the one who says, 'It is anyone from whom he has gained the greater part of his learning.' "

[DD]   (Now why did he not simply interpret the Mishnah-pericope by saying "The law is in accord with R. Judah"?

[EE]   [Because there are] repeaters of traditions who will get confused and switch [matters about].)

[FF]   R. Eliezer would make a tear in mourning on the demise of someone who had simply opened his education at the outset [but was not his principal teacher (= Z)].

[GG]   Samuel removed his phylacteries on the news of the demise of one who had enlightened his eyes in his learning of the Mishnah [= BB].

[HH]   And what is the case of one's "enlightening his eyes in his learning of the Mishnah"?

[II]   It is one who taught merely so brief a passage as the following: *[The two keys]—one goes down into the lock as far as its armpit, and one opens the door forthwith [M. Tam. 3:6E].*

[JJ]   (Now what is the meaning of *One goes down into the lock as far as its armpit?* That it would go down for a cubit before it would open the door.)

[KK]   R. Hananiah was walking, leaning on the shoulder of R. Hiyya bar Ba in Sepphoris. He saw all the people running. He asked him, "Why do all the people run?"

[LL]   He said to him, "It is because R. Yohanan is in session and expounding Torah in the schoolhouse of R. Benaiah, and all the people are running to hear what he has to say."

[MM]   He said to him, "Blessed be the All-Merciful, who has shown me the fruits of my labor while I am still alive."

[NN]   For all of the Aggadah had he [Hananiah] laid forth before him [Yohanan], except for Proverbs and Ecclesiastes.

[V.A]   *When both of them are standing in danger of [sexual] defilement, the man takes precedence over the woman [M. Hor. 3:4F].*

[B]   Why is this the rule?

[C]   Because the woman is accustomed to such treatment, but the man is not accustomed to such treatment.

[D]   MᶜSH B: R. Joshua went to Rome. They told him about a child from Jerusalem who was ruddy, with beautiful eyes and a handsome face, and his locks were curled, and he was in danger of being put to shame. R. Joshua went to examine him. When he came to the door, [standing outside] he recited this verse: "Who gave up Jacob to the spoiler, and Israel to the robbers (Is. 42:24)?"

[E]   **That child answered and said, " 'Was it not the Lord against whom we have sinned, in whose ways they would not walk, and whose law they would not obey' (Is. 42:24)?"**

[F]   **At that instant R. Joshua's eyes filled with tears, and he said, "I call the heaven and the earth to testify against me, that I shall not move from this spot until I shall have redeemed this child!"**

[G]   **He redeemed him for a huge sum of money and sent him to the land of Israel.**

[H]   **And concerning him [Ishmael] Scripture has said, "The precious sons of Zion, worth their weight in fine gold, how they are reckoned as earthen pots, the work of a potter's hands" (Lam. 4:2) [T. Hor. 2:5L–G].**

The Talmud's units systematically follow and complement the elements of the Mishnah, with unit **I** explaining M. 3:4B–C, and unit **II**, M. 3:4D, unit **IV**, M. 3:4D–E, and unit **V**, M. 3:4F. To be sure, each unit develops its own materials, sometimes moving in a direction independent of the Mishnah. But the fundamental principle of organization is clear. Unit **I** introduces a number of fresh questions of the precedence of one animal offering over some other. The analysis is acute. Unit **II** proceeds to the matter of the relative precedence of man and woman, beginning with the established issue, sacrifice. I see no reason for the insertion, whole, of unit **III**, a set of stories illustrative of Prov. 18:16. The analytical mode next is applied, at unit **IV**, to the relative precedence of man and woman in areas generated by the examples of the Mishnah. The detail introduced into the formulation of **IV**.K is curious. The mother is divorced, since, if she were not, both she and the son would owe respect to the father; the father has provided half the son's learning. If he had provided the whole of it, the father would be in the status of the master. If he has provided none of it, the father would have no precedence over the (divorced) mother. So the way in which the problem is phrased takes account of issues that the formulator does not wish to explore, but of which he must make account. The rest of the cases present no surprises. The definition of the master (X and following) raises interest in the story of Ḥananiah, who saw Yoḥanan as his student, even though he had taught him less than the bulk of his learning. Unit **V** treats the problem of sodomy, illustrated by a story about Joshua at all costs rescued Ishmael from such a fate (**V**.D–H). So, in all, the materials of the Talmud are well chosen and carefully laid forth.

3:5

[A] *A priest takes precedence over a Levite, a Levite over an Israelite, an Israelite over a mamzer, a mamzer over a Natin, a Natin over a proselyte, a proselyte over a freed slave.*

[B] *Under what circumstances?*

[C] *When all of them are equivalent [in other regards].*

[D]   *But if the mamzer was a disciple of a sage, and a high priest*
        was an ignoramus, the mamzer who is a disciple of a sage takes
        precedence over a high priest who is an ignoramus.

[I.A]   A sage takes precedence over a king; a king takes precedence
        over a high priest; a high priest takes precedence over a
        prophet; a prophet takes precedence over a priest anointed for
        war; a priest anointed for war takes precedence over the head
        of a priestly watch; the head of a priestly watch takes prece-
        dence over the head of a household [of priests]; the head of a
        household of priests takes precedence over the superintendent
        of the cashiers; **the superintendent of the cashiers takes prec-**
        edence over the Temple treasurer; the Temple treasurer
        takes precedence over an ordinary priest; an ordinary [T.
        Hor. 2:10F–H] *priest takes precedence over a Levite; a Levite*
        takes precedence over an Israelite; an Israelite takes precedence
        over a mamzer; a mamzer takes precedence over a Natin; a Na-
        tin takes precedence over a proselyte; a proselyte takes prece-
        dence over a freed slave.
            Under what circumstances?
            When all of them are equivalent.
            But if the mamzer was a disciple of a sage, and a high priest
        was an ignoramus, the mamzer who is the disciple of a sage
        takes precedence over a high priest who is an ignoramus [M.
        Hor. 3:5A–D].

[B]   **A sage takes precedence over a king.**

[C]   **[For if] a sage dies, we have none who is like him.**

[D]   **[If] a king dies, any Israelite is suitable to mount the throne**
        [T. 2:8].

[E]   Said R. Yoḥanan, "All those forty days that Moses served on
        the mountain, he studied the Torah but forgot it. In the end it
        was given to him as a gift. All this why? So as to bring the
        stupid students back to their studies [when they become dis-
        couraged]."

[F]   When R. Simon bar Zebid died, R. Hili went up to take leave
        of him: " 'Surely there is a mine for silver, and a place for gold
        which they refine. Iron is taken out of the earth, and copper is
        smelted from the ore . . . (Job 28:1–2).' These, if they are lost,
        can be replaced. But a disciple of a sage who dies—who will
        bring someone to take his place?
            " 'But where shall wisdom be found? And where is the

place of understanding? Man does not know the way to it, and it is not found in the land of the living (Job 28:12–13).' "

[G]   Said R. Levi, "If the brothers of Joseph, because they found something, their hearts failed them, as it is written, 'At this their hearts failed them' (Gen. 42:28), we, who have lost R. Simeon bar Zebid, how much the more so!"

[H]   **A king takes precedence over a high priest,**

[I]   **as it is said, "[And the king said to them,] 'Take with you the servants of your lord, and cause Solomon my son to ride on my own mule, and bring him down to Gihon.' "**

[J]   **And the high priest takes precedence over the prophet, as it is said, "And let Zadok the priest and Nathan the prophet there anoint him king over Israel (1 Kings 1:33–34)."**

[K]   **[David] gave precedence to Zadok over Nathan [T. Hor. 2:9A–D].**

[L]   R. Jonah in the name of R. Hama bar Hanina: "A prophet [quietly] folds his hands and feet and sits himself down before a high priest."

[M]   What is the scriptural basis for this notion?

[N]   **[Scripture] says, "Hear now, O Joshua the high priest, you and your friends who sit before you, for they are men of good omen (Zech. 3:8)."**

[O]   **Is it possible that he speaks of ordinary men?**

[P]   Scripture says, "For they are men of good omen,"

[Q]   **and omen refers only to prophecy, as it is said, "And he gives you a sign or an omen (Deut. 13:2)" [T. Hor. 2:9E–H].** [This proves that the prophet sits humbly before a high priest.]

[R]   **[A high priest anointed with oil takes precedence over one dedicated through many garments.]**

[S]   **A prophet takes precedence over the high priest anointed for battle,**

[T]   **and the high priest anointed for battle takes precedence over the prefect,**

[U]   and the prefect takes precedence over the head of the weekly course [of the priests, who take care of the cult in a given week],

[V]   and the head of the priestly course takes precedence over the superintendent of the cashiers,

[W]   and the superintendent of the cashiers takes precedence over the treasurer.

[X]   And the treasurer takes precedence over an ordinary priest.

[Y]   And an ordinary priest takes precedence over a Levite [T. Hor. 2:10A–I].

[Z]   *A priest takes precedence over a Levite.*

[AA]   *A Levite takes precedence over an Israelite [M. Hor. 3:5A].*

[BB]   Is not a Levite the same as an Israelite [so why specify precedence]?

[CC]   Said R. Abun, "It is for the time of the singing on the platform that they taught this passage [in which case the Levite is superior to the Israelite]."

[DD]   Said R. Abun, "[If awaiting conversion to Judaism] there are a proselyte and an apostate to idolatry, the apostate takes precedence, because of a precedent."

[EE]   On what account does everybody exert himself to marry a woman who is a proselyte, and everyone does not exert himself to marry a freed slave-girl?

[FF]   Because a woman who has become a proselyte is assumed to have guarded herself [sexually],

[GG]   while a freed slave-girl has the status of one who has been freely available [T. Hor. 2:11].

[HH]   Why does everybody run after a rat [to kill it]?

[II]   Because it is a pest for people.

[JJ]   Said R. Yoḥanan "Do not trust a slave for sixteen generations: 'But in the seventh month Ishmael the son of Nethaniah, son of Elishama, of the royal family, came with ten men and attacked and killed Gedaliah and the Jews and the Chaldeans who were with him at Mizpah' (2 Kings 25:25)."

[**II**.A] R. Joshua b. Levi said, "[If there] are a head [not a sage] and an elder [a sage], the elder takes precedence. For there is no head if there is no elder."

[B] What is the scriptural evidence for this position?

[C] "You stand this day all of you before the Lord your God: the heads of your tribes, your elders, and your officers, all the men of Israel (Deut. 29:10)."

[D] And it is written, "Then Joshua gathered all the tribes of Israel to Shechem, and summoned the elders, the heads, the judges, and the officers of Israel (Joshua 24:1)."

[E] Thus Moses gave precedence to the heads over the elders, while Joshua gave precedence to the elders over the heads.

[F] Moses, because all of them were his disciples, gave precedence to the heads over the elders. Joshua, because all of them were not his disciples, gave precedence to the elders [who were sages] over the heads [who were not sages].

[G] Moses, because he did not yet have need of them [48c] for conquering the land, gave precedence to the heads over the elders. Joshua, because he needed them for conquering the land, gave precedence to the elders over the heads.

[H] Moses, because he was not fatigued by the study of the Torah [having divine help], gave precedence to the heads over the elders. Joshua, because he was fatigued by study of the Torah, gave precedence to the elders over the heads.

[I] R. Joshua of Sikhnin in the name of R. Levi: "Moses, because he foresaw through the Holy Spirit that the Israelites were destined to be imprisoned by the [gentile] kingdoms, and their heads would be standing over them [to deal with the gentiles], gave precedence to the heads over the elders."

[**III**.A] It was taught in Tannaitic tradition: The arranger [of the Mishnah traditions] takes precedence over the one capable of analyzing them.

[B] R. Samuel brother of R. Berekiah asked, "Even such as R. Ami?"

[C] He said to him, "How can you ask about R. Ami? He has a first-class analytical mind."

[D]   This is what has been said: The Mishnah takes precedence over Scripture.

[E]   And the following supports this tradition:

[F]   For R. Simeon b. Yoḥai taught, "He who takes up studies in Scripture—it is a good quality that is no good quality."

[G]   Rabbis treat Scripture as equivalent to the Mishnah.

[H]   R. Samuel bar Naḥman said, "The Mishnah takes precedence over the Talmud."

[I]   What is the Scriptural basis for that opinion?

[J]   "Get wisdom [Mishnah], get insight [Talmud]" (Prov. 4:5).

[K]   R. Yoḥanan said, "The Talmud takes precedence over the Mishnah."

[L]   What is the scriptural basis for this opinion?

[M]   "To get wisdom is better than gold, to get understanding is to be chosen rather than silver" (Prov. 16:16).

[N]   How does R. Yoḥanan interpret the scriptural basis for the position of R. Samuel bar Naḥman? Water [silver/Talmud] is cheap, wine [gold/Mishnah] is costly. Still, it is possible for the world to live without wine, but it is not possible for the world to live without water.

[O]   And how does R. Samuel bar Naḥman interpret the scriptural basis of R. Yoḥanan's position?

[P]   Salt is cheap, and pepper is dear. It is possible for the world to live without pepper, but it is not possible for the world to live without salt.

[Q]   One should always pursue the Mishnah more than the Talmud.

[R]   That is to say, "[following Jastrow II, p. 1624A] What you say (that the study of the Mishnah is preferable) refers to the time before Rabbi had embodied and abridged most of the Mishnah-traditions in his edition, but since then, run at all times after the Talmud (where the discussions are quoted in their original form)."

[S]   R. Samuel b. R. Yosé b. R. Bun explained the following verse: " 'A rich man is wise in his own eyes, but a poor man who has understanding will find him out' (Prov. 28:11).

[T]   " 'A rich man is wise in his own eyes'—this refers to the one who is a master of the Talmud.

[U]   " 'But a poor man who has understanding will find him out'— this refers to a master of aggadah.

[V]   "[It is to be compared] to two who entered a city. In the hand of this one are bars of gold, and in the hand of that one is small change. This one who has in hand bars of gold does not get to spend it and sustain himself, while that one who has small change gets to spend it and sustains himself."

[W]   R. Aḥa interpreted the following verse: " 'A just balance and scales are the Lord's; all the weights in the bag are his work' (Prov. 16:11).

[X]   " 'A balance'—this refers to Scripture.

[Y]   " 'Scales' refers to the Mishnah.

[Z]   " 'Just' refers to the Talmud.

[AA]   " 'Are the Lord's' refers to the Supplement [Tosefta].

[BB]   " 'All the weights in the bag are his work'—all of them take their reward from one bag."

[CC]   R. Abba bar Kahana went to a certain place. He found R. Levi sitting and interpreting the following verse: " 'A man to whom God gives wealth, possession, and honor, so that he lacks nothing of all that he desires, yet God does not give him power to enjoy them, but a stranger enjoys them' (Qoh. 6:2).

[DD]   " 'Wealth'—this refers to Scripture.

[EE]   " 'Possessions'—these are laws.

[FF]   " 'Honor'—this is the Supplement.

[GG]   " 'So that he lacks nothing at all that he desires'—these are the great collections of the Mishnah, for instance, the Mishnah of R. Huna, and the Mishnah of R. Hoshaiah, and the Mishnah of Bar Qappara.

[HH]   " 'Yet God does not give him power to enjoy them'—this refers to a master of aggadah who never gets to declare something prohibited or to declare something permitted, to declare something unclean or to declare it clean.

[II]   " 'But a stranger enjoys them'—this refers to a master of the Talmud."

[JJ]   R. Abba bar Kahana got up and kissed him on his head [and] said, "You have had the merit of saying [a teaching] while standing up [as a disciple]. May you have the merit of saying something while sitting down [as a master]."

[KK]   If they want to appoint elders, whence do they appoint them? From Tiberias or from the south?

[LL]   Said R. Simon, " 'Judah will go up [from the South]' (Judges 1:2), [so judges should come from the South, Lydda]."

[MM]   Said to him R. Mana, "That which you cited applies to going up to war [as in context]. But as to appointing them: 'The man next to him . . . who saw the king's face and sat first in the kingdom (Esther 1:14).' [Those who see (RW'Y) are the worthy ones (R'WY). Hence nearby authorities, from Tiberias, take precedence.]"

[NN]   R. Jacob bar Idi in the name of R. Joshua b. Levi: MᶜSH Š: "Elders entered the second-story room in the house of Gediyya in Jerico, and an echo issued forth and said to them, 'There are among you two who are worthy to receive the Holy Spirit, and Hillel the Elder is one of them.' They then gazed upon Samuel the Small.'

[OO]   "Once again the elders entered the second-story room in Yabneh, and an echo issued forth and said to them, 'There are among you two who are worthy to receive the Holy Spirit, and Samuel the Small is one of them.' And they all gazed upon Eliezer b. Hyrcanus.

[PP]   "And they were delighted that their opinion proved to be the same as that of the Holy Spirit."

[QQ]   Members of the household of Bar Pazzi and members of Bar Hoshaiah would go up and greet the patriarch every day. And the members of the house of Bar Hoshaiah went in first [before those of the house of Bar Pazzi].

[RR]   The house of Bar Pazzi went and intermarried with the house of the patriarch. Then they wanted to go in first [to greet the patriarch, before the ones who had traditionally done so first]. So they appealed the matter of R. Imi.

[SS]   [He said to them,] " 'And you shall erect the tabernacle according to its judgment' (Ex. 26:30: According to the plan for
it that has been shown you on the mountain). Now is there
such a thing as 'judgment' for pieces of wood? But this beam
has gotten the merit of being placed at the north, so let it be
placed at the north; the other had the merit of being placed at
the south, let it be placed at the south."

[TT]   Two families in Sepphoris, Balvati and Pagani, would go up
and greet the patriarch every day. And the Balvati family would
go in first and come out first. The Pagani family went and attained merit in learning. They came and sought the right to enter first. The question was brought to R. Simeon b. Levi. R.
Simeon b. Levi asked R. Yoḥanan. R. Yoḥanan went and gave
a talk in the schoolhouse of R. Benaiah: *"But if the mamzer
was a disciple of a sage and a high priest was an ignoramus, the
mamzer who is a disciple of a sage takes precedence over a high
priest who is an ignoramus"* [M. Hor. 3:5D].

[IV.A]   Now they considered interpreting the Mishnah passage to refer
to the matter of redemption [in the case they were taken cap-
tive], or to providing food or to giving garments [as are speci-
fied]. But to status in the session it should not apply, [so in a
session of the school the *mamzer* is not given priority even if he
is learned].

[B]   Said R. Abun, "It also applies to status in the session of the
court."

[C]   And what is the scriptural basis for this opinion?

[D]   It is in the following verse: "Happy is the man who finds wisdom, and the man who gets understanding, for the gain from it
is better than gain from silver, and its profit better than gold.
She is more precious than jewels" (Prov. 3:13–15).

[E]   And [wisdom] is more precious even than this [priest] who enters the Holy of Holies [cf. T. Hor. 2:10P–R].

Unit **I**'s materials seem to me to form a distinct group because
they concentrate on the exposition of the list of priorities given
in the Mishnah, augmenting the list, and explaining the precedence given to the sage. The striking shift effected by the Talmud, compared to the Mishnah's version, is the insertion of
the sage at the head of the list (**I**.A). This contrasts with the

Mishnah's priest-Levite-Israelite sequence. The sage enters the Mishnah's consideration only as a secondary development of the theme of priority, and then it is only to place knowledge of the Torah into the sequence of precedence. For the Talmud it is the principal point of interest. The priority of the sage is not only over the high priest. Indeed, for the Talmud's materials, the chief figure is the king (patriarch). The analytical mode of exegesis, taking up the Mishnah's topic and unpacking its principles, characterizes unit **II**. But there is no really sharp break between the first and the second units. What unit **II** contributes is the comparison of the precedence owing to the sage and the head. Unit **III** then moves still further from the interests of the Mishnah, by raising the question of the relative priority of learning in Scripture, the Mishnah, and the Talmud. The final unit, **IV**, which reverts to the interpretation of the Mishnah, closes with the expected homily.

Niddah

5 Introduction to Niddah

The Mishnah-tractate Niddah is devoted to two principal themes, secretions of the body that are deemed unclean and impart uncleanness, and doubts in connection with these same excretions. Most of the body fluids under discussion derive from the woman, though the *zab* makes his appearance as well. The logical and conceptual framework of the tractate is formed by the application to the stated theme, body fluid that imparts uncleanness, of the problematic of matters of doubt and their resolution. The Palestinian Talmud serves the first three chapters of the tractate, with a cursory treatment of chapter 4, but we shall briefly consider the topic of the entire document, since the whole serves as an amplification of relevant Scriptures pertinent even to the fraction of the Mishnah-tractate under discussion here. The primary set is Lev. 15:19–30 (note also Lev. 18:19, 20:18; translation: Revised Standard Version):

[19] When a woman has a discharge of blood which is her regular discharge from her body she shall be in her impurity for seven days, and whoever touches her will be unclean until the evening.
[20] And everything upon which she lies during her impurity shall be unclean; everything also upon which she sits shall be unclean. [21] And whoever touches her bed shall wash his clothes and bathe himself in water and be unclean until the evening. [22] And whoever touches anything upon which she sits shall wash his clothes and bathe himself in water and be unclean until the evening, [23] whether it is the bed or anything upon which she sits, when he touches it he shall be unclean until the evening. [24] And if any man lies with her, and

her impurity is upon him, he shall be unclean seven days; and
every bed on which he lies shall be unclean.

In the present group of chapters, the sole point important for
our tractate is the opening statement (15:19): the menstrual period imposes uncleanness for seven days.

[25] If a woman has a discharge of blood for many days, not
at the time of her impurity, or if she has a discharge beyond
the time of her impurity, all the days of the discharge she shall
continue in uncleanness; as in the days of her impurity she
shall be unclean.
[26] Every bed on which she lies, all the days of her discharge, shall be to her as the bed of her impurity; and everything on which she sits shall be unclean as in the uncleanness
of her impurity. [27] And whoever touches these things shall be
unclean and shall wash his clothes and bathe himself in water
and be unclean until the evening. [28] But if she is cleansed of
her discharge, she shall count for herself seven days and after
that she shall be clean. [29] And on the eighth day she shall
take two turtledoves or two young pigeons and bring them to
the priest, to the door of the tent of meeting. [30] And the
priest shall offer one for a sin offering and the other for a
burnt-offering; and the priest shall make atonement for her before the Lord for her unclean discharge.

What is important in the second unit is that a discharge of
blood not during the menstrual period or going on after the
seven days of menstruation, which continues over "many
days"—understood to mean three days—imposes upon the
woman the uncleanness of the *zabah*. Our tractate takes for
granted the menstrual period lasts for seven days; then comes
an intervening period during which discharge of blood may impose the state of the *zabah*. This period, deemed to continue
for eleven days, from one menstrual period to the next, is
called the *zibah*-period. Alternatively, the days are called "the
clean days," in that blood appearing on them is not held to be
unclean by reason of menstruation. This matter is linked to
that of childbirth; a woman who gives birth during the eleven
days of *zibah* may give birth as a *zabah*. Accordingly, we also
find the language, "Lo, she gives birth BZWB," that is, in the
status of a *zabah*.
This brings us to the second major scriptural pericope relevant to our tractate, Lev. 12:1–8:

[1] The Lord said to Moses, [2] Say to the people of Israel: If a woman conceives and bears a male child, then she shall be unclean seven days; as at the time of her menstruation, she shall be unclean.

[3] And on the eighth day the flesh of his foreskin shall be circumcized.

[4]Then she shall continue for thirty-three days in the blood of her purifying: she shall not touch any hallowed thing, nor come into the sanctuary, until the days of her purifying are completed.

[5] But if she bears a female child, then she shall be unclean two weeks, as in her menstruation, and she shall continue in the blood of her purifying for sixty-six days.

[6] And when the days of her purifying are completed, whether for a son or for a daughter, she shall bring to the priest at the door of the tent of meeting a lamb a year old for a burnt-offering and a pigeon or a turtledove for a sin offering; [7] and he shall offer it before the Lord and make atonement for her; then she shall be clean from the flow of her blood. This is the law for her who bears a child, either male or female. [8] And if she cannot afford a lamb, then she shall take two turtledoves or two young pigeons, one for a burnt-offering and the other for a sin offering; and the priest shall make atonement for her, and she shall be clean.

The point of principal interest is in the seven or fourteen days during which blood that exudes is deemed unclean, and the thirty-three or sixty-six days "of purifying." In our tractate this is understood to mean that blood that exudes from the woman who has given birth on these days "of purifying" is deemed to be clean. This generates some interesting but undeveloped problems, e.g., is the blood of purifying of a woman unclean with ṣaraᶜat, whose body fluids in general are deemed unclean, regarded as unclean also? It is self-evident that the inclusion of the present unit in our tractate is required by Lev. 12:2, which compares the woman in the week or two weeks after childbirth to the woman in her menstrual period.

The tractate begins, at chapter 1, with the problem of retroactive contamination. Once a woman's period is discovered to have begun, has she imparted uncleanness to objects she has touched before she realized that the period was at hand? If so, for how long a period of time? The pericope presents interesting formal problems. Then the rule of retroactive contamination is contravened. There is no retroactive contamination if a woman has a fixed period. As is common, the opening unit is

not large and does not attend to the logically prior and primary
issue of the tractate at all.

That comes with the second unit, which deals with unclean
excretions, M. 2:5–5:2 (broken off here in the middle). Here
we review all the sorts of bloody excretions that may signify
that a woman is unclean, as a menstruant, or as one who has
given birth or as one who has aborted. We then consider special sorts of women, Samaritans, Sadducees, gentiles, and their
status; the rule applying to blood produced in labor, to blood
that appears during the *zibah*-period, and to blood attendant
upon a Caesarean birth. The final problem is the point at
which any sort of the aforelisted unclean fluids imparts uncleanness—a neat summary to the whole. Let us now examine
in detail the topical sequence of Mishnaic pericopes treated in
the Palestinian Talmud.

Retroactive contamination (1:1–2:4).

1:1   We reckon that objects touched by a woman before the time
       that her period started are clean (Shammaites). Hillelites: Ob-
       jects a woman touched from the time she last examined herself
       and found herself clean and until the time she found her period
       has begun are unclean. If a woman has a fixed period, her pe-
       riod of uncleanness begins only with the discovery that the pe-
       riod has begun. Test-rags are equivalent to an examination.

1:2, 3,
4, 5, 6   Expansion of M. 1:1.

2:1   Continuation of examination rules.

2:2–3   *Re* use of test-rags, continuation of examination rules (2:3 ex-
         pands 2:2).

2:4   All women are assumed to be clean for their husbands. Test-
       rags are required.

Unclean excretions (2:5–5:2).

A. The unclean blood (2:5–3:7).

2:5   Sages' parable *re* sources of blood.

2:6–7   Colors that denote blood is unclean (2:7 expands 2:6).

B. **Status of abortions as to uncleanness.** 3:1–7

3:1   She who aborts—with blood, unclean as menstruant; without blood, clean. Judah: Unclean.

3:2   She who aborts something like a rind, hair, dust, red flies, etc. She who aborts something like fish, etc. She who aborts something like a beast, etc., if male, unclean, clean for period of male birth, etc., so Meir. Sages: Anything which does not bear human form is not deemed a fetus.

3:3   She who aborts a sac filled with water, etc. If limb was formed, she observes uncleanness, cleanness of both male and female.

3:4   She who aborts a sandal, placenta, observes uncleanness of male, female.

3:5   She who aborts a *tumtom* or androgyne observes uncleanness, cleanness of male, female, etc.

3:6   She who aborts and the nature of the abortion is not known observes uncleanness, cleanness of male, female. If it is not known whether it was human, she observes for male, female, and menstruating woman.

3:7   She who miscarries on fortieth day does not take account of possibility that it is a human fetus. On forty-first day, she observes uncleanness, cleanness of male, female, and menstruation.

6 Yerushalmi Niddah
Chapter One

1:1

[A]   *[48d] Shammai says, "[For] all women it is sufficient [to reckon menstrual uncleanness from] their time [of discovering a flow]."*

[B]   *Hillel says, "[They are deemed unclean retroactively] from [the time of] an examination [at which the flow of menstrual blood was discovered] to the [last] examination [made beforehand, at which no flow of menstrual blood was discovered],*

[C]   *"even for many days."*

[D]   *And sages rule not in accord with the opinion of this one nor in accord with the opinion of that one but:*

[E]   *[the woman is held to have been unclean only] during [the preceding] twenty-four hours [when] this lessens the period [of uncleanness demarcated by the span] from examination to examination.*

[F]   *[And she is held to have been unclean only] during the period from [one] examination to [the preceding] examination [when] this lessens the period of twenty-four hours [of retroactive uncleanness].*

[G]   *Any woman who has a fixed period—sufficient for her is her fixed period [in which case there is no retroactive uncleanness at all].*

[H]   *And she who makes use of test-rags—lo, this [form of examination] is equivalent to an examination [and so marks the point before which the woman is assumed to have been clean],*

138

[I]   *which lessens either the period of twenty-four hours [of retroac-*
tive contamination] or the period from examination to examina-
tion.

[I.A]   What is the meaning of the phrase, *"It is sufficient [to reckon*
menstrual uncleanness from] their time [of discovering a
flow]"?

[B]   [Such women] do not retroactively impart uncleanness to food
subject to the laws of cleanness.

[II.A]   *And sages rule not in accord with the opinion of this one nor in*
accord with the opinion of that one.

[B]   Not in accord with the opinion of Shammai, who placed no
limit to his view of the matter [in entirely dismissing the possibility of retroactive uncleanness].

[C]   Nor in accord with the opinion of Hillel, who took an extreme
position.

[III.A]   *But [the woman is held to have been unclean only] during [the*
preceding] twenty-four hours [when] this lessens the period [of
uncleanness demarcated by the span] from examination to ex-
amination, and [she is held to have been unclean only] during
the period from [one] examination to [the preceding] examina-
tion [when] this lessens the period of twenty-four hours [of ret-
roactive uncleanness].

[B]   *How does a period of twenty-four hours diminish the period*
from one examination to the next examination?

[C]   [If] a woman examined herself on Monday [finding no evidence
of the advent of her menstrual period], and produced menstrual blood on Thursday, the [retroactive] contamination applies only back to the hour, on Wednesday, twenty-four hours
[before the time at which, on Thursday, the woman discovered
the menstrual blood].

[D]   *How does the period from one examination to the next exami-*
nation diminish the period of twenty-four hours?

[E]   [If] a woman examined herself in the morning [finding no evidence of the advent of her menstrual period], and produced
menstrual blood at dusk, the [retroactive] contamination applies only back to the morning [and not for the antecedent
twenty-four hours].

[**IV**.A]   There have we learned the Tannaitic teaching: *A dead creeping thing that was found in an alleyway imparts uncleanness retroactively [M. Nid. 7:2].*

[B]   R. Ammi asked [whether] the cited passage of the Mishnah might not be contrary to the position of Shammai.

[C]   Said R. Yosé, "If it is not in accord with the position of Shammai [who rejects the possibility of retroactive contamination entirely], then [the cited passage of the Mishnah also] is not even in accord with the position of Hillel.

[D]   "For does Hillel not concur in the case of an alleyway that is [daily] swept out, and through which a water-course runs, that it is deemed clean [retroactively, in case a dead creeping thing is found therein]?"

[E]   Shammai maintains this: In the case of a woman, because she customarily [examines herself when she] urinates, sages have treated her as comparable to an alleyway that is swept out from day to day and through which a water-course runs, so that it is deemed clean [under normal conditions, until proven otherwise].

[**V**.A]   Up to now [we have assumed that we deal with a case] in which a woman examined herself and found herself wholly dry.

[B]   [But what is the law] if a woman examined herself and found blood that [in fact] is clean [and not a source of uncleanness at all]?

[C]   R. Ammi in the name of Rab, R. Ba in the name of R. Judah: "[If] a woman examined herself and found clean [blood], she is [in any case] prohibited from having sexual relations until the source [of her blood] is [entirely] dried up."

[D]   (ḤD) R. Tobi said in the name of R. Abbahu, "She is prohibited from having sexual relations for twenty-four hours."

[E]   Said R. Jacob bar Aḥa when he came up here [to the land of Israel], "I heard from all the rabbis that she is permitted to have sexual relations forthwith [and need not wait for twenty-four hours]."

[**VI**.A]   They contemplated ruling:

[B]   The party who rules that she is permitted to have sexual relations [maintains that it is comparable to a case in which] an examination serves to limit the period of contamination established by the presumptive uncleanness during the antecedent twenty-four hours.

[C] The party who rules that she is prohibited from having sexual relations [maintains that it is] not [comparable to a case in which] an examination serves to limit the period of retroactive contamination during the preceding twenty-four hours.

[D] But [in fact] even in accord with the party who holds that she is prohibited from having sexual relations, [it is comparable] to an examination, which indeed serves to limit the contamination to the preceding twenty-four hours.

[E] Then why is the woman prohibited from having sexual relations?

[F] Because since she becomes accustomed [to having sexual relations] at a time of a flow of clean blood, she also may become accustomed to have sexual relations during a flow of unclean blood.

[VII.A] [If] a woman examined herself and found blood the status of which is subject to doubt, it is self-evident that this [examination] does not function as does an examination to impose a limit on the retroactive uncleanness during the antecedent twenty-four hours.

[B] But as to the status of the blood itself: What is the rule as to its imparting uncleanness as a matter of doubt?

[C] We may infer the rule from the following teaching:

[D] **One whose sex is unknown and an androgyne who produced a drop of blood—sufficient for them [to impart uncleanness to objects they have touched] is their time** [of actually having discovered the blood; we do not impose uncleanness, by reason of doubt as to their status as women, on objects they have touched from the last examination, or for the preceding twenty-four hours] [T. Nid. 1:3A].

[E] Now what do you wish to infer from this passage?

[F] Said R. Yosé, "One whose sex is unknown and an androgyne are cases of doubt [as to whether they are women or men], and the matter of imputing retroactive contamination during the antecedent twenty-four hours is a case of [doing so by reason of] doubt. Now [we do not impute uncleanness by adding] one matter of doubt to yet another matter of doubt.

[G]   "Here too her producing a drop of blood is a case of doubt [as to the status of the blood], and imputing uncleanness for the antecedent twenty-four hours is by reason of doubt. Now [we do not impute uncleanness by adding] one matter of doubt to yet another matter of doubt."

[VIII.A]   Huna bar Ḥiyya said, "The imputation of retroactive uncleanness for a period of twenty-four hours of which they have spoken applies in a case of [food in the status of] Holy Things, but not in a case of [ordinary] food [merely] subject to the laws of cleanness."

[B]   Responded Rab Ḥisda, "And [do we] not [have] the following Tannaitic teaching (TNY): MᶜŚH B: **A young girl in ᶜAitalu [whose time had come to produce menstrual blood] missed three periods and did not produce blood, and afterward she produced blood. And the case came before sages, and they ruled, 'Sufficient for her is her time [of actually observing a flow, but there is no retroactive uncleanness imputed to objects she touched beforehand]' [T. Nid. 1:9J].**

[C]   "Now are there Holy Things in ᶜAitalu? [Obviously not.]"

[D]   Now [in this case] we are dealing with a situation in which the food was prepared in accord with the cleanness-rules applying to the cleanness of Holy Things, and not in accord with the cleanness-rules applying to ordinary food.

[E]   Now [if you go so far as that,] you may as well interpret the case as one in which the food was prepared in accord with the rules applying to purification-water, for the rules of cleanness required for purification-water are still more stringent than those applying to Holy Things.

[IX.A]   TNY: In a case of retroactive contamination for a period of twenty-four hours [49a] of which the sages have spoken, they suspend [the status of food prepared in a state of cleanness], but they do not burn it.

[B]   And R. Zeᶜira looked into (ḤDY) the matter, and found it taught:

[C]   **She who produces a bloodstain imparts uncleanness retroactively. And to what does she impart uncleanness? Food,** drink, and things used for lying and sitting. And she is in disarray [as to setting her fixed period], and retroactively imparts uncleanness to the one who has intercourse with her [T. Nid. 9:6].

[D]   She who produces blood imparts uncleanness [to objects that she touched] retroactively. And to what does she impart uncleanness? Food, drink, and objects used for lying and sitting. But she is not in disarray [as to setting her fixed period], and she does not impart uncleanness retroactively to one who has had intercourse with her.

R. ʿAqiba says, "She does retroactively impart uncleanness to the one who has intercourse with her."

[E]   And in the case of this one [who produced a bloodstain] and that one [who produced blood], they suspend [the status of food she has touched], but they do not burn [as definitely unclean food she has touched] [T. Nid. 9:6, 9:5. This settles the question of A.]

[X.A]   There they say: the contamination effected for the preceding twenty-four hours, of which they spoke, is such that an object on which such a woman has lain is unclean, as is an object that she has touched.

[B]   One who has had sexual relations with her [during this period of doubt] has the status of one who has had sexual relations with a[n actually] menstruating woman.

[C]   But he is not deemed to impart uncleanness through merely shifting an object, so he does not impart uncleanness to a clay utensil.

[D]   It is found taught, He does impart uncleanness to a clay utensil through shifting it [so L].

[XI.A]   In a case of retroactive contamination during the preceding twenty-four hours of which they have spoken: As to that which such a woman touches in the public domain [in which case a doubt normally is resolved as clean]—what is the law [so L]?

[B]   We shall infer the answer from the following case:

[C]   A woman who is pregnant and a nursing mother [are assumed to be] clean for their husbands, and so a woman who has a fixed time.

[D]   And all other women are deemed to be clean for having sexual relations, but impart uncleanness to things that they touch [in a period of twenty-four hours retroactive upon an appearance of blood]. [This answers A.]

[E]   Thus one must rule that things that she touches in the public domain are deemed certainly unclean [even in a case of doubt, just as at D].

[XII.A]   R. Yudan asked about a case in which a woman examined her shift at dawn and found it clean, at dusk and found a blood-stain on it.

[B]   It is obvious that her shift is unclean only from the moment at which she last had examined it.

[C]   But what is the status of the woman herself? Is she deemed unclean for the preceding twenty-four hours?

[D]   Now in fact, do you not declare the woman herself unclean only on account of her shift? But her shift is unclean only from the moment at which she examined it. So will the woman herself be deemed unclean for the whole of the preceding twenty-four hours? [Obviously not!]

[XIII.A]   *And she who makes use of test-rags—lo, this [form of examination] is equivalent to an examination [and so marks the point before which the woman is assumed to have been clean].*

[B]   What would be a concrete case?

[C]   [If] a woman examined herself at dawn [finding no blood], and had sexual relations toward noon, making use of a test rag, and then produced blood at dusk—unclean [are only those objects that she touched] retroactively to the time of her having had sexual relations [but not earlier].

[D]   Levi said, "Concerning the test rag used after having sexual relations [the Mishnah] speaks, but the test-rag used before having sexual relations is swept clean by her vagina, so it does not effect a good examination."

[E]   R. Abun in the name of R. Zeira [said], "The Mishnah speaks of a test rag used before sexual relations, but as to the test rag used after sexual relations, it is discolored on account of semen."

The principal issue is the status of objects touched by a woman immediately prior to her discovering that her period has begun; at that point, of course, Scripture specifies that whatever the woman touches is deemed unclean. Since we do not know for sure that the woman was unclean prior to her producing a drop of menstrual blood, we deal with resolving cases of doubt. There are three positions. Shammai resolves all such cases of doubt in favor of cleanness; to him there is no issue at all. We do not scruple about contamination before we have solid evidence that the woman is unclean. Hillel resolves such cases in favor of uncleanness, retroactive to the last point at which we know for sure the woman was clean. This of course is exactly the opposite view. Sages take up a position vis-à-vis Hillel's, ignoring Shammai's view entirely. They allow for a period of twenty-four hours of retroactive contamination, limited by the moment, in that interval, in which the woman last examined herself and found that she was clean. All of this is nicely spelled out in the Mishnah, which contains ample interpretation of its own ideas. The problem of the discontinuity between sages (D) and Shammai (A) need not detain us. Sages clearly have a conflict between two criteria for retroactive contamination, and Shammai is not party to that version of the dispute.

I see thirteen independent units of discourse, as indicated. The progression from one unit to the next superficially is choppy, since there is no clear effort at establishing formal or literary continuity. But the sequence of exercises reveals a quite logical principle of arrangement. First we have an effort to gloss verbatim and explain the principal elements of the Mishnah's discourse. This is done through citations of the Mishnah's language and brief interpretations thereof. The work of glossing is at units **I, II, III**. Second, at **IV**, we proceed to take up the underlying principles expressed at M and compare these principles to those governing other cases, relevant or parallel in principle. **V** amplifies the Mishnah's rule, remaining well within the framework of exegesis of the Mishnah, and **VI**, **VII**, and **VIII** complete the disciplined exegesis of the Mishnah's language and principles. Only at **IX** do we raise questions essentially secondary to the Mishnah's interests, leaving the frame of discourse defined by the Mishnah. Units **X** and **XI** carry forward the exegesis of **IX**, just as **V—VIII** have carried forward their predecessors' exegesis of the Mishnah. **XII** returns us to the matter of doubt, that is, **IV**. Whether or not **XII** should have been placed earlier in the discussion, however,

is not in doubt, because, in fact, it is continuous with **XI**. So
the order, over all, is (1) the exegesis of the Mishnah, (2) expansion of discourse to encompass underlying principles of the
Mishnah, then (3) the exegesis of this range of expanded discourse. **XIII** is essentially distinct from the continuous discussion which has preceded and takes up a separate stich of the
Mishnah. It does what we expect on the basis of the earlier materials, that is, it begins by simply amplifying the Mishnah's
main point with relevant facts.

Let us now turn to a brief account of the Talmud's materials, of which only **IX–X** pose difficulty. The close glossing of
the Mishnah at **I**, **II**, and **III** leaves no room for comment at
all. Everything is fully articulated. The exercise at **IV** is interesting, because the underlying issue of the dispute of the Mishnah, the matter of retroactive contamination, here is made
explicit. Clearly, Shammai cannot concur with the presupposition of **IV**.A (= M. Nid. 7:2), that retroactive contamination
to begin with is a possibility. What is interesting is Yosé's view
that Hillel also will not accord with the cited pericope of the
Mishnah. The reason is that, in the stated case (**IV**.D), there is
no clear likelihood of contamination prior to the actual discovery of the dead creeping thing, because the alleyway is kept
clean. There are no grounds to suppose the dead creeping thing
was present for a long time prior to its discovery. Superfluously, E then explains why Shammai has the same view of the
woman. What is clarified is Hillel's position, a first-rate piece
of exegesis.

V undertakes a different sort of secondary expansion. It
raises a question not contemplated in the Mishnah, namely, a
case in which, while the woman does find blood, it is the sort
of blood that is not deemed to signify uncleanness. That is, it
is not menstrual blood but some other type. So, the issue now
shifts from retroactive contamination (**V**.C, D, E), a mark of
significant turning to broader issues than those dealt with either
in the Mishnah or in its initial exegesis. What we want to know
is whether the woman may have sexual relations during the
coming day, not whether she has contaminated objects she
touched during the preceding one. The answer to this fresh
question (E) is itself expanded at **VI**. But **VI** also brings us
back to the issues of the Mishnah, that is, to the consideration
of retroactive contamination, and it may be that **VI** should be
deemed an integral part of the discussion of **V**. The inclusion
of **VI** marks a careful effort at presenting a coherent discussion.

VII continues this secondary expansion of the Mishnah, now raising to the forefront of discussion the matter of doubt. What is at issue is the multiplication of reasons for doubt, that is, the intrusion of more than one ground for our not being certain about the facts of the matter. Since **V–VI** have asked about blood that is clean, the interest of **VII** in blood the status of which is uncertain is a logical next step. It again indicates how carefully the whole has been put together. The point of **VII** then is neatly expressed and requires no amplification.

The secondary expansion of the Mishnah concludes at **VIII**, which asks an essentially forced question about the circumstance or purpose of uncleanness. There are, after all, several distinct purposes for cleanness, first, to preserve the cleanness of ordinary food as if it were sanctified, e.g., as heave-offering; second, to preserve the cleanness of food deriving from the altar (Holy Things); and, third, to preserve the cleanness of food or objects used for the purification-rite (M. Hag. chapters 2–3, M. Par. chapter 10). The proposal of **VIII**.A is that we deal with food having the status of Holy Things. The relevance to what has gone before is then obvious. Since we deal with imputing uncleanness in a case of doubt, Huna bar Ḥiyya suggests that such an extreme position should be taken, specifically, when the doubt concerns Holy Things, subject to a more stringent rule than ordinary food or heave-offering. Ḥisda's reply invokes a case cited also in the Tosefta, but used in the Tosefta for a purpose other than the present one. I am inclined to see **VIII**.D and E as secondary expansion of A–C.

IX simply presents a thesis, A, and an extensive citation of materials also found in the Tosefta in support of that thesis. **X** continues the interest of **IX** in the way in which the uncleanness of the woman under discussion is transmitted and the objects to which it is transmitted. The main point of **X** is the status of the one who has sexual relations with her. He has entered into her status of uncleanness (B). C's point is that while a woman who is unclean as a menstruant imparts uncleanness through merely shifting an object, without actually touching it, the man who has sexual relations in this regard differs. A clay utensil will not be susceptible to uncleanness through his touch on its outer surfaces, since a clay utensil does not receive uncleanness through its outer surfaces. Now if such a man shifts a clay utensil, he too makes that clay utensil unclean. He thus has exactly the same status as the woman. D holds the opposite view.

XI, **XII**, and **XIII** pose no problems of interpretation. The established principle is that, in a case of doubt, objects found in public domain are deemed clean. Here at M. Nid. 1:1, of course we have a case of doubt about the status of objects during the preceding twenty-four hours (**XI**.A). D–E prove that, in a case of doubt, in the present matter objects are deemed unclean. This view then is challenged by Yudan at **XII**. The cited case yields the opposite conclusion. Objects subject to doubt are deemed clean, so too the woman will be deemed clean. **XIII**, as I said, simply amplifies a matter of fact, with the two possible, contrary opinions fully spelled out and explained. In all, therefore, the Talmud's treatment of the Mishnah is systematic, coherent, and entirely cogent.

1:2   [In Leiden MS and *editio princeps:* 1:3]

[A]   *What [is the case in which] her [having a] fixed period suffices for her [as at M. Nid. 1:1A, G]?*

[B]   *[If] she was sitting on a couch and occupied with the preparation of food subject to the laws of cleanness,*

[C]   *[and] she got up and saw a spot of blood [where she had been sitting],*

[D]   *she is deemed to be unclean.*

[E]   *But all the food [that she had been preparing up to that moment] is deemed to be clean.*

[F]   *[Thus] even though they have ruled that she imparts uncleanness [to objects she has touched] over the preceding twenty-four hours, [because she has a fixed period] she counts [her time of uncleanness, hence of having imparted uncleanness to food with which she has just had contact] only from the very moment at which she discovered [the drop of blood].*

[G]   *R. Eleazar [sic!] says, "For [only] four sorts of women, sufficient is their fixed time [for having a period without retroactive contamination]: a virgin, a pregnant woman, a nursing mother, and an old lady."*

[H]   *Said R. Joshua, "[For that tradition] I heard only [that the rule applies to] a virgin."*

[I]   *But the law is in accord with the opinion of R. Eliezer.*

[I.A]   Said R. Joshua, "I heard only [that the rule applies to a virgin."

[B]   But the law is in accord with the opinion of R. Eliezer.

[C]   **[T. Nid. 1:5C: Said to him R. Eliezer], "They do not say to him who has not seen the new moon to come and give testimony, but to him who has seen it does one say to come and give testimony.**

[D]   **"You have not heard, but I have heard." [T. Nid. 1:5C]**

[E]   So long as R. Eliezer was alive, the law was in accord with R. Joshua. Once R. Eliezer had died, Joshua made the rule accord with the position of R. Eliezer.

[II.A]   Now how shall we interpret this matter [I.E]?

[B]   If it is a case in which R. Eliezer had heard the tradition from a single authority, while R. Joshua had heard it from two, whether [Eliezer was] alive or dead, the law should be in accord with R. Joshua. [On the other hand,] if it is in a case in which R. Joshua had heard it from a single authority, while R. Eliezer had heard it from two authorities, whether [Eliezer was] alive or dead, the law should be in accord with R. Eliezer.

[C]   This accords with that teaching which we have learned in a Tannaitic saying:

[D]   [If] one says, "I have heard from two authorities," and two say, "We have heard the tradition from a single authority," greater is the probative value of the tradition stated by the one who had heard from two authorities than that of the two who had heard from a single authority.

[E]   But thus should we interpret the matter: [It was] a case in which both are equal. This one had heard from a single authority, and that one had heard from a single authority, [or] this one had heard from two authorities, and that one had heard from two authorities.

[F]   While [Eliezer] was alive, [Joshua] did not concur in his opinion. After [Eliezer] had died, [Joshua] did concur in [Eliezer's] opinion.

[III.A]   Now what did [Joshua] perceive [after Eliezer's death] to give the ruling as he did?

[B]   It was in accord with the following Tannaitic teaching:

[C]   "As to the four sorts of women [M. Nid. 1:2F] concerning whom sages have ruled that their fixed period suffices [so that we do not impute uncleanness for the antecedent twenty-four hours, or up to the last examination at which the woman found herself to be clean],

"their bloodstain [also] imparts uncleanness retroactively,

"except for the case of the girl whose time for having a period has not yet come.

"For such a girl does not produce bloodstains [anyhow]," the words of R. Meir.

And sages say, "As to the four sorts of women concerning whom sages have ruled that their fixed period suffices, their bloodstain does impart uncleanness retroactively.

"And as to a girl whose time for having a period actually has come, a bloodstain produced by her is tantamount to a drop of blood produced by her' [T. Nid. 3:1].

[D]   Just as, in the case of a drop of blood produced by her, sufficient for her is her fixed period [so that she does not impart uncleanness retroactively], so in the case of a bloodstain produced by her, sufficient for her is her fixed period.

[E]   Said R. Yannai, "It is because it is common for her to produce excretions."

[F]   Now [reverting to A] if in the case of this one, who regularly produces excretions, you have ruled that it is sufficient for her to be deemed unclean from the time of her fixed period, these, who do not commonly produce excretions, all the more so should be subject to that same rule.

[G]   It is on the basis of this reasoning that [Joshua ultimately] accepted the opinion of [Eliezer].

M. 1:2's secondary expansion of M. Nid. 1:1 leads to the special point of interest in the Talmud. Once a woman has a fixed period, then, as B–F explain, there is no question of retroactive contamination. At issue for the Talmud is Eliezer's tradition that four sorts of women rely on a fixed period. Joshua has a distinct tradition, that only a virgin is eligible. The Tosefta's expansion of the matter, I, is what the Talmud then amplifies at II and III. In fact, the whole of the Talmud is a continuous unitary discussion. The main point comes at III. What we have here is not a claim that Joshua knew what Yannai would say so much later on, but rather that Joshua knew the same kind of reasoning that, later on, Yannai would articulate. This is not farfetched. For the main point of **III**.F is that, if one can concede that the virgin is deemed to enjoy a fixed period, then there is no reason to deny that the other woman on the list also are going to enjoy the same advantage. That is the operative point.

1:3   [In Leiden MS and *editio princeps:* 1:4]

[A]   *Who is a virgin [among the four women who fall into the category of those for whom the time of first seeing blood suffices, without scruple as to prior contamination by reason of doubt]?*

[B]   *Any girl who has never in her life produced a drop of [menstrual] blood,*

[C]   *even though she is married.*

[D]   *A pregnant woman?*

[E]   *From the moment at which the fetus is known to be present [three months].*

[F]   *A nursing mother?*

[G]   *Up to the time at which she will wean her child.*

[H]   *[If] she handed [the child] over to a wet-nurse, weaned [the child], or [the child] died,*

[I]   *R. Meir says, "She imparts uncleanness [to objects she has touched] during the twenty-four hours [preceding the point at which she discovered the menstrual blood]."*

[J]   *And sages say, "Sufficient for her is [contamination] from the time [at which she discovered the drop of blood, and there is no question of retroactive contamination]."*

[**I**.A]   Thus is the teaching of the Mishnah: *Any girl who has not seen menstrual blood in her life, and even though she is married.*

[B]   They [thus] spoke of a virgin as to blood[, that is, a girl who had never menstruated], not a virgin as to the hymen.

[C]   There are cases in which a girl is a virgin as to blood and not virgin as to the hymen. There are cases in which she is a virgin as to the hymen but is not a virgin as to blood.

[D]   [A girl is] a virgin as to the hymen [Leiden MS, *editio princeps,*
and printed text: blood] when she produced a drop of blood
and afterward was married.

[E]   [She is a] virgin as to blood [Leiden MS, *editio princeps,* and
printed text: the hymen] when she was married and afterward
produced a drop of blood.

[II.A]   It was taught in a Tannaitic saying:

[B]   **There are three kinds of virgins: a virgin woman, a virgin sycamore, and virgin soil. A virgin woman is any woman who
has never been laid [L drops: by a man]. A virgin sycamore
is any that has never been chopped down. Virgin soil is any
that has never been worked. Rabban Simeon b. Gamaliel
says, "It is any in which there is not a single sherd" [T.
Sheb. 3:14H, 15].**

[III.A]   [The law (M. Nid. 1:3B) that a girl who has not produced a
drop of blood does not impart retroactive uncleanness even
when she does produce a drop] applies even if she was married,
even if she became pregnant, even if she gives suck [to her
baby], and even if she excretes blood for all seven days for a
male or all fourteen days [of clean blood] for a female.

[B]   And does she have a divining tool in hand [to know whether it
will be a male or a female]?

[C]   When [the child] is a male, it is for seven days, and when it is
a female, it is for fourteen days [after birth, that the stated rule
applies].

[IV.A]   And that is the rule [only] when she has ceased to produce
blood of purifying [that is not menstrual blood and thus is not
unclean. But she has not yet produced a drop of menstrual
blood].

[B]   That is in accord with the following Tannaitic teaching:

[C]   [A girl] ceased to produce blood of purifying and yielded no
more blood, but afterward she produced a drop of blood—

[D]   and the case came before the sages, who ruled, "Sufficient for
her is her time [of actually producing a drop of blood, and
there is no question of retroactive contamination]" [cf. T. Nid.
1:12D].

[E]   Now in the view of Rab, who maintains that [the source of blood of purifying and the source of menstrual blood] are one and the same, but the Torah has declared [that single source] to be clean [during the days of purifying], this ruling is wholly in order[, since it maintains that there must be a clear division between blood of purifying and menstrual blood, marked by a space of time in which there is no excretion at all. Hence sages approve such a case, because the blood of purifying came to an end before the other sort of blood began. Thus all are from a single source].

[F]   In the view of R. Yannai, who maintains that it is a single source [for both types of blood], but [the character of the blood] changes [at the period after birth], it also is satisfactory.

[G]   But so far as Levi is concerned, who maintains that they are two distinct sources of blood, even if the blood of purifying had not [yet] come to an end, [we should nonetheless invoke the principle of] sufficiency of the moment at which the blood actually appears [without scruple as to prior contamination, since, as we see, in his view the two kinds of blood are unrelated and derive from two distinct sources in the woman's body].

[H]   Said R. Mana, "The reason of Levi [for concurring in the cited ruling differs from the reason of Rab and Yannai for accepting the same ruling. It is that] once she becomes accustomed [to having sexual relations during a time at which she is producing] clean blood, she may just as well get used to having sexual relations during a time at which she produces unclean blood." [Thus requiring a bloodless interval is for a reason other than that imputed by Rab and Yannai. cf. 1:1 **VI**.F.]

[I]   Said R. Yosé b. R. Bun, "Levi can solve the problem on the basis of yet another Tannaitic teaching, which we have learned:

[J]   " 'R. Yosé says, 'A pregnant woman and a nursing mother who passed three periods [without producing menstrual blood]—sufficient for them is their time [of actually producing blood, to contaminate objects they may touch. There is no question of retroactive contamination].'

[K]   " 'And we have a Tannaitic comment on this same teaching:

[L]   " 'The time of her pregnancy and the time of her nursing join together and add up to the three periods [in which the period is missed. That is to say, if the woman missed one period while pregnant, and two while nursing, they are deemed to be three].'

[M]   "Thus [this authority] maintains that they are a single source. [The cited teaching thus takes for granted that the different sorts of blood derive from a single source. Levi can then answer, in Yosé b. R. Bun's view, that the authority behind the cited teaching holds that they are a single source, while he follows an authority who does not concur in that view, but who holds that the blood comes from two distinct sources.]"

[V.A]   **When is the presence of the fetus recognized?**

[B]   **Sumkhos says in the name of R. Meir, "In three months.**

[C]   **"Even though there is no clear proof of that proposition, there is at least an indication of it: 'And it came to pass at the end of three months' (Gen. 38:24)" [T. Nid. 1:7A–C].**

[D]   Said R. Yudan, "And even if she is pregnant only with air: 'We were with child, we writhed, we have as it were brought forth wind' (Is. 26:18) [cf. T. Nid. 1:7E].

[E]   " 'You conceive chaff, you bring forth stubble' (Is. 33:11)."

[VI.A]   R Zeira, R. Ba bar Zutra, R. Ḥaninah in the name of R. Ḥiyya the Great: "Even if [the fetus is discernible] in the greater part of the first month, and for the greater part of the last month [if] the middle [month] is complete[, we deem the three months' rule to apply—that is, after only sixty-two days]."

[B]   Assi says, "Ninety days, complete."

[C]   And Samuel says, "They and their intercalated days [that is, three months, whether they are ninety days or even more than ninety days, by reason of adding additional days through late sightings of the moon]."

[D]   A case [of paternity] came before the rabbis over there [in the east], and they did not know whether [the conception of the child had taken place] within the thirteen days assigned to the first month, or the seventeen days assigned to the second one, or seventeen of the first and thirteen of the latter, with five complete [months] in the middle. [In this paternity case, the woman lost her husband and remarried soon thereafter. In this case, the woman gave birth in six complete solar months, but seven lunar months, after the death of the first husband and the remarriage. There were then five complete months, and the status of days in the first and last months—that is, seven in all—is unclear, with the possibility of thirteen days of the first month and seventeen of the final one, or vice versa, contributing to the six full months.]

[E]   They considered imputing genealogical invalidity to the fetus, by reason of *mamzerut*. [That is, the mother's status was not such that she was free to remarry when she did, so the child may have been born of a married woman and a man other than the husband.]

[F]   Said to them R. Naḥman bar Jacob, "A similar case came before Abba bar Ba, and he declared the fetus to be valid" [thus deeming the greater part of a month tantamount to a whole month, as at **VI.A**].

[G]   Now did Abba bar Ba take issue with Samuel, who was his son [who wants complete months (**VI.C**)]?

[H]   Said R. Ba, "There is a distinction to be drawn between [49b] perceiving the presence of the fetus and the actual birth.

[I]   "Recognizing the presence of the fetus is a matter of complete months [as Samuel has said].

[J]   "But [when we consider assigning the paternity of the child, once it is] born, we deal with abbreviated months."

[K]   There we have learned in a Tannaitic tradition:

[L]   *How long is protracted labor [for a woman in protracted labor who produces a drop of blood is deemed to be a menstruant and not a Zabah]? R. Meir says, "Even forty or fifty days." R. Judah says, "Sufficient for her is her ninth month." R. Yosé and R. Simeon say, "Hard labor continues no longer than for two weeks" [M. Nid. 4:5].*

[M]   R. Yosé in the name of R. Ba: "That is to say that a woman counts [reaching of term to give] birth in abbreviated months, for has it not been taught 'thirty days' [and not a whole month, inclusive of the intercalated days]?"

[N]   R. Yosé b. R. Bun (L:) in the name of Samuel: "That is to say that a woman [counts the giving of birth in] complete months, as we have learned, 'Sufficient for her is her [complete] month [inclusive of the intercalated days].' "

[O]   R. Yudan inquired, "In the end, does [the rule apply] only if she actually gives birth?"

[P]   No, even if she aborted [the rule applies].

[Q]   Said R. Mana, "I heard in the name of Samuel, 'There is no difference [in the time required] for recognizing the presence of the fetus and for [completing term and] giving birth.' But I do not know from whom I heard that teaching."

[R]   Said R. Ba, son of a priest, before R. Yosé, "R. Jeremiah stated that tradition."

[S]   Said R. Hezekiah to him, "R. Jeremiah did not state that teaching."

[T]   Now R. Yosé scrupled about accepting [what Mana had said]. He said, "If Joshua, who was so close to Moses, would not have said thus, but do you [lit.: he] say thus [in a case in which the source of the teaching in Samuel's name is not certain]!"

[U]   He retracted and said, "To be sure, he may have said it, but it was said as someone who has heard a ruling but is having difficulties with it."

[V]   And Abba bar Ba [indeed] did differ from Samuel, his son.

[W]   R. Berekiah in the name of Samuel: "A woman gives birth only on the 271st, 272nd, 273rd, or 274th day of her pregnancy [thus requiring nine complete months]."

[X]   Said to him R. Mana, "Whence did my master hear this saying?"

[Y]   Said to him, "From R. Ba."

[Z]   There is then confusion in the attributed opinions of R. Ba. There [H–J] he said, "There is a distinction between [measuring months for] recognizing the presence of the fetus and [reaching term for actually] giving birth. But here he said thus."

[AA]   R. Ba bar Zutra in the name of Samuel: "Whatever is subject to HRBH (= 212), lo, it is subject to 'RBH (208) [that is, seven months, as at D–E]."

[VIII.A]   R. Hiyya bar Ashi was in session before Rab. He observed that he was preoccupied.

[B]   He said to him, "Why so?"

[C]   He said to him, "My ass is pregnant and is coming to term, and I wanted to cover her so that she should not be chilled."

[D]   He said to him, "When did the male mount her?"

[E]   He said to him, "On such and such a day, and I reckoned from there."

[F]   He said to him, "If so, she will require [waiting a few more days]."

[G]   And so is it taught in a Tannaitic teaching: [The ass] who gives birth in less than term does not give birth in less than the days of the moon [354], and the one who gives birth beyond term does not give birth in more than the days of the sun [365 days].

[H]   A teaching of R. Joshua is at issue with this saying [of Rab's, that there is little variation in term], for R. Joshua b. Levi said, "Cows belonging to Antoninus were to be impregnated.

[I]   "And the servants of the court of Rabbi had oxen mount. Some of them gave birth now, and some of them gave birth later on [so there was much variation]."

[J]   Here [G] we speak of the case of an unclean beast and there [H–I] we speak of the case of a clean beast [which produces variation in the term of pregnancy].

[K]   And is it not written, "Do you know when the mountain goats bring forth? Do you observe the calving of the hinds? Can you number the months that they fulfill? And do you know the time when they bring forth, when they crouch, bring forth their offspring, and are delivered of their young?" (Job 39:1–3) [This indicates that there is a fixed term even for clean beasts.]

[L]   He said to him, "A clean wild beast is just like an unclean domesticated beast [in giving birth between 354 and 365 days after impregnation]."

The first three units, I–III, cite and then complement the Mishnah. The work is rather indifferent, compared to what is done at M. 1:1. The one clarification at I.A is the insertion of *menstrual*, as though that were not self-evident. The rest clarifies what is already clear. II simply cites a relevant passage

found in the Tosefta, as indicated. **III** serves as a bridge to
what is, in fact, an essentially autonomous discussion, **IV**, on
whether there is a distinct source for menstrual blood on the
one side and for blood of purifying on the other. That long discussion is clear as amplified. **V** then follows exactly the same
literary pattern. That is, the Tosefta is cited, verbatim, as an
introduction to yet another sizable, autonomous discussion.
The issue of the length of time that must pass for the fetus to
be recognized is joined with a parallel one, namely, the length
of time it takes for the fetus to be fully formed and reach term.
This discussion is phrased, not surprisingly, in terms of contradictory opinions of authorities (**VI**.A–C). Then the position of
Samuel's father vis-à-vis the issue on which his son takes a
stand is investigated. The issue is drawn at F. Then (H and
following), an effort is made to distinguish the interval, that for
the fetus, from the other, that for the term of pregnancy. This
exercise produces a protracted discussion, leading, at Z, to the
recognition that, in fact, there are contradictory traditions in
Samuel's name. The concluding unit, **VIII**, is tacked on because of its general relevance to the matter of the length of
pregnancies, now those of beasts.

1:4   [In Leiden MS and *editio princeps:* 1:5

[A]   *Who is an old woman?*

[B]   *Any woman who has missed three periods near the time of
menopause.*

[C]   *R. Eleazar says, "Any woman [not only an old one] who has
missed three periods—sufficient for her is her time [of actually
discovering blood, without scruple as to retroactive contamina-
tion]."*

[D]   *R. Yosé says, "[Only] a pregnant woman and nursing mother
who have missed three periods—sufficient for them is their
time."*

[**I**.A]   R. Meir says, "On account of [the need of producing] milk,
blood ceases" [= D].

[B]   R. Yosé says, "On account of pain [of giving birth], blood
ceases" [= D].

[C]   You turn out to rule in both a lenient and a strict way in accord with the opinion of R. Meir, [and] in both a lenient and a strict way in accord with the opinion of R. Yosé.

[D]   A lenient ruling in accord with the opinion of R. Meir is as follows: If the infant went on nursing for four or five years, [L: it is forbidden], sufficient [for the nursing mother] is her time [of finding the blood, for that entire interval].

[E]   And a strict ruling: If [the mother] gave her child over to a wet-nurse, weaned him, or he died, [blood discovered by her at the outset of her period means that she] imparts uncleanness [by reason of doubt] for the antecedent period of twenty-four hours.

[F]   And a lenient ruling in accord with the opinion of R. Yosé is as follows: If [the mother] gave her child over to a wet-nurse or weaned him or he died, [nonetheless] sufficient for her is her time [of finding blood].

[G]   A strict ruling: If he went on nursing for four or five years, it is forbidden [to deem sufficient the moment of discovering the flow of blood] beyond the first twenty-four months.

[H]   Now in regard to R. Meir's ruling that [the woman] imparts uncleanness for the antecedent period of twenty-four hours [under the stated circumstances]—what is the rule? Does it take effect forthwith, or is it only once the infant will cease to suck and be unable to go back to the teat? [Do we invoke the rule of twenty-four hours' antecedent contamination forthwith upon weaning, so that once the woman sees a drop of blood, she imparts antecedent contamination, or does the matter depend upon the condition of the infant?]

[I]   We may infer the ruling from the following:

[J]   **"An infant continues to suckle all twenty-four months. From that point onward, he is like one who sucks [from] an abomination," the words of R. Eliezer.**

[K]   **And R. Joshua says, "The infant continues to suck even for four or five years and he is permitted [to do so]. If he separated from the teat they do not return him to it" [T. Nid. 2:3I–J].**

[L]   How long [a time is deemed to mark the child's actually separating from the teat and giving up nursing, so that the child then is prohibited from returning to nursing]?

[M]   R. Jacob b. R. Aḥa, R. Ḥiyya in the name of R. Yoḥanan: "After twenty-four hours."

[N]   R. Ḥezekiah, R. Abbahu in the name of R. Simeon b. Laqish: "No longer than three days, reckoned from the moment of the last feeding." [So, in regard to G, it depends on the status of the infant.]

[O]   Under what circumstances? In a case in which he gave up the teat while in a state of good health. But if he did so while in a state of illness, they do bring him back to the teat forthwith.

[P]   [Now this rule applies, moreover] in the case of an infant who is in no danger [by reason of sickness], but in the case of an infant whose life is endangered [by sickness], forthwith do they return him to the teat even after some time as soon as [the need is recognized].

[II.A]   *An old lady.*

[B]   What is the definition of an old lady?

[C]   R. Simeon b. Laqish said, "Any woman who does not protest when they call her 'Madam.' "

[D]   Does the matter then depend on the woman's own [private] opinion?

[E]   Said R. Abin, "Any who is appropriately called 'Madam.' "

[F]   It was taught in a Tannaitic teaching: People are not to call slaves "Mister So-and-so" or "Madam So-and-so."

[G]   The staff of Rabban Gamaliel's house did refer to male and female slaves of the household as "Mister Ṭabi," and "Madam Ṭabitha."

[III.A]   R. Hoshaiah taught (TNY): "[If a woman] gave birth and then converted [to Judaism], she is not subject to the rule of producing blood of purifying[, and all blood produced after birth, for seven or fourteen days, is deemed unclean]."

[B]   Said R. Yosé, "And is that a suitable [teaching? It is self-evident and hardly requires articulation.] If R. Hoshaiah had not taught it, it would have been [logically] required [anyhow].

[C]   "Since such a woman [while a gentile] does not produce unclean blood, she also is not going to produce clean blood." [So
we learn that after conversion, she will produce unclean blood
in the stated circumstance.]

[D]   TNY: "A convert, a captive, or a slave-girl, who was redeemed, converted, or freed, has to wait for three months
[before marrying, lest she be pregnant beforehand]," the words
of R. Judah.

[E]   R. Yosé says, "They need not wait for three months" [T.
Yeb. 6:6N–O].

[F]   And as to the matter of menstrual blood?

[G]   R. Judah says, "She is subject to the rule of the sufficiency of
the time [at which the blood is found, thus is deemed to have a
fixed period from the time of her prior status, and she then
does not impart retroactive uncleanness for twenty-four
hours]."

[H]   R. Yosé says, "She imparts uncleanness for the antecedent
twenty-four hours. [The period fixed beforehand now is null.]"

[I]   Said Rabbi, "The opinion of R. Yosé appears appropriate in
the case of menstrual blood[, so there is no fixed period], and
the opinion of R. Judah in the matter of a possible pregnancy[,
and they must wait three months]."

[J]   R. Ḥiyya in the name of R. Yoḥanan: "The law is in accord
with the opinion of R. Yosé."

[K]   R. Ba, son of a priest, raised the question in session with R.
Yosé, "Do we not rule as follows: 'In a case of dispute between
R. Judah and R. Yosé, the law is not in accord with the opin-
ion of R. Yosé'?

[L]   "But since Rabbi said, 'The opinion of R. Yosé appears appropriate,' [in this dispute we do follow the opinion of R. Yosé]."

[M]   Now has not R. Ba in the name of R. Zeirah stated, "In every
case in which Rabbi ruled, 'The opinion [of so-and-so] appears
appropriate,' the dispute remains moot, except for the case of
the circle of pressed figs, in which this party concurs with that
party, and that party concurs with this party?" [The reference
is to T. Ter. 5:11.]

[N]   Said R. Yosé the Elder in session before R. Ḥanina son of R. Abbahu, "And [does the law follow R. Yosé] even if it is certain that [the women] indeed had sexual relations [immediately prior to their change in status, so there are solid grounds for supposing they should wait three months to see whether they have become pregnant]?"

[O]   He said to him, "And do not gentile women ordinarily have sexual relations? [But, nonetheless, these women do not have to wait three months, for they are assumed to take prophylactic measures.]"

[IV.A]   *R. Eliezer says, "Any woman [not only an old one] who has missed three periods—sufficient for her is her time [of actually discovering blood, without scruple as to retroactive contamination]."*

[B]   [Now it was taught in a] Tannaitic [tradition] on the [foregoing passage of the Mishnah]:

[C]   They said to him, "Sages have listed only the old lady."

[D]   Now has it not been taught in a Tannaitic tradition:

[E]   **Said R. Eleazar, "MʿŚH B: A young girl in ʿAitalu whose time had come to produce a flow of menstrual blood missed three periods, and afterward she produced menstrual blood. The case came before sages. They ruled, '[She is subject to the rule that] sufficient for her is her time.' "**

[F]   They said to him, "You then were a minor, and a minor is not competent to give testimony."

[G]   On one occasion Rabbi gave instructions in accord with the opinion of R. Eleazar [Eliezer], and he was distressed about it.

[H]   Said R. Mana in session before R. Yosé, "When he gave instructions in accord with the lenient rulings of R. Meir and in accord with the lenient rulings of R. Yosé, he was not distressed. So here should he have been distressed?"

[I]   He said to him, "In that case [of Yosé and Meir], we are dealing with the opinions of individuals. So one may take the position to join his opinion with that of R. Meir and his master, as against that of R. Yosé, or join his opinion with that of R. Yosé and his master, as against that of R. Meir. But do you have the possibility of ruling in this case, 'Let him join his opinion with that of R. Eleazar and his master over that of sages' [who are, after all, the majority]"?

[J]   "And moreover, it has been taught in a Tannaitic teaching, **'They said to him, It was an interim ruling [and not meant as established law]' " [T. Nid. 1:9K].**

[**V**.A]   R. Yosé [49c] says, "A pregnant woman and nursing mother who have missed three periods—sufficient for them is their time."

[B]   And [it has been taught in a] Tannaitic [teaching] on the [foregoing citation of the Mishnah]:

[C]   The period in which the woman is pregnant and the period in which she is nursing join together to establish the three missed periods.

[D]   For [Yosé] is of the opinion that [the blood derives from] a single source.

The secondary amplification of the Mishnah precedes the close citation and glossing. That is, **I** does not link up to the Mishnah's interests, while **II**, **IV**, and **V** first cite and then gloss the Mishnah. The issue of **I** is to augment the opinions of Meir and Yosé. Since the Mishnah's Yosé includes both the pregnant woman and the nursing mother, and **I**.A–B presents a dispute on whether the one or the other belongs on the list of those subject to the rule of the sufficiency of the time of finding blood, there is a clear disjuncture. So the whole of **I** is essentially a supplement. **II**, **IV**, and **V**, as noted, require no comment. Like **I**, **III** is essentially autonomous of the Mishnah's specific interests, though the point of relevance, **III**.H, should be noted.

1:5   [In Leiden MS and *editio princeps:* 1:6]

[A]   In what case did they lay down the ruling, "Sufficient for her is her time [of first discovering the drop of menstrual blood, so that there is no prior contamination]"?

[B]   In the case of [a virgin's, a pregnant woman's, a nursing mother's, or an old lady's] first producing a drop of blood [after missing the period in the latter three instances].

[C]   *But in the instance of the second [or later] producing of a drop of blood, [the blood] imparts uncleanness for the antecedent period of twenty-four hours [by reason of doubt as to when it first occurred].*

[D]   *But if [the woman] produced the first drop of blood by reason of constraint [that is, through an abnormal cause], then even in the case of the second drop of blood, [we invoke the rule of] sufficiency of the time [of finding the blood for demarcating the commencement of the woman's contaminating power].*

[I.A]   Samuel said, "This teaching [of A] applies only to a virgin and an old lady. But as to a pregnant woman and a nursing mother, they assign to her the entire period of her pregnancy or the entire period of her nursing [respectively, for the blood ceases, and what does flow is inconsequential, so there is no retroactive contamination at all]."

[B]   Rab and R. Yoḥanan—both of them say, "All the same are the virgin, the old lady, the pregnant woman, and the nursing mother [= B]."

[C]   Said R. Zeira, "The opinion of Rab and R. Yoḥanan accords with the position of R. Ḥaninah, and all of them differ from the position of Samuel."

[D]   For R. Eleazar said in the name of R. Ḥaninah, "On one occasion Rabbi gave instruction in accord with the lenient rulings of R. Meir and in accord with the lenient rulings of R. Yosé."

[E]   What was the nature of the case?

[F]   [If] the fetus was noticeable, and then [the woman] produced a drop of blood—

[G]   R. Meir says, "She is subject to the rule of the sufficiency of her time [of actually discovering the blood]."

[H]   R. Yosé says, "She imparts uncleanness retroactively for twenty-four hours."

[I]   [If] she produced many drops of blood, then missed three periods, and afterward produced a drop of blood,

[J]   R. Meir says, "She imparts uncleanness retroactively for twenty-four hours."

[K]   R. Yosé says, "She is subject to the rule of the sufficiency of her time [of actually discovering blood]."

[L]   Now if you say that they assign to her the entire period of her
       pregnancy or the entire period of her nursing, what need do I
       have for the lenient ruling of R. Yosé? The teaching of R. Meir
       [in such a case] produces a still more lenient ruling than does
       that of R. Yosé. [For so far as Meir is concerned, if we read his
       view in the light of Samuel's opinion (A), the nursing mother
       and the pregnant woman enjoy the stated leniency throughout
       the period of nursing or pregnancy. The issue, then, is that
       Meir deems this drop of blood (I) as a second one. Yosé re-
       gards the cessation of the period as consequential.]

[M]   Said R. Mana before R. Yosé, "Or perhaps we should assign
       [Rabbi's ruling] to the case of the milk [dealt with above, in
       which Meir and Yosé dispute about whether the woman who
       hands over her son to a wet-nurse retains the stated leniency.
       At issue then is whether the matter depends upon the status of
       the woman's milk or on the status of the child]."

[N]   He said to him, "The matter was explicitly stated in regard to
       the present issue."

[II.A] Up to this point [in the discussion], we have dealt with a girl
       who has reached the time to produce menstrual blood.

[B]   As to a girl who has not yet reached her time for producing
       menstrual blood, but produced a number of drops of blood,
       the first time this happens, she is subject to the rule of the suf-
       ficiency of the time [of discovering the blood, so that there is
       no retroactive contamination]. At the second appearance of
       blood, we similarly invoke the rule of the sufficiency of the
       time of discovering the blood. And so too at the third appear-
       ance of blood. But thenceforward, she imparts uncleanness for
       the antecedent twenty-four hours [until she establishes a regu-
       lar period for herself].

[C]   R. Jeremiah in the name of Rab: "The third appearance of
       blood itself imparts uncleanness for the antecedent twenty-four
       hours."

[III.A] **An old lady who missed three periods—sufficient for her is
       her time [of discovering the blood].**

       **[If] she went and again missed three periods, and after-
       ward produced a drop of blood, sufficient for her is her time.**

This is the case if she has not established an accurate count for a fixed time, for instance, if she diminished or added to it.

But if she had accurately counted her period, she would have established a fixed time [and would then be subject to the rule governing all other women] [T. Nid. 1:11].

[B] R. Yudan asked: "[If] she produced a first drop of blood and a second, and then missed three periods and produced no blood, but then produced a drop of blood, [do we treat this] as a protracted period, so that she imparts uncleanness for the antecedent twenty-four hours, or [do we regard it] as a break in her periods, so that she should be subject to the rule of sufficiency [of the time at which the blood actually is discovered]?"

[C] Said to him R. Yosé, "If at the time at which you treat [the woman] as a jug full of liquid[, when she *is* producing drops of blood], you invoke for her the rule of the sufficiency of the time of the actual appearance of blood [so that there is no retroactive contamination], in this case, in which she is in no way to be treated as a jug full of liquid[, since she has missed three periods], is it not an argument *a fortiori* [that we should invoke the same lenient rule]?"

[D] He said to him, "But if so, even if she were to produce a single drop of blood, she should not impart uncleanness during the antecedent twenty-four hours, unless she in fact had produced three periods after a cessation of her period."

[E] He said to him, "It is comparable to a protracted period."

[IV.A] How long is her menstrual cycle?

[B] They assign to her a medium period.

[C] R. Simeon b. Laqish in the name of R. Yudan, the Patriarch: "They assign to her a medium period, that is, thirty days."

[D] Then let them assign to her a fixed period?

[E] Since she has not clarified her period through a regular blood-flow, she is not deemed to have a fixed period.

[F] And what is the rule as to her producing bloodstains?

[G] Hezekiah said, "Since you have treated her as a jug full of liquid, she most certainly is subject to the rule of bloodstains[, for she does produce menstrual blood]."

[H]   Samuel said, "Even if the entire sheet were full of drops of blood, she does not produce bloodstains [until a regular period is established]."

[I]   R. Yoḥanan in the name of R. Yannai, "Even if she had produced blood a hundred times, she is not subject to the rule of bloodstains."

[V.A]   Until what time [does the law of the Mishnah apply to a virgin]?

[B]   Until she reaches puberty. And what is puberty? When she produces two pubic hairs.

[C]   R. Ba, R. Ḥiyya, R. Yoḥanan in the name of R. Simeon b.Yoṣedeq, "Her spit [liquid produced during the antecedent time before her blood flowed] is deemed clean. What she steps or sits on is deemed clean. What she touches in public domain is deemed clean."

[D]   They theorized that the foregoing ruling applies to retroactive contamination [effected in the various ways and fluids of C. That is, since this girl is not subject to the expectation of producing blood, even though she now has produced blood twice in two periods, we do not invoke the rule of retroactive contamination in the specified circumstances].

I and II are devoted to the explication and secondary expansion of the Mishnah. The point of I.A is to explore the position of Samuel. Once Zeira alludes to Ḥaninah's position, the relevant materials are cited. (I do not think we should regard them as part of what is assigned to Zeira.) The lenient rulings are at G and at K. Rabbi is supposed to have adopted them both. The inserted language at L, following Pené Moshe, explains the relevance of the whole. M–N then close the discussion, posing no difficulty. II proceeds to the matter of the virgin. The dispute is clear as given. III takes up a relevant pericope located at T. Nid. 1:11. The issue is this matter of missing three periods, and, as expected, we want to know whether the periods must only be contiguous or may extend over a long period of time. That is the question of Yudan at III.B. The answer is that if the woman is producing blood—the first two periods—we are willing to impose the lenient ruling. When she has ceased to do so for a long time and then begins again, we surely should invoke that same lenient rule. For formerly she was full of liquid, and now she has been shown to be empty of liquid for some time, thus D. D then prepares the way for the answer of the question asked at B and supplied at E. **IV** takes up the status of these women who have missed their regular periods and who have once more begun to menstruate (**IV**.A). Their cycle is not yet fully established, so they are assumed to have a period of intermediate length, thirty days. The next question has to do with whether such a woman is subject to the law of bloodstains. That is, do we deem a bloodstain on an object in contact with such a woman to be unclean, as it would be if the woman were in her period and had yielded a drop of blood, e.g., on a sheet? The position of Samuel and Yannai is that we do not. Since the woman as yet has no regular period (**VI**.A–E), she also is not going to be subjected to the stated law. The concluding unit returns to the categories of the Mishnah, now dealing in a predictable way with the virgin of M. 1:5B. It is surely out of place, since it continues **II**.

1:6   [In Leiden MS and *editio princeps*: 1:7]

[A]   *Even though they have said, "Sufficient for [the woman who has a fixed period] is her time [of actually discovering a flow of menstrual blood, so that there is no question of retroactive contamination]," nonetheless such a woman must keep on inspecting herself,*

[B]   *except in the case of an [already] menstruating woman;*

[C]   *and a woman who is sitting out "the blood of her purifying" after having given birth[, for all blood produced by such a woman is deemed clean].*

[D]   *And [even though a woman has a fixed period], she is to [literally: and she who . . .] makes use of test rags,*

[E]   *except for a woman who is sitting out "the blood of her purifying" [after having given birth],*

[F]   *and a virgin,*

[G]   *whose blood is clean.*

[H]   *And twice a day must the woman [who has a fixed period] examine herself: morning and dusk;*

[I]   *and [also] when she is preparing to have sexual relations.*

[J]   *Yet a further examination beyond these [is required of] women of the priestly caste, when they are preparing to eat food having the status of heave-offering [for which cultic purity must be attained].*

[K]   *R. Judah says, "Also when they cease eating food having the status of heave-offering [to make sure that what is left over retains the status of cultic cleanness]."*

[I.A]   Does the Mishnah mean to refer to *a menstruating woman* [who is unclean anyhow and surely should not require an examination]?

[B]   [The reference is to a woman the time of whose period has come but] who has not yet ceased to be in a state of cleanness[, for the blood has not flowed, so she therefore has to examine herself to determine when her actual flow begins].

[C]   Does the Mishnah mean to refer to her *who makes use of test-rags* (HMŠMŠT . . .)?

[D]   [The meaning is that] she must make use of test-rags (ŠTŠMŠ).

[E]   *And a virgin, whose blood is clean.*

[F]   The reference of the Mishnah is to *a girl who has not yet reached the time of menstruation, who got married* [M. Nid. 10:1A].

[G]   [What follows is a comment on a later passage of this same pericope, that is, M. Nid. 10:1, which is as follows: *If she produced menstrual blood before marriage while still in her father's house and then got married, the House of Shammai say, "They give her [only] the coition of obligation[, and blood produced on that account is assumed to be unclean as menstrual blood." The House of Hillel say, "All the night is hers."* Samuel's comment then is on the saying of the House of Hillel.] Samuel said, "The night and following day constitute a complete cycle, and part of the cycle is tantamount to the whole of it [so the House of Hillel mean to allow not only the night but also the following day as free of taint of menstrual blood]."

[II.A]   *[And a virgin, whose blood is clean].* [If, then] she ceased to produce blood [because of sexual relations, but] afterward produced blood, [this latter blood is deemed] unclean.

[B]   [If after the first act of intercourse] the color of her blood changed, [this latter flow of blood is deemed] unclean.

[C]   Said R. Zeira, "That is so if the color of the blood did not change because of the sexual activity. But if it changed because of the sexual activity, it is deemed clean."

[D]   Said R. Yosé, "And the Mishnah itself has stated that same rule, for it has said, *'And a virgin, whose blood is clean.'* "

[E]   Now the rule has been stated, "If [the color of the blood] changed on account of sexual activity, it is clean." And if you should rule, "If it changed on account of sexual activity, it should be deemed unclean, and let her make use of a test-rag," is it possible that the color of the blood should change on account of sexual activity and the blood be deemed unclean? [Surely not.]

[III.A]   *And twice a day must the woman [who has a fixed period] examine herself: [morning and dusk].*

[B]   Said R. Yosé b. R. Bun, "These two examinations are the counterpart to the two times that the day changes [from dark to light, from light to dark]."

[IV]   [The introductory passage for what follows at C must be supplied by B. Nid. 60b: Bar Pada said, "Whenever her husband is liable to a sin-offering, that is, where menstrual blood has been found immediately after intercourse, foods requiring cultic cleanness belonging to her [also] are unclean; where the husband is liable to a suspensive guilt-offering, when blood is discovered after enough time for the woman to get out of bed and wash, so that it is not certain that she was menstruating during intercourse, foods requiring cultic cleanness belonging to her are in a suspended state of uncleanness; where the husband is exempt, foods requiring cultic cleanness belonging to her are clean." R. Hoshaiah ruled, "Even where the husband is actually liable for a sin-offering, foods requiring cultic cleanness are deemed to be in a state of suspension."]

[A]   R. Eleazar in the name of R. Hoshaiah: "Whenever sages have ruled that her husband is liable for an offering, as to her part, foods requiring cultic cleanness belonging to her are deemed unclean. [If] her husband is exempt from an offering, for her part foods requiring cultic cleanness belonging to her are clean. [If] her husband is subject to an offering by reason of doubt, for her part foods requiring cultic cleanness are deemed to be in a state of suspension."

[B]   [The saying that follows assumes and questions the ruling that, even when the husband is liable for a sin-offering for having had sexual relations with a menstruating woman, the foods requiring cultic cleanness are kept in a state of suspension. We thus take for granted that there was blood in the vagina, but not outside it.] R. Samuel bar Rab Isaac asked, "This is [to be compared to a case of] an old man [the penis] and a child [the blood] who were walking in a reception room. [For this reason the husband is unclean, while the food is deemed not unclean. The penis has had contact with blood, the food has not.] Now is it not certain that the elder [the penis] passes first [and so the husband is surely unclean? But we cannot be certain that the blood also has passed.] And if the child [the blood] comes, it also passes through. [So why is there not certainty that, if the husband is certainly unclean and liable for an offering, the food also should be unclean?]"

[C]   R. Abun in the name of R. Yudan: "I say that, in that case, there was an act of sexual intercourse that closed off [the passage to the blood, so that the blood remained inside and did not exude to affect the food, and, in that case, there is no reason to deem the food to be unclean].

[D]   "But here [in regard to the clean food], if the blood had been present, what would have stopped it from coming out? [So we thus assume it did not come out.]"

[E]   The following Mishnah passage differs from the position of R. Hoshaiah [A]: *"If she was sitting on a couch and occupied with the preparation of food subject to the laws of cleanness, and] she got up and saw a spot of blood [where she had been sitting], she is deemed to be unclean, but all the food [she had been preparing] is deemed to be clean"* [M. Nid. 1:2B–D]. [Hoshaiah says the status of the food is held in suspense, while the Mishnah-pericope declares it to be clean.].

[F]   The following Mishnah passage differs from the position of Bar Pedaiah [who declares the food to be unclean if the husband is liable for an offering by reason of having had sexual relations with a menstruating woman].

[G]   *R. Judah says, "Also when they cease eating food having the status of heave offering"*—with regard to what matter?

[H]   Is it not in reference to a case in which, if the woman produced a drop of blood, she will so retroactively have imparted uncleanness to the food? [But here the husband will *not* be liable for a sin-offering, and, it must follow, Bar Pedaiah cannot accord with the stated rule of the Mishnah's R. Judah.]

[I]   Said R. Ezra before R. Mana, "Interpret the passage to refer to a woman who is not [yet] subject to a fixed period."

[J]   He said to him, "Thus did R. Yosé say, 'In each case in the present matter, we speak about a woman who does have a fixed period.' "

[K]   Said R. Yosé b. R. Bun, "The Mishnah passage should then be divided. Up to this point [A–J], the Mishnah speaks of a woman who is subject to a fixed period. But from this point [of R. Judah's saying (K)] and beyond, [the Mishnah speaks] of a woman who is not subject to a fixed period."

[L]   Even if you rule that the Mishnah should not be so divided, we may still interpret the passage as referring to a woman who has a fixed period. And what Bar Pedaiah does in this passage [is to concur with] those who differ from R. Judah.

The Talmud here poses textual difficulties at a number of points, in part because of a faulty text, in part because of the difficulty of interpreting what is said. The discussion of the cited passage of the Mishnah opens with the expected glossing of the Mishnah's language (**I**). The only point of difficulty is at **I.G**, which clearly was attached before the passage as a whole— that is, E–F + G—entered into the framework of discussion of the framers of this unit. That is necessarily so, for Samuel's reference is wholly irrelevant to the purposes for which M. Nid. 10:1A is cited. It therefore joined M. Nid. 10:1 before that entire pericope entered into the present discourse. **II** continues this work of glossing, and its points are clear. If there has been sexual activity, then we assume that the change in the color of the blood is on that account; if not, then we assume otherwise. **III** concludes the work of glossing

The second half of the Talmud is relevant to the cited passage of the Mishnah only because the Mishnah-pericope itself figures in the argument as it is worked out. But the discussion is essentially independent of our pericope of the Mishnah. The real problem of **IV** is not so much the necessity to draw upon

B. Nid. 60b's version of the sayings. To be sure, if we do not cite that version, we lose Bar Pedaiah, and, it is clear, he must be cited, in the setting of A, so that F–L can make sense. What I find difficult is to interpret B and C–D. I have done the best I can with that passage. The critical part of the whole, E–L, happily poses no problems of interpretation, and the text is clear and accessible. So the relationship of the Talmud to the Mishnah, and the proposed utilization of the Mishnah for the Talmud's own purposes, are entirely clear.

7 Yerushalmi Niddah
Chapter Two

2:1

[A]   *[49d] Any hand that makes many examinations*

[B]   *in the case of women is to be praised,*

[C]   *and in the case of men is to be chopped off.*

[D]   *A woman who is a deaf-mute, imbecile, blind, or mentally unbalanced—*

[E]   *if women of sound senses are available, they take care of them, so such a woman may eat food having the status of heave-offering [which requires protection from uncleanness].*

[F]   *It is the way of Israelite women to make use of test-rags, one for him and one for her.*

[G]   *The pious women get yet a third ready, to attend to the 'house' [to examine themselves before, as well as after, intercourse].*

[I.A]   Thus is the Mishnah passage's meaning: whoever puts his finger in his eye a lot brings out a lot of tears [and likewise the consideration of M. Nid. 2:1C is masturbation].

[B]   **[In the case of men the hand is to be chopped off]: R. Ṭarfon says, "It is to be chopped off while lying on his navel."**

[C]   **They said to him, "Lo, his belly will be split open."**

[D]   **He said to them, "That's exactly what I meant [T. Nid. 2:8B–D].**

[E]   **"Death is better for him than life!"**

[F]   The associates say, "R. Ṭarfon curses him with a curse that touches his very body."

[G]   Said R. Yosé, "[Rabbi Tarfon's intent] is only to explain that it is prohibited to feel around below the navel."

[H]   This teaching [A–B] that you have presented applies to the matter of masturbation. But as to examining oneself for signs of zibah-flow [that is, semen-flow not at the time of an erect penis, Lev. 15:1ff], whoever examines himself more than his fellow is more to be praised than his fellow.

[I]   Pious women [M. Nid. 2:1G] would examine themselves on account of each jug [of wine having the status of heave-offering] and each loaf [having the status of heave-offering].

[J]   M'SH B: Tabitha, the serving-girl in the household of Rabban Gamaliel, was carrying wine for drinks. She inspected herself [before lifting up] each jug of wine.

[K]   She said to [Rabban Gamaliel], "My lord, I have noted a bloodstain [on my garment]."

[L]   Then Rabban Gamaliel was disturbed [at the possibility that all the wine had been made unclean].

[M]   She said to him, "But I was inspecting myself [before lifting up] each jug of wine, and I became unclean only on the occasion [of lifting up] this jug alone."

[II.A]   They said in the name of R. Yannai, "The blind woman [does] not [belong] here [at M. Nid. 2:1D, for she can inspect herself by touch]."

[B]   And one said (QMT) in the name of R. Haninah, "The blind woman [does] not [belong] here."

[C]   [And said] R. Ila, R. Yosé b. Hanina in the name of the house of R. Yannai, "The blind woman [does] not [belong] here."

[III.A]   Said R. Yannai, "Also the first [woman listed earlier, at M. Nid. 1:6H–K] is called pious. We have learned in the cited Mishnah-pericope that they are *required* to examine themselves, and will you declare [them to be especially pious]?"

[B]   Said R. Ila, "[The fact that they are called pious for doing merely what is in fact required of them] is to let you know that whoever carries out the teachings of sages is called pious."

[IV.A]   R. Jeremiah in the name of Rab: "[If] a woman examined her [vagina] with a hand that had not been inspected [and that might have contained blood originating other than in the vagina], or if she set herself down in a filthy place [from which she might have picked up a drop of blood, she nonetheless is deemed unclean and may not attribute the blood to other than the vagina], because the body is presumed to have been inspected[, so whatever is found comes from a source of bodily uncleanness]."

[B]   Said R. Zeira, "The Mishnah itself has said exactly the same thing: *If [a drop of blood] is found on the man's [rag], [the husband and wife are unclean and liable for a sacrifice [M. Nid. 2:2A].* Is it not because [of the prevailing assumption that] the body is presumed to have been inspected[, so blood that is found is menstrual]?"

[C]   Said R. Ḥaninah, "Interpret the cited Mishnah to speak of a case in which the man had inspected [his body in advance and had found no blood, so the cited passage does not indicate the presence of the stated presupposition at all]."

[D]   Then R. Zeira angrily exclaimed, "And does a man usually do such a thing[, that is, examine himself to see whether there is blood on his penis]?"

[E]   R. Zeira in the name of R. Jeremiah: "[If a drop of blood is found on a sheet,] a drop up to the size of a bean is attributed [to a dead louse, and is not deemed a sign of uncleanness. This is contrary to the view of Jeremiah in Rab's name at IV.A]. If it is larger than that size, a woman has to find a reason [for the presence of the bloodstain,] other than her having menstruated; and if she can find no such reason, then she is deemed unclean]."

[F]   They say that R. Jeremiah retracted his opinion. They say that when he heard what the rabbis [below, V] had to say, he retracted his opinion. [That is, in the stated case, the woman is unclean not by reason of a bloodstain, but by reason of having produced menstrual blood.]

[V.A]   Rabbi [Judah the Patriarch] praised R. Ḥ, father of R. Hoshaiah, in the presence of R. Ishmael, the son of R. Yosé.

[B]   R. Ḥama father of R. Hoshaiah asked in session before R. Ishmael b. R. Yosé, "If a woman examined herself with a hand that had not been inspected, or if she sat herself down in a filthy place[, what is the law]?"

[C]   He said to him, "In accord with whose opinion do you ask me
this question? Is it in accord with the opinion of the master [R.
Yosé, the teacher of Judah the Patriarch], or in accord with the
opinion of the disciple [Judah the Patriarch himself]?"

[D]   [Ishmael] said to him, "Father [Yosé] said it is deemed to have
the status of a bloodstain [**IV.E**], while Rabbi [the disciple of
Yosé] says it is deemed tantamount to a drop of menstrual
blood [so the woman is unclean, not merely in a state of doubt
as to her status] [**IV.A**]."

[E]   [Ishmael] said to [Rabbi], "Is this the one you were praising?"

[F]   Said R. Zeirah, "It is easier for someone to heed the reasoning
of his master [Rabbi in the dispute that follows]."

[G]   If a woman examined herself and put [the rag] in a box made
of glass [and found blood]—

[H]   R. Ḥiyya says, "It is deemed a bloodstain [= **IV.E**]."

[I]   And Rabbi [Judah the Patriarch] says, "It is tantamount to a
drop of menstrual blood [= IV.A]."

[J]   R. Ḥiyya replied to Rabbi, "And do you not allow her to find
some excuse [for the drop of blood, e.g., blaming it on some
source of blood other than menstrual blood]?"

[K]   Said R. Bun bar Ḥiyya, "The reasoning of Rabbi is that it is
usual for boxes to be inspected and cleaned of dead creeping
things. But it is not usual for them to be inspected on account
of lice.

[L]   "If it is up to the size of a bean, she may attribute the blood to
a louse. But if it is larger than that dimension, what can she
claim to be the source of the bloodstain anyhow?"

I, II, and **III** systematically work through the Mishnah's materials, as indicated. The exposition varies, from stories that illus-
trate or augment the Mishnah, e.g., **I.**J–M, to corrections of
the Mishnah's contents (**II**). The discussion of the Mishnah
concludes with the homily of **III.**B. I see no problems in the
interpretation of this set. The issue of **IV–V,** one extended
unit, is closely tied to the Mishnah. Specifically, the Talmud
wishes to explain the result of finding a bloodspot or stain, that
is, upon making the examination of which the Mishnah speaks.

At issue is the status of a bloodstain or spot discovered under less than ideal conditions (**IV**.A). The alternatives are (1) to regard the blood as certainly vaginal and unclean, or (2) to deem it possibly to derive from some other source, e.g., a crushed louse. Jeremiah citing Rab takes the former position. Zeira (B–D) rejects this view. Then Zeirah cites Jeremiah himself in the opposite view (E). **IV**.F attempts to harmonize the two teachings in the name of Jeremiah (A, E), as indicated. The purpose of the final unit, **V**, then, is to spell out what is alleged at **IV**.F, that is, Jeremiah retracted at E the view he affirmed at A. As is clear, **V**.A–F, are fully formed independent of **IV** and go over the same materials without reference to the authorities of **IV**. The main point for this context is that Rabbi backs up the view that, in the stated case of **IV**.A, **V**.A–F, the woman is unclean beyond doubt. G–J show Rabbi in the same position. How all of this explains the retraction of **IV**.F is not specified. Perhaps the point is that Jeremiah accedes to Rabbi's position. It seems to me that K–L explain the reasoning of Ḥiyya, Bun's father, not that of Rabbi. Since it is possible that there may be lice in the glass box, it has to be taken into account that the blood comes from a crushed louse, contrary to the view of **IV**.E, **V**.B–D, J. (To be sure, Pené Moshe interprets K–L as the reason cited at **IV**.F; I do not follow his reading of the matter.) It would appear to me that the two units of **V**, A–E + F and G–J + K–L, are joined to the foregoing essentially because they go over the same ground, and not because they are distinctly relevant to **IV**.F. I also suppose that, to begin with, they are juxtaposed to one another because they go over a common theme, Rabbi's opinions on a single issue, and then are placed with **IV** because of the congruity of Rabbi's and Rab's opinions. So, in all, the probability is that **IV**.F is not the reason for the addition of **V** and should be regarded simply as an uncompleted thought, a phenomenon so common in this Talmud.

2:2

[A]   *[If blood] is found on [the husband's] test-rag, they are unclean, so liable for an offering [for having had sexual relations during the wife's period].*

[B]   *[If] it is found on hers—*

[C]   *[if the discovery takes place] forthwith, they are unclean and so liable for an offering.*

[D]   *[If blood] is found on hers after a while, they are unclean on account of doubt [as to the possibility that indeed the blood originated in menstruation], but they are exempt from an offering.*

[I.A]   It was taught in a Tannaitic tradition on this Mishnah-pericope:

[B]   Whether it is forthwith or not forthwith, *[if blood] is found on his [test-rag]* [delete: forthwith], *they are unclean.*

[C]   [The consideration of] immediate discovery, they did say, applies to the matter of drying off [the sexual parts after having sexual relations], and it does not apply to making the inspection, [which may even take place later on, not forthwith].

[D]   R. Huna said, "That interval of an immediate inspection is] sufficient so that the wife may dry off the mouth of the 'utensil' on the outside, but not what is in the inner chambers or in the cracks."

[II.A]   They asked in session before R. Naḥman bar Jacob, "What is the law as to [the wife's] being required to make an inspection [not merely drying off] during the interval specified for immediate inspection?"

[B]   Said R. Ba, "If you rule that [the wife] should be required to make an inspection during the interval specified for immediate drying off, you nullify the entire concept of such an interval."

[C]   Said R. Yosé b. R. Bun, "If you rule that [the wife] should be required to make an inspection during the specified interval, would this not be equivalent to an inspection that serves to diminish the period of twenty-four hours? [That is, would there not be a conflict, in that the inspection during the stated interval would replace the inspection of which M. Nid. 1:1 has spoken?] And we have learned in the Mishnah, *An inspection limits the uncleanness for the antecedent twenty-four hours.*"

[III.A]   Said R. Yosé b. R. Bun, "**It may be compared to a servant and a witness who were standing at the threshold of the court. Once the servant goes out, the witness enters in**" [T. Nid. 3:5M–P].

[B]   This is the interval that is deemed "immediate [inspection]."

[**IV**.A]   *And they are exempt from a sacrifice.*

[B]   And they are exempt from a sin-offering.

[C]   But they are liable to a guilt-offering for an unverified offense [by reason of doubt, and not wholly exempt, as the Mishnah's phrasing would suggest].

The clarification supplied at **I** poses no problems. The Talmud's principal contribution at **I**.D, Huna's instructions on what constitutes immediately drying off. **I**.D, then sets up the inquiry of **II**, that is, about the possibility of requiring an actual inspection, not merely a drying off. **II**.A raises this possibility, and **II**.B dismisses it on the grounds that by definition it is excluded. II.C presents a second argument for the same proposition, namely, that the Mishnah already has made provision for an examination—the one that limits the interval of retroactive uncleanness—and it comes after, not during, the specific brief interval for drying off. **III** contributes yet another definition of "forthwith." **IV** revises the Mishnah's view that no sacrifice at all is required, bringing M. 2:2D into conformity with what, in fact, is the prevalent law.

2:3

[A]   *What is meant by "after a while" [M. Nid. 2:2D]?*

[B]   *Sufficient time for the woman to get out of bed and wash off her "face" [sexual organs].*

[C]   *And [if a drop of blood should appear] after [the stated interval], she imparts uncleanness [by reason of doubt] to objects she has touched for the antecedent twenty-four hours.*

[D]   *But she does not impart uncleanness to her lover.*

[E]   *R. ᶜAqiba says, "She does impart uncleanness to her lover."*

[F]   *But sages concur with R. ᶜAqiba in the case of a woman who produces a bloodstain that she does impart uncleanness to her lover.*

[**I**.A]   Said R. Yosé b. R. Bun, "What is the meaning of *after a while* [M. Nid. 2:3A]? It can only be, 'After after-a-while.' "

[B]   And what is this interval?

[C]   It is sufficient time for the woman to put out her hand and take the test-rag from under the pillow.

[D]   But after 'after-a-while' [if she should make the inspection and discover a drop of blood], her lover [nonetheless] is deemed clean.

[II.A] R. Eleazar in the name of Rab, "The theory of sages accords with the view of R. Meir [who says at T. Nid. 3:1: '**All women concerning whom sages have said, Their time suffices [for them to impart uncleanness, and there is no retroactive uncleanness]—their bloodstain does cause them to impart uncleanness retroactively. . . .'].**"

[B]   R. Yohanan said, "This is the view of those very same sages [50a] [who differ from Meir on the bloodstain as to retroactive uncleanness but maintain it imparts uncleanness once it is found]."

[C]   Why so? [Perhaps we do deal with Meir, as A has said].

[D]   Associates in the name of R. Yohanan: "Let us derive this teaching of rabbis from the position of R. 'Aqiba [with whom sages of M. 2:3F concur], in accord with that which R. 'Aqiba said, 'She imparts uncleanness to her lover, but is not in disarray as to the reckoning of her period.' Thus do rabbis rule: "She imparts uncleanness to her lover and is not in disarray as to the reckoning of her period.' "

Having explained the matter of an immediate drying off, the Mishnah proceeds to spell out the other possibility, a thorough examination "after a while." Yosé b. R. Bun's clarification of M. 2:3A–B is a quibble. What he wishes to say is that B refers to the point that begins "*after* a while" has passed. That is, if, after a while, a woman gets out of bed and washes, and a drop of blood appears, then she is deemed to have begun her period, so that she imparts uncleanness by reason of doubt to objects she has touched during the preceding twenty-four hours. But, the Mishnah proceeds to point out, this same doubt is such that she does not also impart uncleanness to her lover (D). What Yosé b. R. Bun has done, therefore, is to read A–B in the light of C–D. 'Aqiba, for his part, maintains a more consistent position that, if the woman imparts uncleanness to objects touched during the antecedent twenty-four hours, she also imparts uncleanness to the lover. That view leads the Talmud to attempt to identify the theory of sages with a named authority of the Mishnah itself, and at **II**.A the view of Meir is invoked. The pericope as a whole thus proceeds as expected from a glossing of the Mishnah's language to an exploration of the Mishnah's principles in the context of other relevant rules.

2:4

[A]   *All women are assumed to be clean for their husbands [even without examination, until the time for their period has come].*

[B]   *Those [husbands] who come home from a trip—their wives are assumed to be clean for them.*

[C]   *The House of Shammai say, "A woman requires two test-rags for each act of intercourse [one before, one afterward].*

[D]   *"Or she should have intercourse by a light [to allow immediate examination of the single test-rag used after intercourse]."*

[E]   *And the House of Hillel say, "She may suffice with two test-rags for the entire night [one before the sequence, one after the sequence of numerous successive acts of sexual relations]."*

[**I**.A]   Abba bar Jeremiah, a priest, in the name of Samuel: "Any woman who has not got a fixed period is forbidden to have sexual relations without an examination [prior to the act]."

[B]   Now have we not learned in the Mishnah-pericope, *All women are assumed to be clean for their husbands?*

[C]   Interpret [Samuel's statement] to refer to a case in which the husbands have come home from a trip [at which point an examination is called for in Samuel's view].

[D]   But have we not learned in the Mishnah-pericope: *Those [husbands] who come home from a trip—their wives are assumed to be clean for them?*

[E]   Said R. Bun bar Ḥiyya, "Interpret [the saying of Samuel to refer to a case in which the husband] came and found her awake [so she has to examine herself, while the Mishnah refers to a case of finding the wife asleep, in which case he will not bother her to examine herself]."

[F]   And has it not been taught, "Whether he found her awake or whether he found her asleep [she is deemed clean]"?

[G]   Said R. Ba, "Interpret [the Mishnah's rule, that the woman is assumed to be clean, to apply to a case in which] he left the wife at a time at which she was assumed to be clean [and if she had a period, one simply reckons with the time of the fixed period. If there is no fixed period, as Samuel says, an examination nonetheless is necessary]."

[II.A]   And [if the husband calculates periods while away] how long a menstrual cycle do they assign to her?

[B]   R. Simeon b. Laqish said, "They assign her an average cycle, thirty days."

[C]   R. Yohanan said, "I repeat the tradition [as follows]: Even [if the husband returns] after three years, it is permitted [to have intercourse, should the period not have begun], so long as the wife does have a fixed period. [So the rule applies without regard to the length of the period, so long as a period is calculated.]"

[D]   Said R. Abbahu, "And [we assume] this law applies to one who has refrained [from having sexual relations] for seven days after [the end of the wife's] period.

[E]   "And one may not say she has not [in addition] immersed herself. [We assume she has done so.]"

[F]   Said R. Hanina, "That is to say that it is forbidden for a woman to remain in her condition of uncleanness [after the specified interval of her period, that is, to remain without immersing herself and so reentering a state of cleanness]."

[G]   Samuel bar Abba asked, "[Does the statement of Yohanan (C) apply] even in the case in which a woman gave birth to a healthy child? [That is, do we take for granted that the woman has completed her process of purification prior to the husband's return?]"

[H]   Said R. Yosé, "Thus do we say the rule even if the woman has become unclean! [Obviously not. So Yosé rejects C.]

[I]   "But if the woman did give birth, the supposition that she is clean is nullified. So too here: since she has become unclean, the supposition that she is clean is nullified."

[**III**.A]   *The House of Shammai say, "A woman requires two test-rags for each act of intercourse, or she should have intercourse by a light."*

[B]   But has it not been taught: "He who has sexual relations by a light—lo, that is disgusting"?

[C]   Thus does the Mishnah-passage teach: Let her have sexual relations and [*then*] examine herself by a light.

[**IV**.A]   R. Zeira, R. Ḥiyya bar Ashi in the name of Rab: "If a woman had sexual relations using a test rag [and the rag is lost], she is prohibited from having sexual relations [any more, until another test-rag is provided]."

[B]   Said R. Zeira "When there is evidence that it is available, it is permitted [to continue to have relations], and when there is no evidence that it is available, lo, is it not an argument *a fortiori* [that we should *assume* that she is clean, contrary to the foregoing teaching]!"

[C]   Said R. Yosé, "[On the contrary], in the case [described in the Mishnah-pericope], you can depend on [the test-rag, that is, the next day you can examine it, and therefore you may rely on it and assume the woman clean, since there will be ample evidence in due course to test that assumption]. But in the case in which the rag is lost you will not be able to rely on it[, she is prohibited from having sexual relations without an examination, such as the Mishnah has required]."

Once more the interests of the Talmud focus upon the specific materials of the Mishnah. **I** brings into alignment the cited teaching of Samuel and the clear statement of the Mishnah. Samuel imposes a condition where the Mishnah specifies none, thus A–B. The effort to harmonize the two begins with a needless and obvious quibble, C–D, and E–F do not do much better. The third, G, then gives a definitive answer. **II** carries forward the interest in the length of a fixed period. But the real point has to do with M. Nid. 2:4B. What Yoḥanan wants to stress is that if there is a fixed period, that remains subject to calculation, however long the husband is away. Even after three years the husband is permitted to assume the period has been regular. Abbahu adds the obvious point that, of course, the woman's calculations must include her ritual immersion to complete the rite of purification. Yosé challenges Yoḥanan's position by pointing out that, where there has been a birth while he was away on his trip, the husband's calculations may be thrown off. So the husband may not take for granted the wife is clean, merely because of his prior knowledge of her schedule, when there is an event, such as a healthy birth, which can have thrown her period off its prior schedule. **III** takes up the exegesis of the Mishnah once more. **IV** provides a secondary expansion of the rule of the test-rag. If the required rag is misplaced, Zeira invokes the rule that the wife is assumed to be clean. Yosé does not. Yosé wants the supposition to be subject to the test of evidence, if not now, then later on.

2:5   [In Leiden MS and *editio princeps*: 2:4]

[A]   *Sages have employed a metaphor in regard to women:*

[B]   *the inner room, front hall, and second-story room [upstairs].*

[C]   *Blood in the room is unclean [as menstrual blood].*

[D]   *[If] it is found in the front hall, a matter of doubt concerning it is ruled to be unclean, since it is assumed to have come from the fountain [uterus].*

[I.A]   So does the Mishnah-pericope teach: *Blood in the inner room is unclean* [as menstrual blood]. And blood in the upstairs room is clean.

[B]   R. Judah in the name of Samuel: "The room is further in than the front hall, and the upstairs room is located on top of the room, halfway over the front hall. And the door of the upstairs room opens into the front hall."

[II.A]   R. Naḥman b. R. Isaac proposed to R. Huna, "The Mishnah-pericope [at D] refers to blood that is found from the door of the upper room and inside [and so comes from the uterus]."

[B]   He said to him, "If it is found from the door of the upstairs room and inward, it is a matter of certainty [that the blood is unclean]. But thus do we interpret the Mishnah [D], to apply to a case in which [blood] is found from the door of the upstairs room and outward."

[III.A]   The opinions of rabbis are at variance [with Huna, **II.**A–B], for R. Yoḥanan said, "There are three that are subject to doubt,

but that [sages] have treated as a matter of certainty [of un-
cleanness], and these are they: [1] She who aborts a cut-off
hand or a cut-off foot, and [2] [she who aborts] a mass of veins
and blood, and [3] *blood that is found in the front-hall* [M.
2:5D]."

[B]   Now how shall we interpret [the matter of (3) to apply to] the
case in which the blood is found from the door of the upstairs
room and inward? It is a matter of certainty [that this is unclean blood and not of doubt, as Yoḥanan has claimed].

[C]   But thus must we interpret the matter: When it is found from
the door of the upstairs room and outward, [it is a matter of
doubt, = **II.B**, Huna].

[D]   R. Abba, son of R. Papi, exclaimed in session before R. Yosé,
"We have learned many more matters of doubt than you teach
in this matter!"

[E]   He said to him, "What R. Yoḥanan had said [applies only to]
cases involving [doubt and cleanness of] women."

I.A's gloss is important, since the Mishnah's formulation at M.
Nid. 2:5C lacks the expected and necessary complementary
contrast. **I.**B then explains the rule of M. 2:5D. Because the
front hall is connected to the room (uterus) itself, blood in the
front hall will be unclean. **II** and **III** take up the facts supplied
at **I.**B and so carry forward the exegesis of the Mishnah.
Naḥman suggests that at D the Mishnah-pericope refers to
blood found in the front hall from the opening to the upper
room and inward, that is, toward the room itself. This is the
sort of blood that may or may not be unclean. If it comes from
the room, it is; if it comes from the upstairs room, it is not.
Huna corrects this impression, pointing out that if the blood is
found inward from the point at which the entry to the upstairs
room joins the front hall, the blood assuredly derives from the
room and is unclean. The uncertainty comes when the blood is
found from the door and outward. Now the blood may come
either from the inner room or from the upstairs room. **III** is
continuous with **II**. **III.**A adduces the view of Yoḥanan, which
conflicts with **II.**B and maintains that a matter of doubt, not of
certainty, is deemed *as if* it were certain. Huna has maintained
there is no doubt at all about the specified case. B–C respond
in Huna's behalf. D–E conclude the matter, explaining that

Yoḥanan's list, to begin with, enumerates three sorts of doubt in one kind of case only, since there are many other matters of doubt that sages have treated as certainly unclean.

2:6   [In Leiden MS and *editio princeps*: 2:5]

[A]   Five [colors of] blood are unclean in a woman:

[B]   red, black, [blood of a] bright crocus color, [blood] like water mixed with earth, and [blood] like wine mixed with water.

[C]   The House of Shammai say, "Also :blood the color of water in which fenugreek has been soaked, and blood the color of gravy from roast meat."

[D]   The House of Hillel declare [these two] clean [since they are not red].

[E]   [Blood that is] yellow—

[F]   ʿAqabya b. Mehallel declares unclean.

[G]   And sages declare clean.

[H]   Said R. Meir, "If it does not impart uncleanness by reason of being a bloodstain, it is unclean as a liquid [that has exuded from a menstruating woman, like her urine or spit]."

[I]   R. Yosé says, "Neither thus nor so."

[I.A]   Rab and R. Yoḥanan—both of them say, "There are four kinds of blood [and not five].

[B]   "[Black colored blood does not count because it] is red that has faded and turned black."

[C]   Said Samuel, "Black [colored blood] may derive from any one of them."

[II.A]   Whence do we derive evidence that there are five varieties of unclean blood specified by the Torah?

[B]   Said R. Joshua b. Levi: " 'And she has uncovered the fountain of her bloods' (Lev. 20:18) [= two], 'And she will be clean from the source of her bloods' [= two], a discharge of blood from her body (Lev. 15:19) [= one, thus five]."

[C]   And lo: "And if a woman has a discharge of blood" (Lev. 15:25)—this blood [too] should be part of that number.

[D]   [It is blood from those other sources,] but it came upon her
during the *zibah*-days and turned into a *zibah*-flow [not reckoned with those listed at M. Nid 2:6A–B].

[**III**.A]   And how do we know that there is unclean blood, and there is
clean blood[, so not all blood is unclean, but only the five
which are listed]?

[B]   R. Ḥama bar Joseph in the name of R. Hoshaiah: "It is written, *If any case arises requiring a decision . . . (Deut. 17:8).*
Now 'between blood and (W) blood' is not written, but *of one
kind of blood from (L) another.*
    "On this basis there is proof that there is blood that is un-
clean, and blood that is clean."

[**IV**.A]   *The House of Shammai say, "Also: blood the color of water in
which fenugreek has been soaked, and blood the color of gravy
from roast meat."*

[B]   Lo, there are then seven [colors of blood that are unclean in a
woman].

[C]   [The two enumerated by the House of Shammai are] like blood
mixed with earth.

[**V**.A]   R. Yosé in the name of Rab, the associates in the name of R.
Yoḥanan: "R. Meir [M. 2:6H] declared [blood] unclean only in
a case to which ʿAqabya['s opinion applied, that is, yellow
blood]."

[B]   Then let it impart uncleanness as does blood the color of water
in which fenugreek has been soaked, and blood the color of
gravy from roast meat, to which the House of Shammai['s
opinion applied].

[C]   [The House of Shammai] say, "They are like water mixed with
earth [and blood like wine mixed with water]."

[D]   Clean blood [of such an appearance as is specified by the House
of Shammai] imparts susceptibility to uncleanness. Unclean
blood does not impart susceptibility to uncleanness [to dry produce on which it falls]. [So the issue raised at B does not apply,
and Meir refers only to ʿAqabya's view, as A has said.]

The exegesis of M. 2:6A–B at **I**.A–C produces a minor dispute
on the source of black blood. **II** proceeds to supply an exegeti-

cal basis for the Mishnah's claim that there are five types of blood that are unclean. This is done by finding references to the matter adding up to five (two plurals, one singular). The challenges to Joshua's florilegium of verses, C, are turned away (D). **III** asks for a more fundamental proof-text. The Mishnah takes for granted that there are types of blood that are not unclean at all. Proof of that proposition is therefore to be adduced. **IV** raises the the obvious question of how the House of Shammai can accord with the enumeration of the superscription at M. 2:6A, since they will want to count seven kinds of unclean blood. **V** brings us to the exposition of Meir's opinion. **V.A** makes the important claim that Meir refers, to begin with, only to the yellow blood declared unclean by 'Aqabya. This blood, Meir says, should have the capacity as a liquid to impart uncleanness to dry foodstuffs. Perhaps, it is suggested (B), Meir speaks also of the Shammaite liquids. The opinion of the House of Shammai is invoked. The types of blood to which they refer in fact impart uncleanness. There is no point in such a case in invoking the matter of imparting susceptibility too. For, as C–D reply, if blood is unclean, it imparts directly; it does not merely impart susceptibility to uncleanness. Only if blood is clean does it impart solely susceptibility to uncleanness. So Meir's distinction will not hold up, within the position of the House of Shammai. But it will serve, as proposed at the outset (A), to clarify the position of 'Aqabya.

2:7   [In Leiden MS and *editio princeps:* 2:6]

[A]   *What is the red color [to which reference has been made at M. Nid. 2:6A]?*

[B]   *It is [a red] like that of blood flowing from a wound.*

[C]   *Black?*

[D]   *Like ink sediment.*

[E]   *[If the blood] is lighter than this, it is clean.*

[F]   *And bright crocus color?*

[G]   *Like the brightest [shade of crocus] that there is.*

[H]   *And the color of earthy water?*

[I]   *[Like a color produced when] over dirt from the valley of Beth Kerem water is run.*

[J]   *[A color like] water mixed with wine?*

[K]   *Two parts water to one part wine,*

[L]   *[using] wine of Sharon.*

[I.A]   R. Jacob bar Aḥa, R. ʿUlla of Caesarea in the name of R. Ḥaninah, R. Ba in the name of R. Simeon b. Menassia: "*[It is red] like blood flowing from a wound* [M 2:7B] that has faded more than once [repeatedly]."

[B]   Said R. Jacob bar Sosai in session before R. Yosé, "And the Mishnah-pericope itself has said the same thing: *Red like blood flowing from [an already existing] wound* [hence a wound that has received more than a single blow]."

[C]   R. Isaac bar Naḥman and R. Abudama of Haifa were in session. Someone came along [bearing a bleeding wound]. Said R. Isaac bar Naḥman to R. Abudama, "That [color] is close to [the color or red] that comes from menstrual blood."

[D]   What [is the point of this observation]? Does he differ [from Simeon b. Menassia]? [No. The point of the observation is that] if [the blood had] faded yet again, [the blood would have been like menstrual blood [in color].

[II.A]   *Black like ink sediment.*

[B]   What does one do [to compare the color of the blood with the specified shade of black]?

[C]   R. Ba in the name of R. Judah: "One takes ink sediment and puts it on white skin [near the wound]."

[D]   R. Yosé b. R. Bun said, "[Even] on spotty skin."

[E]   R. Zeira in the name of our rabbis: "[The shade of] black is like that of a raven. [If it is] black as a grape, [or] black as pitch, it is clean."

[F]   Associates in the name of R. Yoḥanan: "[If it is] black as ink, it is clean [blood]."

[G]   R. Ammi in the name of R. Yoḥanan: "[If it is as black as] imported aromatic leaves, it is unclean."

[H]   R. Zeira asked in session before R. Ammi, "Are all of these [different shades] applied in practice?"

[I]   He said to him, "Yes."

[J]   R. Simeon b. Laqish said, "In the case of all of them, [if the shade of black] is lighter than the specified [shades], [the blood] is clean. [If it is] deeper than they, [the blood is] unclean" [cf. M. 2:7E].

[K]   R. Yoḥanan said, "In the case of all of [the colors listed in M. 2:6–7], [if the shade of black is] lighter than the specified shades], [the blood] is clean. [If it is] deeper than they, [the blood also is] clean, except in the case of black."

[L]   The Mishnah-pericope supports the position of R. Yoḥanan, for we have learned [in the cited pericope]: *Black? Like ink sediment. [If] it is lighter than this, it is clean. Lo, if it is deeper than this, [it is] unclean.* [We give such a ruling] only in the case of a black shade. But lo, in the case of all of the others, even though the shade is deeper [than the ones specified in the Mishnah], the [blood] is clean.

[M]   [In] the town of R. Judah [the law followed the opinion of] R. Simeon b. Laqish [J], [even though] R. Judah was in accord with the opinion of R. Yoḥanan [L].

[N]   Bar Qappara repeated [the tradition] and sustained the opinion of R. Simeon b. Laqish [J], but he did not carry out the law in practice in accord with him [but in accord with the position of R. Yoḥanan].

[O]   [A servant] of R. Ḥanina made a mixture [of the specified elements] for Bar Qappara.

[P]   He said to him, "What [is the law that applies to a blood of a shade] such as this?"

[Q]   He said to him, "Unclean."

[R]   It grew lighter.

[S]   He said to him, "Clean [= J]."

[T]   He said to him, "May peace come on a man who erred in what he said but did not err in what he saw."

[U]   They contemplated ruling, "The one who rules that it is clean does so in a case in which it is clear. The one who rules that it is unclean does so in a case in which it is turbid."

[V]   Let us then infer the law from the following case, concerning a woman of the household of Rabbi, who produced black blood.

[W]   The case came before R. Jacob bar Zabedi and before R. Isaac bar Ṭablai. They contemplated declaring her unclean.

[X]   Said to them R. Ḥelbo, "Thus said [50b] R. Huna in the name of Rab: '[If] it is a dull black color, it is clean. [If it is a] bright one, it is unclean.' "

[Y]   [Thus the Mishnah-pericope has referred] only to black. Lo, all of [the rest of them], even if they are clear, are clean [= K].

[III.A]   *Bright crocus color? Like the brightest shade of crocus that there is.*

[B]   **[Like a leaf] that is wet, not dry.**

[C]   **On top, not on the bottom.**

[D]   **As one examines it in the shade, and not as one examines it in sunlight [T. Nid. 3:11F–G].**

[E]   R. Abbahu brought [for comparison] to the session of R. Eleazar various sorts of blood contained in [blood-letters'] vessels.

[F]   He said to him, "The color has already dimmed."

[G]   R. Jacob bar Zabedi brought before R. Abbahu blood of a goat in the case of red blood, and blood of fish in the case of black.

[H]   He said to him, "The color has already dimmed."

[IV.A]   *And the color of earthy water? Like a color produced when over dirt from the valley of Beth Kerem water is run.*

[B]   R. Ḥaninah and R. Jonathan—both of them say, "[The flow of water must be equivalent to] running water over a strip of cloth [that is, in substantial volume]."

[V.A]   *A color like wine mixed with water? [Two parts water to one part wine, using wine of Sharon].*

[B]   Abba bar Ḥanah in the name of R. Yoḥanan: "A cup of mixed wine as it appears from the outside."

[C]   They contemplated ruling: "Like Tiberian [glass] cups."

[D]   [But] said R. Abudama of Sepphoris in session before R. Mana, "Like a flat bowl that does not cast a shadow onto its own sides."

[VI.A] Samuel said, "Whoever does not know how to discern clean blood should not take upon himself to examine unclean blood."

[B]   Rab said, "[One should do so] only if he is an expert in them and in their names."

[C]   A teaching of R. Yohanan makes the same point: "I am able to discern all shades of clean blood and all shades of unclean blood. If a shade of blood is clean as red blood, it may be unclean among those shades of blood matching water mixed with earth. Whoever does not know that fact does not know how to discern [the differences among shades of blood]."

[D]   And furthermore we [infer the same viewpoint] from the following teaching: [As to dirt that is like the color of blood: they examine the mixture when it is turbid, and they do not examine it when it is clear. If] the mixture becomes clear, they do not go and make it turbid [a second time, for there is no limit to the mixture of water and dirt] [T. Nid. 3:11M–0].

[E]   R. Hanina would make them turbid again.

[F]   They said before R. Yohanan, "R. Haninah made [the water and dirt] turbid again, and you did not make them turbid again?"

[G]   He said to them, "R. Hanina drank old wine, R. Yohanan did not drink old wine. [The former was experienced, the latter not experienced.]"

[H]   R. Hanina [indeed] drank the best vintage wine,

[I]   [for,] said R. Hoshaiah, "Since R. Haninah's eye had been nourished on many cases, even turbid mixtures did he not declare invalid."

[J]   R. Shemi in the name of R. Aha, "R. Haninah would make an estimate [of the required color of dirt and water] based on a clump of dirt [without actually mixing it, because of his exceptional experience in judging such cases]."

[K]   R. Abun, R. Shemi in the name of R. Aha, "Since we know that R. Haninah is suitable, shall we therefore rely on his judgment?"

[L]   R. Ḥaninah was living in Sepphoris, and cases would come be-
fore him. And two times cases went forth [from his court].
Now R. Yoḥanan and R. Simeon b. Laqish were living there.
But he did not add them to his court.

[M]   They said, "That old man is wise, and his knife is sharp."

[N]   One time he joined them [to his court].

[O]   They said, "Why does Rabbi [after ignoring us so long] pay
attention to us today?"

[P]   He said to them, "May [something bad] come upon me, if it is
not so that every case that I bring forth from my court I do
judge in accord with a law that I learned from my teacher as a
valid law, as many times as there are hairs on my head [and if
in addition I did not see my teacher apply these laws] in practice at least three times. And on that account I rely on my own
teaching. But this particular case did not come before my
teacher as a matter of law or practical decision more than two
times. On that account I have joined you with me to make the
decision."

[Q]   R. Isaac bar Naḥman learned from R. Eleazar to recognize
clean blood.

[R]   And lo, did he not [learn] unclean blood [= **VI.A**]?

[S]   And did not R. Isaac bar Naḥman say to R. Abudama of
Haifa, "The wound on this one is nearly like that of menstrual
blood" [= **I.C**]?

[T]   But whoever learned this from him would also learn that from
him.

[U]   Iṣaac bar Jonathan and Rab [Huna, thus W] were sitting in session. A woman came and asked them [about the condition of
her blood].

[V]   Said to her R. Isaac bar Jonathan, "I have seen a dimmer
[color] than that."

[W]   Said to him R. Huna, "Thus said Rab: 'In accord with the case
before you must you give judgment.' "

[X]   Said R. Jacob bar Aḥa in the name of R. Simeon b. Abba,
"How many basketfuls of cases would come before R. Ḥaninah
[H–P], and for whatever came before him did he give a deci-
sion."

[VII.A] What is the law as to inspecting bloodstains by night?

[B] Rabbi examined one of them by night and declared it unclean. He decided to leave it for the morning. He examined it by day and declared it clean.

[C] He said, "Great are the teachings of sages, who ruled that [judges] are not to examine bloodstains by night."

[D] He decided to leave it for the night. He examined it by night and declared it clean.

[E] He said, "But it is not I who made an error, but [the bloodstain] grew dim."

[VIII.A] [If a woman] saw a [drop of blood] on the bolster, what is the law as to her being deemed a credible witness to report, "I saw a drop of blood of this sort" or ". . . of that sort"?

[B] R. Ba in the name of R. Judah, R. Ḥelbo, R. Ḥiyya in the name of R. Yoḥanan, "[If] she saw [a drop of blood] on the bolster, she is deemed a credible witness to report, 'I saw a drop of blood of this sort' or '. . . of that sort.' "

[C] And so it was taught in a Tannaitic teaching: She is deemed a credible witness.

[D] Is it possible to maintain that the examination of a bloodstain is equivalent to examinations of negaᶜ-spots [so that a woman may testify to a priest what she has seen]?

[E] Scripture says, "And it will be brought to Aaron, the priest, or to one of his sons, the priests (Lev. 13:2)" [so the negaᶜ-spot must itself be brought for inspection to a priest, and a description of it will not suffice].

The Mishnah carries forward the established theme, and, for its part, the Talmud undertakes a fairly close exegesis of the law and language of the Mishnah. Illustrative stories do not move far from the matter subject to sustained discussion. The one point of interest at **II** is the dispute of Simeon b. Laqish and Yoḥanan (J–K and following). The dispute focuses upon the close interpretation of the language of the Mishnah. The discussion is sustained and fairly well organized; the materials are consistently relevant to the basic point. **III, IV,** and **V** follow a single pattern, citing the Mishnah and then providing some clarifying information. **VI** then goes on to the more general issue of procedures of sages in examining menstrual blood. This topic allows for the inclusion of somewhat more discursive materials. The main point has to do with the expert knowledge of Ḥanina, subject of several sayings and stories. That that is the principal purpose of the whole is shown at **VI.X**, which reverts to the main theme after a mass of inserted materials. **VII** and **VIII** at the end raise questions not invited by the Mishnah, but entirely relevant to the theme of the chapter as a whole, namely, the rules for undertaking the adjudication of the status of blood and bloodstains. The two issues, doing so by night and relying upon a woman's description of what she has seen, are entirely pertinent. So, in all, the Talmud is well put together and follows a consistent pattern, first dealing with the Mishnah-pericope, then expanding the range of discourse while remaining essentially within the framework of the Mishnah's topic, if not of its concrete law.

8 Yerushalmi Niddah
Chapters Three and Four

3:1

[A] *[50c] She who aborts a shapeless object, if there is blood with it, is unclean, and if not, she is clean.*

[B] *R. Judah says, "One way or the other, she is unclean."*

[I.A] [The position of the sages of A, who make the matter depend on the presence of blood, is because] the rabbis maintain that it is the source [uterus] that produces the shapeless object [so the woman is clean so far as having given birth, and so if she produces blood, it is menstrual blood, and she is unclean as a menstruant. When there is no blood, there of course is no reason to declare her unclean].

[B] R. Judah says, "It is blood that has congealed and been turned into a shapeless object."

[C] Said R. Yoḥanan, "R. Judah declares unclean only in a case in which there are four sorts of blood [in the shapeless object]."

[D] R. Jacob b. Aḥa, R. Simeon bar Ba in the name of R. Yosé, son of Nehorai: "The law is in accord with the opinion of R. Judah."

[E] R. Eleazar heard [this statement] and said, "I do not accept the authority of that judgment."

[F] Samuel said, "The law is in accord with the position of R. Judah."

[G] Said R. Zeirah, "It is not that he stated that the law is in accord with R. Judah, but he noted that rabbis are accustomed to follow the law in accord with R. Judah."

197

[H]   R. Yoḥanan in the name of R. Simeon b. Yoḥai, **"One cuts it
       open, and if blood is found inside it** collected together, **she is
       unclean, but if not, she is clean"** [T. Nid. 4:1A–B].

[I]   R. Eliezer b. Jacob taught as a Tannaitic tradition and took is-
       sue with R. Simeon b. Yoḥai: " 'When a woman has a dis-
       charge of blood that is her regular discharge from her body
       [she shall be in her impurity seven days]' (Lev. 15:19—[in her
       body, blood signifies menstrual uncleanness, but] not in an
       abortion or in a shapeless object."

The issue of the Mishnah is whether or not we impute menstrual uncleanness in the case of the stated sort of abortion. Judah holds that we do, because of the source, blood, of the
abortion itself. The sages behind A maintain otherwise, for the
reason stated by the Talmud at A. After a statement of the
basic issue of the Mishnah, the Talmud focuses upon the position of Judah, which is declared to prevail. Yoḥanan (H) adduces in support of his opinion (C) that there are several sorts
of blood collected together. Eliezer b. Jacob (I) takes issue with
Simeon b. Yoḥai and also, it must follow, with sages and Judah. In his opinion menstrual uncleanness is limited to the
woman's period and has nothing to do with abortions.

3:2

[A]   *She who aborts something like a rind, hair, dust, or red flies
       should put them into water. If they dissolve [into blood] she is
       unclean.*

[B]   *She who aborts something [shaped] like fish, locusts, insects, or
       creeping things, if there is blood with them, is unclean. And if
       not, she is clean [= sages, M. 3:1A].*

[C]   *"She who aborts something in the shape of a domestic beast,
       wild animal, or bird, whether unclean or clean, if it is male,
       should sit out the days of purifying of a male; if it is female,
       she should sit out the days of purifying for a female. [Male:
       seven unclean days, thirty-three days of purifying, in which all
       blood that exudes is deemed clean; female: fourteen unclean
       days, sixty-six days of purifying.] [If] it is not known [whether*

it is male or female], she should sit out the days of purifying
for a male and an female," the words of R. Meir.

[D]   And sages say, "Whatever does not bear the form of a human
being is not deemed a fetus."

[I.A]   R. Ḥaninah in the name of R. Simeon b. Laqish: "She should
put them [M. 3:2A] into warm water."

[B]   And have we not learned in the Mishnah [M. 3:2B]: She who
aborts something like fish, locusts, insects, or creeping things,
if there is blood with them, is unclean. And if not, she is clean.
Now let her put them into warm water [until they dissolve, and
if then there is blood, she should be unclean, just as is stated at
M. 3:2A].

[C]   [We must] apply the rule applying in the one case to the other,
and the rule applying in the other case to the one.

[D]   We apply the rule applying in the one [M. 3:2A] to the other
[M. 3:2B]: If they dissolve, she is unclean, and if not, she is
clean.

[E]   And the rule applying in the other [M. 3:2B] to the one [M.
3:2A]: If there is blood with them, she is unclean, and if not
she is clean. And she should put them into warm water.

[F]   There [M. Nid. 7:1] we have learned in the Mishnah: [The
blood of the menstruating woman and the flesh of a corpse impart uncleanness when they are wet, and impart uncleanness
when they are dry. But the Zab's flux, phlegm, spit, and the
creeping thing, carrion, and semen impart uncleanness when
wet but do not impart uncleanness when dry. If they can be
soaked and return to their former bulk, they impart uncleanness when wet and when dry.] And how long are they to be
soaked? In lukewarm water, for twenty-four hours.

[G]   **Judah b. Naqosa says, "It must be in likewarm water for
twenty-four hours" [T. Nid. 6:11E].**

[H]   What does one do? He puts it on the ashes or puts hot water
into it in any amount whatsoever.

[II.A] She who aborts dry blood—

[B]   R. Eleazar says, "She is unclean."

[C]   R. Yosé b. Ḥanina said, "She is clean."

[D]   The teaching of the Mishnah is at variance with the view of R. Yosé b. Ḥaninah: *The blood of the menstruating woman and the flesh of a corpse impart uncleanness when they are wet and impart uncleanness when they are dry.* [Yet Yosé says dry blood is clean.]

[E]   Interpret [the Mishnah to refer to a case] in which the blood had been wet and then dried up.

[F]   The teaching of the Mishnah is at variance with the view of R. Eleazar: *She who aborts something like a rind, hair, dust, or red flies, should put them into water. If they dissolve, they are unclean* [and not, as Eleazar says, invariably unclean, e.g., in the case of dry blood].

[G]   Interpret [the Mishnah's view that if the thing does not dissolve, it is clean] since [if it does not dissolve] it is because it is a creature [unto itself, and it is not blood at all].

[H]   Said R. Zeira, "And even if you reply [that on the list is] dirt—dirt also [can constitute] a distinct creature [through parthenogenesis]."

[I]   Said R. Ba, "And even if you say it is sandy matter of dirt, a woman may abort [such too]."

[J]   So you may interpret the Mishnah [to refer to a case of cleanness] because [it constitutes] a creature unto itself [just as G has said].

[K]   The following Mishnah-passage [sic] is at variance with the position of R. Yosé b. Ḥaninah.

[L]   M'ŚH B: **A woman aborted red scabs, and the case came before sages, who sent and called physicians. They told [the sages], "She has a wound inside** [and therefore produces from its crust abortions like red rinds. She thus should put them in water]."

[M]   ŚWB M'ŚH B: **A woman aborted red hairs, and the case came before sages, who sent and called physicians. They said to [the sages], "She has a wart inside [therefore she produces abortions of red hairs]"** [T. Nid. 4:3–4].

[N]   [Now the reason that the woman is deemed clean is that] she has a wart inside or a wound inside. Lo, if she had had no wart or wound inside[, she would have been unclean and here we have dry blood, which Ḥanina would have deemed to be clean.

Sages would have regarded it as unclean except under the stated conditions.]

[O]   [These two cases] indeed are at variance with [Yosé b. Ḥaninah], and there is no way of supporting his position.

[III.A]   Said R. Yoḥanan, "The delivery in this present context is exactly like all other deliveries that are referred to in the Torah. Just as in the case of all deliveries referred to in the Torah, [we deem the delivery to have taken place] only once the head of the greater part of the body will have come forth, so in this case [M. 3:2C–D], [we regard the delivery to have taken place] only once the head and the greater part of the body will have come forth."

[B]   R. Simeon b. Laqish said, "This particular delivery is different from all the other deliveries mentioned in the Torah. In the case of all other deliveries mentioned in the Torah, [the delivery is deemed to have taken place only] when the head and the greater part of the body [will have come forth]. But in this case, [the delivery is deemed to have taken place] once a sufficient [part of the abortion] has come forth to provide evidence for discerning the appearance [of the abortion, that it indeed has human form, in line with M. 3:2D]."

[C]   So what is the difference between [Yoḥanan and Simeon b. Laqish]?

[D]   [If the abortion] went forth chopped up or cut up.

[E]   In accord with the opinion of R. Yoḥanan, once the head and the greater part of the body has come forth [we deem the delivery to have taken place].

[F]   In accord with the opinion of Simeon b. Laqish, once a sufficient [part of the thing] has come forth to provide evidence for discerning the appearance [of the abortion, that it indeed has human form, we deem the delivery to have taken place].

[IV.A]   ["She who aborts something in the sahpe of a domestic beast, wild animal, or bird, whether unclean or clean, if it is male, should sit out the days of purifying of a male; if it is female, she should sit out the days of purifying for a female. If] it is not known [whether it is male or female], she should sit out the days of purifying for a male and a female," the words of R. Meir.

> And sages say, "Whatever does not bear the form of a human being is not deemed fetus."

[B]   In all those cases concerning which we have learned in the Mishnah that a woman must sit out the days of purifying for both a male and a female, [women] have fourteen days of uncleanness [for the female] and twenty-six clean ones [= 33–7]. [That is to say], they assign to her the more stringent rule applying to the male [the lower number of clean days] and the more stringent rule applying to the female [the higher number of unclean days].

[C]   Now this rule that you state applies to sexual relations [that she is assigned only those clean days of a male that remain after we subtract the unclean days]. But as to matters requiring cleanness, let her observe the rules applying to the female [that is to say, the entire period of clean days given after a female birth].

[V.A] Said R. Ḥanina son of R. Abbahu, "The reason of R. Meir is that Scripture refers to these other things with the word *form* just as in the case of man: 'Then the Lord God formed man of dust from the ground' (Gen. 2:7)."

[B]   R. Ami asked, "Now the word *form* [indeed] is written concerning domesticated cattle: 'So out of the ground the Lord God formed every beast of the field and every bird of the air' (Gen. 2:19). But lo, it is written, 'For lo, he who forms the mountains and creates the wind [and declares to man what is his thought, who makes the morning darkness and treads on the heights of the earth—the Lord, the God of hosts, is his name]' (Amos 4:13). On the basis of this verse [by the reasoning just now spelled out], if a woman aborted something in the shape of a mountain, she should be unclean."

[C]   There is a difference in regard to having given birth, for the word *form* is not written concerning the [mountains] from the outset of the creation of the world.

[D]   R. Yosa in the name of R. Yoḥanan, "[The reason of R. Meir for including beasts and the like] is that they watch out before themselves, just like man [having two eyes]."

[E]   Abba bar Ḥannah in the name of R. Yoḥanan: "Because they walk forward, like man."

[F]   Replied R. Bun bar Ḥiyya, "And have we not learned: *That [beast] the eye of which is round like that of a man* [M. Bekh.

6:8H] is a blemish[ed beast] [so Meir cannot possibly concur that the reason beasts come under consideration is that their eyes are like those of man, since in a beast such a trait is deemed a blemish]."

[G] Said R. Yosé, "Now do we learn in the Mishnah [cited just now, listing blemishes in beasts] that they look out before them, or that they go along forward [like man]? What is the point of this similarity to the eye of man? The eyeball of man is round, the eyeball of a beast is long."

[H] Said R. Yosé the son of R. Bun, "In man the white of the eye is more than the dark, and in a domesticated beast, the dark is more than the white."

[I] R. Haggai said, R. Hananiah, associates of rabbis raised the question with regard to that which R. Meir has taught [that if a woman aborted something in the shape of a bird, she should sit out the appropriate number of days of purifying]: If a woman produced an abortion in the shape of a raven, and [lo], the raven flies away and is sitting at the top of a palm tree, [if then the husband's brother dies without his wife's having given birth to a child], does one say [to the raven, which is then surviving brother-in-law of the widow], 'Come and enter into the ceremony of removing the shoe [of Deut. 25:10ff.] or enter into levirage marriage'?"

[J] Said to him R. Mana, "While you are raising such a question with regard to the opinion of R. Meir, you might as well raise the same quesiton of the rabbis [who deem human features adequate]."

[K] For R. Yosa said in the name of R. Yohanan, "[If the abortion is] wholly in the shape of man, but its face is like that of a domesticated beast, it is not deemed to be a viable fetus. But [if it is] wholly in the shape of a domesticated beast, but its face is that of a man, it is a viable fetus.

"[If it is] wholly in the shape of a man, but the face is in the shape of a beast, and it is standing and reading in the Torah, they say to him, 'Come and get yourself slaughtered.' [If it is] wholly in the shape of a beast but its face is in the shape of a man's, standing and ploughing in a field, do they say to it, 'Come and carry out the ceremony of removing a shoe, or enter into levirage marriage!' "

[L]   And R. Yasa in the name of R. Yoḥanan said, "The end of the matter is *not* that all of the specified traits are present. But even if [only] one of the specified traits is present [it is deemed a viable fetus in the definition of sages at M. 3:2D]."

[M]   And what are the specified traits [that signify human form]? The forehead, eyebrows, eyes, ears, cheek, nose, beard, and dimples.

[N]   And R. Yosa in the name of R. Yoḥanan said, "The end of the matter is *not* that all of the specified traits must be present. But even if one of the specified traits is present, [it is deemed a viable fetus, as stated above]."

[O]   R. Ba, R. Jeremiah in the name of Rab: "The opinion of R. [Meir] is preferable in a case in which the entire face is like that of a man, and the opinion of sages is valid when even only one of the traits is present."

[P]   And the opinion of R. Simeon b. Yoḥai applies even when there is only the [human] visage.

[Q]   R. Pinḥas asked, "Perhaps the theory attributed to R. Simeon b. Yoḥai is confused. There he says, [**"Why does Scripture say, Camel, camel (Lev. 11:4, Deut. 19:7)—two times? To encompass a camel born of a cow, which is equivalent to one born of a camel.] And if its head and the greater part of its body are similar to those of its dam, it is permitted for eating"** [T. Bekh. 1:9A–C].

[R]   "But here he says this [so he seems to invoke conflicting criteria]!"

[S]   Here he speaks of man, there he speaks of cattle.

[**VI.**A]   Said R. Ba, "R. Ḥiyya the Great went to the South. R. Ḥama, father of R. Hoshaiah, and Bar Qappara asked him, '[If the abortion looks] wholly like man, but its face is that of a beast, what is the law?'

[B]   "He came and asked Rabbi. He said to him, 'Go and write to them, 'It is not a viable fetus.' [For we require the face to be like that of a man]' " [= M. 3:2D].

[C]   Said R. Jeremiah, "Zuga went out [to the South]. R. Ḥama, father of R. Hoshaiah, and Bar Qappara asked him, 'If the fetus's two eyes are covered over [not discernible], what is the law?'

[D]   "He came and asked Rabbi.

[E]   "He said to him, 'Go and write to them, 'It is not a viable fetus.' "

[F]   [50d] Said R. Yosé b. R. Bun, "Rabbi is consistent in his opinion. For Rabbi said, '[It is not a viable fetus] unless the entire face is similar to that of a man.' "

[G]   [If] its face is mashed, what is the law?

[H]   R. Yosa said, "R. Yoḥanan and R. Simeon b. Laqish differ on this matter. R. Yoḥanan said, 'It is not a viable fetus.' R. Simeon b. Laqish said, 'It is a viable fetus.' "

[I]   Said R. Zeira, "It is not that R. Yoḥanan said it is no viable fetus in any regard. It is not a viable fetus such as to require the mother to sit out the [33, 66] days of purifying. But it is a viable fetus to require the mother to sit out the days of uncleanness by reason of childbearing [7, 14]."

[J]   R. Yoḥanan said in the name of R. Yannai, "And [if] its thigh is unformed, it is not a viable fetus."

[K]   R. Yoḥanan in the name of R. Yosé b. R. Joshua: "[If] its navel is unformed, it is not a viable fetus."

[L]   R. Yoḥanan in the name of R. Zakkai: "[If] its apertures are not open, it is not a viable fetus."

[M]   R. Zeira in the name of Giddul: "[If] the skull is unformed it is not a viable fetus."

This long and interesting expansion of the Mishnah begins (**I**) with an acute and reasonable effort to compare M. 3:2A to M. 3:2B. The Talmud sees no material difference between the items on the two lists and so invokes the criterion imposed upon one for testing the other. The citation of a relevant passage on soaking blood in warm water both provides important information for what has been said and forms a bridge to **II**. The exercise at **II** clearly is an expansion of the Mishnah, which is cited and tested against relevant rulings of other authorities. Then the statements of these other authorities, Eleazar and Yosé b. Ḥanina, themselves come under acute examination. **III** supplements what has gone before; leaving it out would have caused no loss. **IV** affects the transition to the second half of the Mishnah-pericope, the dispute of Meir and sages. The opinion of Meir is clarified at an important and ambiguous point. Having accomplished such exegesis as was deemed necessary, the framers then introduce the question of the basic reasoning of Meir and sages. Meir's position has to be clarified in light of sages, who call for the presence of a human form. Since Meir accepts the form of a beast, animal, or bird, as equally valid evidence of the presence of a fetus, we have to explain why he deems these to be comparable to the human form, and that is what is attempted at **V**. The first exercise is exegetical. Meir's reason is adduced from scriptural usage (**V.A–C**). The second raises the possibility of an empirical comparison (**V.D–H**). Naturally, appropriate facts of the Mishnah will be brought to test in the stated theory. Third comes a test of Meir's position against the logical consequences of that position. If Meir is right, then we have an absurd possibility (**V.I**). This is turned against sages (**V.J–K**). Common sense resolves the matter (L). Then further relevant information is adduced in evidence on those traits that signify a viable human fetus. Tacked on at the end is the position of Simeon b. Yohai and the predictable examination of the consistency of his views of man and beast. The concluding unit, **VI**, takes up the position of sages at M. 3:2D. It asks for definitions of those features that signify the presence of "human form." Listed are those features that, if absent, mean that the human form is not present. There are two stories, **VI.A–B, C–E**, followed by a statement in general terms of the same point as is made in the stories (F). Rabbi thus is shown to concur with the Mishnah's sages. Finally comes a sequence of miscellaneous rulings, all relevant to the basic issue at hand (G–I, J, K, L, and M), five in all. It would be not possible to build a more carefully organized exposition of the Mishnah, through diverse materials, than this Talmud gives us.

3:3

[A]   *She who aborts a sac filled with water, filled with blood, filled with dry matter, does not take into consideration that this is a valid birth [at all, so she is wholly clean, not unclean even as a menstruant].*

[B]   *But if [a limb] was formed, let her sit out [the days of unclean-*
ness and cleanness] for both male and female.

[I.A]   It was taught in a Tannaitic tradition (TNY):

[B]   [If the sac was aborted,] filled with water, she is unclean by
reason of having given birth. [If it was] filled with blood, she is
unclean as a menstruant. [If it was] filled with flesh, she is unclean as a menstruant.

[C]   And lo, we have learned: *She who aborts a sac filled with*
water, filled with blood, filled with dry matter, does not take
into consideration that this is a valid birth.

[D]   R Bibi in the name of R. Simeon b. Laqish: "The Mishnah-
pericope refers to a case in which the liquid is clear. The Tannaitic *baraita* [B] refers to a case in which the liquid is turbid
[so there is the possibility of a fetus that has dissolved]."

[E]   R. Simon in the name of R. Joshua b. Levi: "And even if it
was clear[, the *baraita*'s rule applies], for a sac appears only in
the case of man[, and the Mishnah and *baraita* differ on this
matter]."

[F]   Now this is the meaning of that which is written: "When I
made clouds its garment, and thick darkness its swaddling
band" (Job 38:9). "Its garment" refers to the sac. "And thick
darkness its swaddling band" refers to the abortion.

[II.A]   A sac, the appearance of which was disfigured—what is the
law?

[B]   R. Yohanan said, "It is a viable fetus."

[C]   R. Simeon b. Laqish said, "It is not a viable fetus, [and the
woman is not unclean]."

[D]   R. Simeon b. Laqish objected before R. Yohanan, "What is the
difference between this case and the case of a corpse that rot-
ted, so that the backbone is no longer discernible [which is
deemed no longer a source of uncleanness? In both instances
there is no issue of uncleanness]."

[E]   He said to him, "In that case [of the corpse], it was right that
it should be deemed *not* a source of uncleanness even if the
backbone were there to be discerned. But why did they declare
it unclean? In order to protect the honor [of the corpse, to

keep people from misusing it]. But in the present case, it indeed does constitute a viable fetus."

[III.A]   What is *the formed limb* of which they have spoken [at M. 3:3B]?

[B]   It is any, **at the beginning of the creation of which looks like a rashon-locust [T. Nid. 4:10E].**

[C]   **They do not examine [the fetus, to determine whether it is male or female] with water, because the water is hard and distorts its shape. But they do so with oil, because it is soft and makes it clear. And they examine it only in the sun [T. Nid. 3:11].**

[D]   It is taught in a Tannaitic teaching: Abba Saul says, "Man is formed from the navel and spreads out [in] his growth in all directions."

[E]   It is taught in a Tannaitic teaching: **Its two eyes are like two drippings of a fly. The two nostrils are like two drippings of a fly. The opening of its mouth is like a hair. They discern its two hands like two drippings of a fly. Its navel is like a dripping of a fly. Its body is like a dripping of a fly. And if it is a female, her sexual organ is like the longitudinal split of a barley-grain [T. Nid. 4:10].**

[F]   And it was taught in a Tannaitic teaching: R. Jonathan says, "They recognize that its two arms are like two threads of crimson, and the rest of its limbs are like attached pieces of unformed matter. And it does not yet have a span of hands and feet. And concerning it it is stated explicitly in the received tradition: 'Thy eyes beheld my unformed substance; in thy book were written every one of them the days that were formed for me when as yet there was none of them' (Ps. 139:16)."

[IV.A]   R. Judah asked Samuel, "Since I am a sage, am I well able to examine the traits of sac?"

[B]   He said to him, "The head of the one who is head of you [that is, your teacher, Samuel himself] is scalded in boiling water, and will you not be burned even by lukewarm water?"

[C]   R. Ḥiyya in the name of R. Yoḥanan: "These women who say that [if the placenta is] like a female slug, it is a male fetus, and if it is like a male slug, it is a female fetus—we do not rely on their knowledge."

[D]   R. Jacob bar Zabedi, R. Abbahu in the name of R. Yoḥanan:
"A woman is permitted to testify, 'I have given birth,' or 'I
have not given birth.' But she is not permitted to testify, 'It is
masculine,' or 'It is feminine.' "

As usual, the Talmud, first, presents materials closely relevant
to the Mishnah, then, second, broadens the range of discourse.
I contains contradictory views, attributed to the authorities of
the same period as those of the Mishnah (I.B). These are
shown in fact to disagree with the Mishnah's law. Sticking with
M. 3:3A, II asks about a sac in a case in which we cannot be
sure of its shape or contents, that is, a closely related and complementary question. III proceeds to the exegesis of the next
phase of the Mishnah, M. 3:3B, and a repertoire of materials
on the formed and unformed limbs of a fetus is laid forth. Finally, as at 3:2, we end with materials on the practical application of the law. The point again is how difficult it is to discern
the traits of the fetus and the placenta.

3:4

[A]   *She who aborts [something shaped like] a sandal or a placenta
should sit out [the days of uncleanness and purifying] for both
a male and a female.*

[B]   *[When] a placenta is in the house, the house is unclean—*

[C]   *not that the placenta is the fetus, but that there is no placenta
that does not have part of a fetus with it.*

[D]   *R. Simeon says, "The fetus is crushed before [the placenta]
comes forth[, so there is no issue of uncleanness]."*

[I.A]   R. Ba in the name of R. Judah: "A sandal [occurs] only when
a [second], live [fetus] has pressed on it. But [the fetus] does
not go forth alive but dead."

[B]   [What follows depends upon M. Ker. 1:3A, D: *There are
women who bring a sin-offering after childbirth and it is eaten
by the priests. . . . She who aborts a sandal or an
afterbirth. . . .* The position of R. Ba in the name of R. Judah
is that there is a second fetus. There should then be an obligation for a sin-offering for this other fetus, as well as for the

sandal-abortion, so two sin-offerings. It is to this problem that R. Bun bar Ḥiyya's saying is directed. To the Mishnah-lemma, *There is no placenta that does not have part of the fetus*], replied R. Bun bar Ḥiyya, "And lo, we have learned in the Mishnah: *She who aborts [something shaped like a sandal or a placenta should set out [the days of uncleanness and purifying] for both a male and a female.* So you do have a [whole] fetus!"

[C] Said R. Huna, explaining [the passage] before R. Jeremiah, "Interpret the Mishnah to refer to a case in which the fetus emerged from the side [in a Caesarean birth], while the sandal emerged from the vagina, [or] the fetus emerged during the days [of purifying] and the sandal afterward; [or] the fetus before [the woman] converted, and the sandal afterward. [There is no obligation for an offering if the birth does not take place through the vagina, if it takes place in the days of purifying, or if the woman was not an Israelite. Consequently, in these three cases there is only a single offering, such as is assumed at M. Ker. 1:3.]"

[D] Even if you say, both came from the womb, [or] both came after conversion, you may interpret the Mishnah to refer to a case in which the fetus came forth first, so the woman set aside an animal for an offering on its account. She did not have time to bring [and offer] it before the sandal came forth. So the first offering was postponed, and she turned out to bring an offering on account of the sandal.

[II.A] What is the sandal of which they have spoken? **It is any that is like a sandal, a fish in the sea. Rabban Simeon b. Gamaliel says, "It is any that is like the tongue of an ox."**

[B] Our rabbis voted concerning this issue, stating, "**[It is not deemed unclean] unless it bears human form**" [T. Nid. 4:7B–D].

[III.A] Who are "our rabbis" [of II.B]? They are R. Judah the Patriarch and his court.

[B] In three places R. Judah the Patriarch is referred to as "our rabbis": in regard to [1] divorce, [2] oil, and [3] sandal.

[C] [3] The matter of "sandal" is this one to which we have just now attended.

[D] [2] The matter of oil is the following, which we have learned in a Tannaitic tradition:

[E]   *Rabbi and his court permitted oil [prepared by gentiles] [M. A.Z. 2:6C].*

[F]   [1] As to writs of divorce, the matter is covered in the following, which we have learned there in a Tannaitic tradition:

[G]   *[If the husband says,] "This is your writ of divorce, to take effect when I die," "This is your writ of divorce [if I die] from illness," "This is your writ of divorce [to take effect] after I die," he has said nothing[, and the writ is invalid] [M. Git. 7:3A–D].*

[H]   And our rabbis declared, "Lo, this is a valid writ of divorce" [cf. T. Git. 5:3A–C].

[I]   Who are "our rabbis"? They are R. Judah the Patriarch and his court.

[J]   And they called it a permissive court. For any court that takes a lenient position in three matters is called a permissive court.

[K]   Said R. Yudan, "His court differed from him in the matter of the [validation of] writs of divorce."

[IV.A]   R. Yannai cried out [in reference to II.B]: "You have declared the fetus to be clean[, by saying that only if there is a human form is the fetus a source of uncleanness]."

[B]   R. Simon in the name of R. Joshua b. Levi: "It is a ruling based on the testimony of R. Ḥoniah of Beth Hauran."

[C]   [And that accords with] the following: R. Zeira: "If it is based on the testimony of R. Ḥoniah of Beth Hauran, [then it was] R. Ḥaninah [who] cried out, 'You have declared the fetus to be clean.' "

[V.A]   **What is the placenta of which they have spoken? It is any that is like a thread of the warp, and its head is like a lupine.**

[B]   **Rabban Simeon b. Gamaliel says, "It is any that is like the craw of a hen, and its head is like a stomach.**

[C]   **"And it is hollow like a trumpet. And a placenta is at least a handbreadth"** [T. Nid. 4:9].

[VI.A]   R. Judah sent to R. Eleazar, asking [with reference to M. 3:4A–C], "As to a placenta part of which came out on one day, part on the next—[what is the law? From what point do they reckon the days of uncleanness and the days of purifying?]"

[B]   He said to him, "If it is for the reckoning of the status of
       blood on the days of purifying, one reckons from the first of
       the two days. If it is for reckoning of the status of the blood on
       the days on which the blood is unclean, one counts from the
       second day."

[C]   Said R. Mattenaiah, "That ruling you have given [in a case of
       doubt, taking the more severe of the possibilities] applies in a
       case in which a fetus did not emerge with [the placenta]. But if
       a fetus emerged with the placenta, whether it is for the purpose
       of counting the days of purifying or for the purpose of reckon-
       ing the days in which the blood is unclean, one counts only
       from that moment at which the fetus actually emerged."

[D]   R. Yosé b. Saul asked in session before Rabbi, "What is the
       law as to attributing the presence of a placenta to something
       that is not a fetus at all[, e.g., something in other than human
       form]?"

[E]   He said to him, "They do not attribute the presence of pla-
       centa to something that is not a fetus at all."

[F]   "What if [the placenta] went forth attached to [the fetus]?"

[G]   He said to him, "They do not teach a rule concerning a case
       that is impossible."

[H]   R. Ḥanin taught as a Tannaitic tradition [in the name] of Sam-
       uel, "They do not attribute the presence of placenta to some-
       thing that is not a fetus at all. [If] it went forth attached to it,
       they do attribute [the placenta] to that to which it is attached."

[I]   Samuel asked the disciple of Rab, "What is the law as to at-
       tributing a placenta to a fetus produced in a miscarriage [with-
       out taking account of the presence of another fetus]?"

[J]   They said to him, "They attribute a placenta to the viable fe-
       tus, and [likewise] they attribute the placenta to a fetus pro-
       duced in a miscarriage."

[K]   Now Samuel praised them, for they stated the law in accord
       with the theory of R. Bun [who held the same position].

[L]   [51a] R. Ḥanin taught as a Tannaitic tradition [in the name] of
       Samuel: "They attribute a placenta to a viable fetus, but they
       do not attribute the placenta to a fetus produced in a miscar-
       riage, because it does not separate from [the fetus] before the
       fetus is fully formed. [If it was from this unformed fetus, it

would be attached. So we take account of the possibility of yet another fetus, to which the placenta was attached.]"

[M]   R. Zeira in the name of rabbis: "Now if you say, 'They attribute the placenta to a fetus, for a woman does not become pregnant and then become pregnant a second time [within the same term, so there is no possibility other than to assign the fetus to the placenta in hand], [or] they cannot attribute [the placenta] to a fetus resulting from a miscarriage, for a woman does not abort and go and abort again,' then I shall say that the woman was pregnant with twins, and the placenta of the first dissolved in the placenta of the second. [So we do not attribute the placenta to the fetus in hand.]"

[N]   R. Zeira, R. Judah in the name of Rab: "They attribute the placenta to the fetus within three days [of the birth of the fetus], for one fetus does not delay [in appearing] for more than three days after its fellow. [So if the placenta appears after three days of the earlier birth, we attribute the fresh placenta to a different fetus.]"

[O]   Said R. Zeira, "Whoever holds the one position holds the other, and they who differ in the one case differ also in the other case."

[P]   Said R. Ba, "Interpret the teaching of R. Judah in Rab's name as follows: 'Assign the ruling that they attribute the placenta to the fetus to a case in which the placenta came out within three days of the birth of the fetus, which emerged first of all. And attribute the teaching that the fetus does not delay to emerge more than three days after its fellow to a case in which the sandal came out first [in which case we take account of a second fetus].' "

[Q]   Said R. Mana, "Well spoken! That which is full of life [the fetus] emerges first of all [while the placenta comes out only later on]."

[R]   Said R. Yosé b. R. Bun, "Once it is open for the larger [the fetus], it is open for the smaller [placenta]. If it is open only for the smaller, it will not be open for the larger[, so in this latter case we take account of a second fetus]."

[S]   Said R. Yoḥanan, "[That we take account of corpse-matter in the placenta] follows the view of R. Simeon, *for R. Simeon says, 'The fetus dissolved before it came out.'* "

[T]   Said R. Yoḥanan, "R. Simeon concedes that [the fetus] brings the days of the mother's delivery to an end[, so she then is unclean]."

[U]   If so, the house should be unclean [and at M. 3:4D Simeon does not deem the house unclean!].

[V]   Said R. Bun bar Ḥiyya, "Interpret the Mishnah to apply to a case in which it came forth crushed[, so there is not sufficient corpse-matter to produce uncleanness]."

[W]   Said R. Simeon to sages, "Do you not agree with me that if **one brings the bowl [containing the placenta] from the inner room to the outer one, that [the inner room now] is clean?**"

[X]   **They said to him, "It is because it is mashed" [T. Nid. 4:13C–D].**

[Y]   He said to them, "Also in this case it is as if it were mashed."

[VII.A]   As to utensils that were located there at the moment at which [the fetus and placenta] emerged, what is the law?

[B]   Let us infer the rule from the following, which we have learned in a Tannaitic tradition:

[C]   *R. Eliezer b. Jacob says, "A large beast that discharged a clot of blood—lo, this [clot] is to be buried, and [the beast now] is exempt from the law of a firstling [having produced an abortion]" [M. Bekh. 3:1S].*

[D]   And a Tannaitic tradition has been laid down in connection with this statement:

[E]   **But it does not impart uncleanness to the one who carries it [T. Bekh. 2:13B].**

[F]   Said R. Yoḥanan, "R. Simeon and R. Eliezer b. Jacob—both of them maintain the same position, [and this now answers the question you have raised]: Utensils that were there at the time at which the placenta came forth are clean."

The basic issue faced here is the relationship between the placenta and the fetus. The placenta by itself is not unclean. The fetus is. If the placenta contains bits of the fetus, then it will impart corpse-uncleanness. As before, we shall be especially interested in the problem of multiple excretions, e.g., a fetus and

a placenta not clearly related to each other. The Mishnah ex-
presses this issue at B when it insists that the placenta must
contain bits of corpse-matter. Simeon then holds that the fetus
is thoroughly mashed up and, for purposes of corpse-contami-
nation, is treated as if it were not present at all. Judah does not
concur with Simeon, but offers a theory behind M. 3:4B–C.
He maintains that when we have a sandal-abortion, the reason
is that there was a second pregnancy. The new (second) fetus
has pressed down on the one already present. The sandal, however, is aborted along with this second fetus, and that explains
the position of the Mishnah. Thus, the point of I is Judah's
position that the reason a fetus comes forth is the presence of a
second fetus. Now we have a clear tradition that a woman who
aborts a sandal has to bring an offering. This seems to contradict Judah's view that there is *no* fetus along with the sandal.
At I.C, Huna presents a number of cases in which one might
have to bring an offering on account of a sandal-abortion. D
provides yet another possibility. II provides an exegesis of the
language of the Mishnah, in fact drawn from the Tosefta. III
takes up II.B and provides information on *its* language, a secondary expansion of the whole. IV at the end takes up where
II.B has left off, rejecting the position of Rabbi.

V turns again to the matter of the fetus and placenta, but
the principal discussion is at VI. Judah's question is clear.
What is important is C, Mattenaiah's observation. The point is
that we do *not* assume that the placenta has served a fetus other
than the one that has come out. It is on that basis that Mattenaiah is able to make the point he does, that we assume we have
only a single fetus, the one that has come out. As noted at the
outset, this becomes the center for what is to follow. The issue
is certainly pertinent to the Mishnah's interests. But it also is
obviously secondary to the Mishnah's issues, a typical example
of that expansive exegesis of the Mishnah which our Talmud
makes its specialty. Once the issue is raised by indirection,
moreover, it is made explicit, and that is the force of VI.D. H,
I–K, and L go over the view of Samuel on the same matter. It
appears that L expands and clarifies H. The point of the discussion emerges at S. So far as we are interested in this entire
matter of relating the placenta to a single fetus, it is because of
the theory of Simeon. We take account of the possibility of
corpse-matter in the placenta, Yoḥanan points out, because the
fetus may or may not have dissolved; if it did not, there is the
chance of corpse-matter. Yoḥanan's position is immediately

challenged at U. Why should Simeon regard the house as
clean, if there is a chance of corpse-matter? V provides one reply. W–Y present a second one. **VII** concludes the discussion
by raising a necessary question, namely, the status of utensils in
the room. Once we have maintained that the house is clean, we
have to deem utensils in the room to be clean also, and that
consistent position is assigned to Simeon at C–F.

3:5

[A] *She who aborts a ṭumṭom [a fetus without clearly discernible
sexual traits] or an androgyne [a fetus producing traits of both
sexes] sits out [the days of uncleanness and purifying] for both
male and female[, fourteen unclean days, for the female, and
twenty-six clean days, the minimum number permitted to the
male].*

[B] *[If she aborts] a ṭumṭom and a male, an androgyne and a male,
she sits out [the days of uncleanness and purifying] for both
male and female.*

[C] *[If she aborts] a ṭumṭom and a female, or an androgyne and a
female, she sits out the days of uncleanness and purifying for a
female alone.*

[D] *[If the fetus] emerged in pieces or feet first, once the greater
part of the body has gone forth, lo, this is deemed fully born.*

[E] *[If] it emerged in the normal way, [it is deemed fully born]
when the greater part of the head has emerged.*

[F] *What is deemed the greater part of the head? Once the forehead has emerged.*

[G] *She who aborts [a fetus], and it is not known what it is, should
sit out [the days of uncleanness and purifying] for both a male
and a female.*

[H] *If it is [not] known whether it is a fetus at all [e.g., if it was not
previously assumed that the woman had been pregnant], let her
sit out [the days of purifying] for a male, female, and for a
menstrual period.*

[I] *She who aborts on the fortieth day [of pregnancy] does not
scruple that it is a [human] fetus at all.*

[J]   *[If she aborts] on the forty-first day, she sits out [the days of uncleanness and purifying] for male, female, and for a menstrual period [= H].*

[K]   R. Ishmael says, "*[If she aborts] on the forty-first day, let her sit out [the days of uncleanness and purifying] for male and for a menstrual period. [If it is on] the eighty-first day, let her sit out the days of [uncleanness and purifying] for male, female, and for a menstrual period.*

[L]   "*For the male is completed on the forty-first day, but the female [only later], on the eighty-first day.*"

[M]   *And sages say, "All the same are the formation of the male and the female: both take place by the forty-first day.*"

[I.A]   In all cases concerning which we have learned in the Mishnah, *Let her sit out the days of uncleanness and purifying for a male and a female,* [there will be] fourteen unclean days [those for a female], and then twenty-six clean days [thirty-three for a male, less seven unclean days for the male, on which all blood that is excreted is deemed to be clean].

[B]   [So] they assign to [the mother] the strict rules pertaining to the male and the strict rules pertaining to the female.

[C]   Now this rule that you have given applies to sexual relations. But as to food requiring preparation in conditions of cleanness, let her sit out [the days of uncleanness and of purifying] applying to a female [alone].

[II.A]   *[If she aborts] a ṭumṭom and a male, an androgyne and a male, she sits out [the days of uncleanness and purifying] for both male and female.* And they take account of the possibility that she has produced a male.

[B]   *[If she aborts] a ṭumṭom and a female, or an androgyne and a female, she sits out the days of uncleanness and purifying for a female alone.* And they do not take account of the possibility that she has produced a male.

[C]   This is the further rule: if she gave birth to a male and then a female, or to a female and then a male, let her sit out the days of uncleanness and purifying for a female, [for in whatever order the births took place, we impose the longer of the two periods].

[**III**.A]   A chopped up fetus, the head of which emerged—what is the rule?

[B]   R. Yosa said, "R. Yoḥanan and R. Eleazar differed on this matter.

[C]   "R. Yoḥanan said, 'Its head is equivalent to the greater part of its body,' [so, in line with M. 3:5D, it is deemed fully born].

[D]   "R. Eleazar said, 'Its head is deemed equivalent [merely] to one of its limbs.' "

[E]   The cited Mishnah-pericope takes issue with the position of R. Yoḥanan: "*[If] it emerged in pieces or feet first, once the greater part of the body has gone forth, lo, this is deemed fully born*[, so we require the greater part of the body when it emerges chopped up]."

[F]   Interpret the Mishnah-pericope to refer to a case in which [following Pené Moshe], it came out feet first [but if it came out head first, that suffices].

[G]   The cited Mishnah-pericope takes issue with the position of R. Eleazar: *[If] it emerged in the normal way, [it is deemed fully born] when the greater part of the head has emerged* [so the head is not merely equivalent to a limb, and this without regard to the condition of the fetus]. Thus has it stated that the head is of no consequence?

[H]   Interpret the Mishnah-lemma to refer to a case in which it emerged [Pené Moshe:] head first.

[I]   R. Jonathan and R. Simeon b. Laqish: R. Jonathan accords with the view of R. Yoḥanan, R. Simeon b. Laqish accords with the view of R. Eleazar.

[J]   R. Zeira [in defining the greater part of the head] showed the associates the forehead and skull.

[**IV**.A]   One of the members of the household of Gamaliel, son of Rabbi Leani, asked in session before R. Mana, "Since you say [that a chopped up fetus that is fully born] is a fetus, [is it not so that] the child born thereafter is not deemed first-born for the purposes of inheritance or for [giving to] the priest [the redemption money for the first-born, there now being no obligation whatsoever]?"

[B]   He said to him, "Interpret the Mishnah to apply to a case in which [the fetus was born] dead [so that the one born thereafter remains first-born for purposes of inheritance]."

[V.A]   R. Isaac bar Naḥman in the name of R. Eleazar: "In the case of fowl, the criterion for the head is the greater part of the head."

[B]   R. Zeira in the name of Samuel, "The gullet of fowl is measured by the greater part of it."

[C]   A case came before R. Yosé in the case of [a bird], the [gullet] of which was perforated by the breadth of a pin.

[D]   [He said,] "And do we not know what constitutes the greater part thereof?"

The important fact for understanding this unit is the familiar one that, upon the birth of a male, there are seven days in which all blood that is excreted is deemed unclean, followed by thirty-three in which blood is deemed clean, and upon the birth of a female, fourteen and sixty-six days respectively. The Mishnah's chief interests are cases in which there are no traits in the fetus by which definitively to assign the fetus to one or the other category. The Talmud remains close to the Mishnah's interests. I and II simply gloss the Mishnah, providing a predictable exegesis. III expands the range of discourse by introducing a case to be settled on the basis of the Mishnah's materials. We want to know the point at which the chopped up fetus is deemed fully born, with the consequent imputation of uncleanness to the mother. The critics of the two authorities cite the present pericope of the Mishnah. As noted, I have revised the reading in accord with Pené Moshe's proposal. Closely related to III, IV stands in the same relationship to the Mishnah as does III. The issue now is the legal consequence of declaring the chopped up fetus to be valid. If so, the next child to be born may or may not have the rights of the first-born. V is tacked on because of the general relevance to the criterion specified in the antecedent materials. In fact the unit is wildly out of place.

4:1

[A]   *[51b] Samaritan women are deemed menstruants from their cradle.*

[B]   *And Samaritan men convey uncleanness to the lower and upper parts of the couch because they have intercourse with menstruating women, since Samaritan women observe the rules of uncleanness for any sort of blood, [so they deem clean blood to be unclean and thus a clean day to be one of the seven unclean ones, losing all count and thus not observing the menstrual laws properly].*

[C]   *But they [who have contact with them] are not liable for entering the sanctuary [in a state of uncleanness], nor do people burn heave-offering on their account [as if the food had been contaminated], because the uncleanness pertaining to them is imputed [solely] by reason of doubt.*

[I.A]   Menstrual blood stinks. Hymeneal blood does not stink.

[B]   Menstrual blood is red. Hymeneal blood is not red.

[C]   Menstrual blood derives from the uterus. Hymeneal blood does not derive from the uterus, but from the side.

What the Talmud adds is the distinction between unclean and clean blood, of which Samaritans are ignorant (M. 4:1B).

4:2

[A]   *Sadducean women, when accustomed to follow in the ways of their fathers, lo, they have the status of Samaritan women.*

[B]   *If they abandon those ways to walk in Israelite ways, lo, they have the status of Israel[ite women].*

[C]   *R. Yosé says, "They always are deemed to have the status of Israelites, until they abandon Israelite ways to walk in the ways of their fathers."*

4:3

[A]   *The blood of a gentile woman and the blood of purifying of a woman afflicted with ṣaraʿat—*

[B]   the House of Shammai declare clean.

[C]   The House of Hillel say, "They are equivalent to her spit and urine."

[D]   The blood of a woman who has not immersed after childbirth—

[E]   the House of Shammai say, "It is equivalent to her spit and urine."

[F]   And the House of Hillel say, "It imparts uncleanness both when moist and when dried up."

[G]   But they concur in the case of a woman who gives birth in the status of Zabah that [her blood] imparts uncleanness both when it is moist and when it is dried up.

4:4–5

[A]   A woman in protracted labor [who produces blood] is deemed to be a menstruant.

[B]   "[If] a woman was in protracted labor for three days during the eleven days [between periods, during which a flow of blood is deemed to be flux within the definition of Lev. 15:25], [and if] she enjoyed a respite for twenty-four hours and then gave birth, lo, this woman is one who has given birth in the status of a Zabah [that is, one who has a flux not at the time of her period]," the words of R. Eliezer.

[C]   R. Joshua says, "A night and a day, like the eve of the Sabbath and its day."

[D]   For she has had relief from the pain, but not from the blood.

[A]   And how long is her protracted labor?

[B]   R. Meir says, "Even for forty or fifty days."

[C]   R. Judah says, "Sufficient for her is her [ninth] month."

[D]   *R. Yosé and R. Simeon say, "Hard labor continues no longer than for two weeks."*

4:6

[A]   *She who is in protracted labor during the eighty days [of uncleanness and purifying] after the birth of a female—*

[B]   *any blood that she produces is clean,*

[C]   *until the fetus emerges.*

[D]   *But R. Eliezer declares it unclean.*

[E]   *They said to R. Eliezer "If in a case in which the law is stringent, in the case of blood that appears during a period of respite, the law rules leniently in the matter of blood produced by hard labor,*

    "in a case in which [to begin with] the law ruled leniently, namely, concerning blood produced during a period of respite—

    "is it not logical that we should rule leniently in connection with blood produced through hard labor?"

[F]   *He said to them, "It is sufficient for the inferred law [about giving birth during the sixty-six days of purifying] to be as strict as that from which it is inferred[, which is the law of labor at any other time].*

    "In what respect has the law ruled leniently for her?

    "In respect to the uncleanness of her flux.

    "But she is unclean in respect to the uncleanness of a menstruant."

4:7

[A]   *All the eleven days [following the seven days of menstrual uncleanness], a woman is assumed to be clean.*

[B]   *If she sat down and did not examine herself—*

[C]   *[whether the neglect was committed] accidentally, under constraint, or [if] she willfully did not examine herself, she [nonetheless] is clean.*

[D]   *[Once] the time of her period has come, [if] she has not exam-*
      ined herself, lo, this one is deemed unclean[, for we take for
      granted that the discharge comes at its regular time].

[E]   *R. Meir says, "If she was in hiding and the time for her period*
      had come and she still did not examine herself, lo, this one is
      deemed [still] clean, because a condition of terror suspends the
      flow of blood.

[F]   *"But during the [seven clean] days [that must be counted by]*
      man or woman suffering a flux, or the one day of cleanness to
      be noted by her who awaits day against day [one clean day for
      each unclean one, after there has been a discharge for two
      days]—during that time lo, these [even in the eleven days of A]
      are assumed to be unclean."

Full discussion of M. Nid. chapter 4 will be found in Jacob
Neusner, *A History of the Mishnaic Law of Purities* (Leiden:
E.J. Brill, 1974–77), vol. 15, pp. 62–78.

Abbreviations, Bibliography, and Glossary

Am haares: An Israelite who is not trusted properly to tithe his produce or to observe the rules of Levitical cleanness. The opposite of a *haber.*

Amah: A cubit (pl.: *amot*).

Appointed Times: Neusner, Jacob. *A History of the Mishnaic Law of Appointed Times.* 5 vols. Leiden: E. J. Brill, 1981–.

Ar.: Arakhin.

Asherah: A tree worshipped in idolatry.

A.Z.: Abodah Zarah.

b.: *Babli,* Babylonian Talmud; *ben,* "son of."

B.B.: Baba Batra.

Bek.: Bekhorot.

Ber.: Berakhot.

Bes: Besah.

Bet hammidrash: Schoolhouse (lit., house of study).

Bet Haperas: A field declared unclean on account of crushed bones spread through it from a plowed-up grave.

Bet kor: 75,000 square cubits, the area of land in which a *kor* of seed is planted.

Bet rova: The area of land in which one quarter *kab* of seed is planted, approximately 104 square cubits.

Bet seah: The area of land in which a *seah* of seed is planted, 2,500 square cubits.

Bik.: Bikkurim.

B.M.: Baba Mesia.

Bokser: Bokser, Barunch M. "An Annotated Bibliographical Guide to the Study of the Palestinian Talmud." In *Principat* (*ANRW* II. 19.2), edited by Wolfgang Hesse. Berlin and New York, 1979.

B.Q.: Baba Qamma.

Damages: Neusner, Jacob. *A History of the Mishnaic Law of Damages.* 5 vols. Leiden: E. J. Brill, 1982.

Dem.: Demai.

Demai: Produce about which there is a doubt whether or not the required heave-offering and tithes were removed.

Denar: A coin worth one-half *sheqel.*

Diverse kinds: Heterogeneous plants or animals. These may not be joined together through being planted in the same field, harnessed together, or cross-bred (Lev. 19:19, Deut. 22:9–11).

Dupondium: A coin worth one-twelfth of a *sheqel.*

Editio princeps: Talmud Yerushalmi
. . . Venezia. Reprinted without place or date. Originally printed by Daniel Bomberg, 1523–24.

Ed: Eduyyot.

Eighteen Benedictions: The central prayer of liturgy, recited three times daily, four times on sabbaths and festivals, and five times on the Day of Atonement.

Erub: A deposit of food that is used (1) to amalgamate several distinct domains or (2) to establish a temporary abode. As a result, on the sabbath, individuals freely may cross the boundaries of the distinct domains or move beyond the usual range of 2,000 cubits permitted for movement on the holy day.

Erub.: Erubin.

Etrog: A citron, carried on the Festival of Booths as the "fruit of goodly trees," mentioned at Lev. 23:40.

Francus: Francus, Israel. *Talmud Yerushalmi. Massekhet Besah. Im perush . . . Eleazar Azkari.* New York: Feldheim, 1967.

Ginzberg: Ginzberg, Louis. *Yerushalmi Fragments from the Genizah. I. Text with various readings from the editio princeps.* 1909. Reprint. New York and Hildesheim: Georg Olms Verlag, 1970.

Git.: Gittin.

GRA: Elijah b. Solomon Zalman ("HaGaon Rabbi Eliyahu," or "Vilna Gaon," Lithuania, 1720–1797), Mishnah commentary, in Romm edition of the Mishnah.

Habdalah: The ceremony that marks the conclusion of a sabbath or festival and the beginning of an ordinary day.

Haber: A person who (1) separates all required agricultural offerings from food he grows or purchases and (2) who eats his food in a state of cultic cleanness.

Hag.: Hagigah.

Hal.: Hallah.

Halisah: The ceremony that severs the bond between a man and the widow of his brother who has died childless (see Deut. 25:7–9).

Hallel: A portion of the liturgy, consisting of Psalms 113–18, recited on festivals and new moons.

Halusah: A woman who has undergone the ceremony of *halisah.*

Haroset: A relish made of fruits and pices with vinegar or wine, used to sweeten the bitter herb at the passover meal (see M. Pes. 10:3).

Herem: Something set aside for use of the priests or Temple. The term is used in vows of abstinence, by which an individual prohibits himself from use of a named object.

Holy Things: Neusner, Jacob. *A History of the Mishnaic Law of Holy Things.* 6 vols. Leiden: E. J. Brill, 1978–79.

Hor.: Horayot.

Hul.: Hullin.

Issar: A coin valued at one forty-eighth of a *sheqel*.

Issaron: A measure of volume, equal to one-tenth of an *ephah*.

Jastrow: Jastrow, Marcus. *A Dictionary of the Targumim, the Talmud Babli and Yerushalmi, and the Midrashic Literature.* 2 vols. Reprint. New York: Pardes Publishing House, 1950.

Karmelit: An area of land classified as neither public nor private domain.

Kel.: Kelim.

Ker.: Keritot.

Kerem rebai:: A vineyard in its fourth year of growth, the produce of which is deemed sanctified (see Lev. 19:24).

Ket.: Ketubot.

Ketubah: A marriage contract indicating the sum of money due to the wife upon her husband's death or on being divorced.

Kil.: Kilayim.

Koy: An animal about which there is doubt concerning whether it is in the category of domesticated or undomesticated beasts.

Krauss: Krauss, Samuel. *Griechische und Lateinische Lehnwörter im Talmud, Midrasch, und Targum.* (Berlin, 1899. Repr. Hildesheim, 1964: Georg Olms Verlagsbuchhandlung).

Leiden MS: *The Palestinian Talmud. Leiden MS. Cod Scal. 3. A facsimile of the original manuscript.* 4 vols. Jerusalem: Kedem Publishing, 1970.

Letekh: A measure of volume equal to one and a half *ephah*.

Lieberman, Caesarea: Lieberman, Saul. *The Talmud of Caesarea. Jerushalmi Tractate Nezikin. Supplement to Tarbiz* II 4, in Hebrew. Jerusalem: 1931.

Lieberman, TR: Lieberman, Saul. *Tosefeth Rishonim. A Commentary. Based on Manuscripts of the Tosefta and Works of the Rishonim and Midrashim in Manuscripts and Rare Editions.* 3 vols. Jerusalem: Mossad Rabbi Kook Press, 1939. In Hebrew.

Lieberman[n], YK: Lieberman[n], Saul. *Ha-Yerushalmi Kiphshuto. A Commentary based on manuscripts of the Yerushalmi and works of the Rishonim and Midrashim in Mss. and rare editions.* Volume 1, *Sabbath, Erubin, Pesahim.* Jerusalem: Darom Publishing Co., 1934. In Hebrew.

Litra: A measure of volume equal to 1/144 of an *ephah*.

Log: One seventy-second of an *ephah*.

Lulab: The branches of palm, myrtle, and willow that are bound together and carried along with the *etrog* on the Festival of Booths (see Lev. 23:40).

M.: Mishnah.

Ma.: Maaserot.

Maah: A coin valued at one-twelfth of a *sheqel*.

Maamad: A priestly course, that is, one of the twenty-four groups of priests from districts outside of Jerusalem. These served in the Temple in rotation.

Maddaf: The level of uncleanness conveyed by a *zab* or *zabah* to an object that is located above his or her head.

Mak.: Makkot

Makh.: Makhshirin.

Mamzer(et): The offspring of a man and woman who cannot legally marry.

Maneh: A weight of gold or silver equal to fifty *sheqels*.

Markof: A musical instrument.

Marshall: Marshall, J. T. *Manual of the Aramaic Language of the Palestinian Talmud. Grammar, vocalized text, translation, and vocabulary.* Edited by J. Barton Turner. Leiden: E. J. Brill, 1929.

Me.: Meilah.

Meg.: Megillah.

Melammed: Melammed, E. Z. *An Introduction to Talmudic Literature.* Jerusalem:1973. In Hebrew.

Melog: Property owned by one individual (usually a wife), the income from which accrues to a different person (the husband).

Men.: Menahot.

Mesora: A person unclean with the disease referred to at Lev. 13:3ff.

Mezuzah: A strip of parchment inscribed with Deut. 6:4–9 and 11:18–21. In accordance with Deut. 6:9 it is fastened to the doorpost of an Israelite's house. Pl.: *mezuzot.*

Mid.: Middot.

Midras-uncleanness: The level of uncleanness conveyed by any of the individuals listed at Lev. 12:2, 15:2, 25, to objects on which they exert pressure.

Mil: Two thousand cubits.

Min: A heretic (pl.: *minim*).

Miq.: Miqvaot.

Moshab:: The level of impurity conveyed by an unclean person to a chair or other object normally used for sitting.

M.Q.: Moed Qatan.

M.S.: Maaser Sheni.

M'SH B (W): A formulaic phrase used to introduce a legal precedent.

Naz.: Nazir.

Nazirite: One who has taken a vow neither to cut his hair, drink wine, nor contract corpse-uncleanness (see Num. 6:1–27).

Ned.: Nedarim.

Neg.: Negaim.

Nega: A sore on the body that may indicate that the individual is unclean with the disease *saraat*, referred to at Lev. 13:3ff.

Netin(ah): A descendant of the Gibeonites, designated at Josh. 9:27 as Temple-slaves. They have impaired status within the Israelite community (see M. Qid. 4:1ff).

Nid.: Niddah.

Niddah: A woman unclean through mestruation.

NY: *Noam Yerushalmi.* Joshua Isaac Salonima, *Sefer Noam Yerushalmi. Vehu beur al hayyerushalmi.* 2 vols, 1868. (Vilna, 1868. Reprint. Jerusalem: 1968.

Oh.: Ohalot.

Omer: The first sheaf of the season, which must be harvested and offered in the Temple as a meal-offering. Only when this is done may the rest of the new grain be reaped (Lev. 23:10).

Or.: Orlah.

Orlah: Produce from an orchard in its first three years of growth, which may not be eaten (see Lev. 19:23).

'P: A formulaic word used to introduce a named authority's expansion of a preceding rule.

Par.: Parah.

Parvah-chamber: The name of a particular room in the Temple.

Pe.: Peah

Peah: Produce that grows in the corner of the field and must be left unharvested, to be collected by the poor (see Lev. 19:9ff).

Pené Moshe: Moses Margolies (d. 1780). *Pene Moshe.* Amsterdam: 1754; Leghorn: 1770. Reprinted in the Yerushalmi Talmud.

Perutah: A copper coin of small denomination.

Pes.: Pesahim.

Pondion: One twenty-fourth of a *shekel.*

Prayer: The Eighteen Benedictions.

Prozbul: The legal document that allows creditors to circumvent the usual abolition of debts in the seventh year of the sabbatical cycle (see M. Sheb. 10:4). The debts are assigned to a court, which prevents their being remitted.

Pundium: One-sixth of a *sheqel.*

Purities: Neusner, Jacob. *A History of the Mishnaic Law of Purities.* 22 vols. Leiden: E. J. Brill, 1974–77.

Qab: A measure of volume, equal to one-eighteenth of an ephah.

Qal vehomer: An argument *a minori ad majus.*

Qartob: A liquid or dry measure equal to one sixty-fourth of a *log.*

QE: *Qorban ha'edah.* Elijah of Fulda, *Qorban Ha'edah.* Dessau: 1743; Berlin:1757, 1760–62. Reprinted in the Yerushalmi Talmud.

Qid.: Qiddushin.

Qin.: Qinnim.

R.: Rabbi.

Rabbinowitz: Rabbinowitz, Louis I. "Talmud, Jerusalem." In *Encyclopaedia Judaica* 15:772–79. Jerusalem: 1971.

Rabinovitz, STEI: Rabinovitz, Z. W. *Sha'are Torath Eretz Israel. Notes and Comments on Yerushalmi.* Jerusalem: 1940.

Ratner: Ratner, B. *Ahawath Zion we-Jeruscholaim. Varianten und Ergänzungen des Textes des Jerusalemitischen Talmuds nach alten Quellen und handschriftlichen Fragmenten ediert, mit kritischen Noten und Erlauterungen versehen.* Vilna: Witte and Gebr. Romm et al. I, *Berakhot* (1901). II, *Shabbat* (1902). III, *Terumot, Hallah* (1904). IV , *Shebi'it* (1905). V , *Kilayim, Ma'aserot* (1907). VI, *Pesahim* (1908). VII *Yoma* (1909). VIII, *Rosh Hashshanah, Sukkah* (1911). IX *Megillah* (1912). X, *Besah, Taanit* (1913). XII, *Pe'ah Demai, Ma'aser Sheni, 'Orlah, Bikkurim* (1917). No number, *Sheqalim, Hagigah, Mo'ed Qatan,* Jerusalem: 1967.

Regel: One of the three pilgrimage festivals, Passover, Pentecost, Booths (Tabernacles). (Pl.: *regalim.*)

R.H.: Rosh Hashshanah.

San.: Sanhedrin.

Schwab: Schwab, Moise. *Le Talmud de Jérusalem. Traduit pour la première fois en français.* Reprinted. Paris: 1960.

Seah: One-third of an *ephah.*

Shaatnez: Fabric in which wool and linen are woven together. This is forbidden under the law of Diverse Kinds.

Shab.: Shabbat.

Shebu.: Shabuot.

Shebuah: An oath.

Shema: A section of the liturgy composed of Deut. 6:4–9, 11:13–21, and Num. 15:37–41. It is recited twice daily, morning and evening.

Sheq.: Sheqalim.

Sheqel:: The chief silver coin of the Israelites, weighing between a quarter and a half of an ounce.

Shittuf: A deposit of food placed jointly by neighbors sharing a courtyard in order to transform all of their homes into a single, collective domain for purposes of carrying burdens on the Sabbath. Cf. *Erub.*

Shofar: A ram's horn, blown on set occasions in Temple and synagogue worship.

Sit: The distance between the extended thumb and index finger.

Sot.: Sotah.

Suk.: Sukkah.

Sukkah: A temporary dwelling ("booth") in which Israelites live during the Festival of Tabernacles, in fullfillment of Lev. 23:34–36, 39–43.

Sukkot: Tabernacles.

T.: Tosefta.

Ta.: Taanit.

Tam.: Tamid.

Tebul-yom: A person who has immersed in a ritual bath and awaits the setting of the sun, which marks the completion of the process of purification.

Tefillin: Phylactories, tied on head and arm, containing four passages: Ex. 13:1–10, 11–16, Deut. 6:4–9, 11:13–21.

Tem.: Temurah.

Teqiah: A blast of a *shofar.*

Ter.: Terumot.

Terefah: Meat that is ruined in the process of ritual slaughter through some improper act of the slaughterer.

Terisit: A coin.

Toh.: Tohorot.

Tumtom: One whose sex is indistinguishable.

T.Y.: Tebul Yom.

Uqs.: Uqsin.

Women: Neusner, Jacob. *A History of the Mishnaic Law of Women.* 5 vols. Leiden: E. J. Brill, 1979–80.

Yad.: Yadayyim.

Yeb.: Yebamot.

Yom.: Yoma.

Y.T.: Yom Tob.

Zab.: Zabim.

Zab/zabah: A person who has suffered a flux and is deemed unclean. Pl.: *zabim, zabot.*

Zeb.: Zebahim.

Zuckermandel: Zuckermandel, M. S. *Tosephta. Based on the Erfurt and Vienna Codices with par-*<!---->*allels and variants.* Reprinted. Jerusalem: Wahrmann Books, 1963.

Zussman, Beth Shean: Zussman, Jacob. "An Inscription of a Legal Character from the Beth Shean Valley." In *Tarbiz* 43 (1973–74): 88–158, 193–195. In Hebrew.

Zuz: A coin valued at a *denar,* (i.e., one-half of a *sheqel*). Pl.: *zuzim.*

Index of Biblical and Talmudic References

General Index

Abba, on death offering by priest, 111

Abba bar Ba, on fetus, recognition of, 155–56

Abba b. Hanah: on abortion and uncleanness, 202; on women, examination of, 192

Abba bar Jeremiah, on women, examination of, 182

Abba bar Kahana, on atonement, precedent of offering, 127

Abba b. Papi, on women, examination of, 186

Abbahu: on abortion and uncleanness, 209; on atonement, precedent of offering, 118; on death offering by priest, 110; on menstruants, 140, 160; on women, examination of, 183–84, 192

Abba Saul, on abortion and uncleanness, 208

Abin: on menstruants, 160; on sin-offering, liability for, 59–60

Abortion and uncleanness, 137, 197–219

Abudama of Haifa, on women, examination of, 190, 193–94

Abun: on atonement, precedent of offering, 128; on court error, liability for unwitting sin, 34; on menstruants, 144, 171; on rulers and priests, sin-offering of, 70, 87; on sin-offering, liability for, 60; on women, examination of, 193

Aḥa: on atonement, precedent of offering, 126; on court error, liability for unwitting sin, 20; on rulers and priests, sin-offering of, 71, 95; on women, examination of, 193

Ami [Ammi]: on abortion and uncleanness, 202; on atonement, precedent of offering, 20, 23, 26, 31; on court error, liability for unwitting sin, 124; on menstruants, 140; on women, examination of, 190–91

ʿAqabiah b. Mehallel: on rulers and priests, sin-offering of, 101; on women, examination of, 187–89

ʿAqiba: on atonement, precedent of offering, 114; on court error, liability for unwitting sin, 11–12, 18, 23, 25; on menstruants, 143–44; on rulers and priests, sin-offering of, 100; on sin offering, liability for, 61–63; on women, examination of, 180–81

Asiyan, on sin-offering, liability for, 65

Atonement, precedent of offering, 112–29

Ba: on abortion and uncleanness, 200, 204, 209, 213; on atonement, precedent of offering, 113; on fetus, recognition of, 155–56; on menstruants, 150, 161, 167; on